THE EVOLUTION
OF CAPITALISM

THE EVOLUTION
OF CAPITALISM

Advisory Editor
LEONARD SILK
Editorial Board,
The New York Times

Research Associate
MARK SILK

THE HISTORY OF
ECONOMICS

BY OTHMAR SPANN

ARNO PRESS

A NEW YORK TIMES COMPANY

New York • 1972

Reprint Edition 1972 by Arno Press Inc.

Reprinted by permission of George Allen & Unwin Ltd.

Reprinted from a copy in
The Wesleyan University Library

The Evolution of Capitalism
ISBN for complete set: 0-405-04110-1
See last pages of this volume for titles.

Manufactured in the United States of America

- - - - - - - - - - - -

Library of Congress Cataloging in Publication Data

Spann, Othmar, 1878-1950.
    The history of economics.

    (The Evolution of capitalism)
    Translation of Die Haupttheorien der Volkswirt-
schaftslehre auf lehrgeschichtlicher Grundlage.
    1. Economics--History. I. Title. II. Series.
HB75.S65 1972   330'.09   70-38268
ISBN 0-405-04138-1

THE HISTORY OF ECONOMICS

*Political Economy
is not a Science of Business
but a Science of Life*

THE HISTORY OF
ECONOMICS

by OTHMAR SPANN

PROFESSOR OF SOCIOLOGY AND ECONOMICS
IN THE UNIVERSITY OF VIENNA

*Translated from
the Nineteenth German Edition by*
EDEN AND CEDAR PAUL

NEW YORK
W·W·NORTON & COMPANY INC
Publishers

PREFACE TO THE FIRST EDITION

THE work I now commit to the hands of students of political economy and to those of cultured general readers is designed to supply, not only a history of economic science, but also a concise formulation and critique of the main theories and systems of political economy. My aim has been to discuss, as clearly and succinctly as possible, the basic problems of economics, viewed in the changing light of historical evolution; and at the same time to give the best possible summary of the contemporary doctrines of the science.

In the study of philosophy, this has always been considered the easiest path towards a better understanding of philosophical theory, and I believe it will be found the easiest and most natural path in economics likewise, since in economics no less than in philosophy we are often concerned with passing judgment on extremely intricate and difficult trains of reasoning. These are cases in which we must let the masters speak for themselves. I hope that my modest endeavours will help to satisfy the growing demand for information as regards the types of economic theory, and I trust that critics will be lenient in view of the complicated nature of my undertaking.

OTHMAR SPANN

EXTRACTS FROM THE PREFACE
TO THE FIFTH EDITION

WITH the kind assistance of the publishers, it has at length
become possible to issue my book in an enlarged form. . . .

When I recall how difficult it is to point out the right way
to the novice in the social sciences, how difficult to disclose
the quintessential spirit of these studies, and when after the
lapse of nearly ten years I contemplate my book in its new
incarnation, I cannot but feel that, even now, it remains
inadequate for its task. From the purely historical outlook,
indeed, that task was comparatively easy. There, my aim was
to bring the acquirements of recent science into relation with
those of earlier days, and thus to demonstrate both worlds of
thought. It was, therefore, easy enough for the book to convey
a substantial aggregate of information. But something very
different was required, over and above this. I had to give the
student a deeper grasp of the ultimate nature of the matters
in hand, to make him realise the true relationship between
economics and society. No doubt most professional economists
still believe it possible to communicate the elements of our
science by mere instruction. Nevertheless, political economy
is quite unsuited for a superficial method of instruction. Adam
Müller, List, Ricardo, Marx, Rousseau, Plato—had not each
one of them his own idea, his own intimate understanding, his
own peculiar conception, of the nature and genesis of society?
I am not thinking, in this connexion, of their particular theories
(which were but the expression of their respective ideas), but
of that living and inexplicable inner notion or representation,
such as we carry in the mind as the image of a beloved personality, a landscape, a heroic figure, or a historical epoch.
I can hardly expect this book to provide its readers with anything of the sort. The beginner will not possess such funda-

mental notions at the outset of his studies, will not acquire them in his first flight. He must conscientiously work them out for himself. But my book is designed to give him confident anticipations, to make the first sparks glow. It should enable him to realise that the working concepts it will furnish him with are but the tools he is to use, and that each of these will need a different method of application, will acquire a peculiar significance, according as his knowledge of essentials becomes more profound, and according as his own general philosophy may tend towards individualism or universalism.

Just as the biologist, whose object of study is the living (which lacks unimpeachable objective characteristics), can only discern that object because he is himself a living creature and is therefore spontaneously aware what life is; so the student of economics must discover in himself, must experience in his own being, what society and economics are; and this knowledge must keep him company in all his experience, observation, analysis, and research.

OTHMAR SPANN

Vienna
July 1919

PREFACE TO THE SIXTEENTH EDITION

WHEN I sent this book of mine to the printers more than fifteen years ago, I did not venture to hope that the new scales of measurement which (tentatively) I was applying to the field of economic doctrine, would so quickly secure general approval. Of Adam Müller, at that time, little more was known than the name, as can be learned by an examination of the then leading handbooks by Philippovich, Schmoller, Adolf Wagner, Conrad, Bücher, Böhm-Bawerk, and Pesch; and it was only by a lucky chance that in 1907 I was able to buy from a secondhand dealer a copy of the almost forgotten *Elemente der Staatskunst*. In like manner, Thünen was ignored and misunderstood; List was esteemed by only a few; and no one seemed to be aware that an "organic" system of economics had existed in Germany after the days of romanticism. The fact was that the champions of the Schmollerian school, which had long since fallen away towards positivism, had forgotten that their theories had been born out of romanticism and post-Kantian German idealism.

Nowadays the important part played by romanticism as a foundation in this respect, is being more and more generally recognised. It can no longer be denied that a red thread runs through economic teaching from Adam Müller to the new historical school; that the names of Adam Müller, Fichte, Baader, Baron vom Stein, List, Thünen, Roscher, Hildebrand, Knies, Bernhardi, Schmoller—and even those of Carlyle, Ruskin, and Carey—form, as it were, a single line of descent; and that they incarnate a universalist-organic and idealist doctrine contrasting with the atomist-individualist and materialist doctrine of Smith, Ricardo, Say, Rau, Menger, and Jevons. Herein, however, is implied (indirectly, at least) the antithesis, which I was the first to point out in the present

work, between the individualist and the universalist conceptions of sociology and economics.

Therewith, too, a new light is thrown on the economic
theories of the Middle Ages, when interest centred in the question of the just price; and we see that the doctrine of the just
price was a genuinely universalist one.

This book, however, has encountered opposition as well
as approval. The author has been blamed for reawakening
romanticism, and some critics have expressed indignation at
"the poetising of science" In so far as these adverse critics aim
their shafts at my own teaching, I show in the text (pp. 283-4)
that their arrows are misdirected. In so far as they object to
the contention that romanticism became the foundress of an
organised school of economics, I should like to reiterate that
romanticism was not a mere artistic movement, but, in virtue
of its widespread philosophical affiliations, was the begetter of
a trend in life and culture which involved all the abstract
sciences, and more especially in social and political science
signified the first severance of European culture from the
Renaissance and the Enlightenment. Nay more, I must insist
that this trend, abstract though it may have been, had enough
effective and concrete reality to determine the course of practical politics for two generations. Even to-day, romanticism,
as mother of all the conservative parties, has a far more powerful
influence upon everyday life than is obvious if we confine our
attention to its workings in the superficial strata of consciousness. The general attitude of such critics reminds me of a
story told of Joseph II. When *Die Entführung aus dem Serail*
was first produced in the Vienna of those days, the Emperor
said to the composer: "My dear Mozart, your music would
be very fine if there were not such a monstrous number of
notes in it!" These enlighteners, rationalists, mechanists, and
individualists, miss the fundamental tones of life; they hear

only a confused noise. In the medieval, romanticist, universalist conception of sociology and economics, they can, therefore, discern nothing beyond the fact that there is "a monstrous number of notes"; and, as "reasonable" persons, they confine their attention to externals, to details that can be weighed and measured and reckoned up. But just as Mozart answered, "Not a note too many, Sire!" so we may rejoin that there is nothing supererogatory in linking economic doctrine with the great fundamental outlooks on society and life. Such a procedure is in conformity with both the realities of concrete science and the logical severities of abstract thought. A lower standpoint is always implied and comprised within a higher.

In this edition, the following sections have been once again revised: the theory of credit (John Law); the theory of diminishing returns (Malthus); the theory of landrent (Ricardo); Baader; the theory of localisation (Thünen); force, or economic law? (social reform); the theory of marginal utility; present-day political economy. In addition, the whole text has been scrutinised; and, in the appendix on "How to Study Economics", the references to literature, and the general advice, have been brought up to date.

OTHMAR SPANN

In der Lahn, near Vordernberg, Styria
Easter 1926

CONTENTS

Chapter Nine

CAREY'S OPTIMISM AND ITS COUNTERPARTS ON THE CONTINENT OF EUROPE

Chapter Ten

A SHORT ACCOUNT OF THE EVOLUTION OF SOCIALISM

B

CONTENTS

INTRODUCTION

A SCIENCE as unfinished as the science of economics must, first and foremost, be considered historically.

In the following work, therefore, the reader will be made acquainted with the teachings of the great economists of earlier days, that he may gain a general view of the problems they set themselves to solve and the solutions they proposed. A brief exposition of the theories of each school of economists will be followed by a critical discussion of these theories. In this way the present-day condition of our science will spontaneously disclose itself to us. Thus, in studying the mercantile system, we shall learn the mercantilists' views regarding money and the balance of trade; when we examine the doctrines of the physiocrats and those of Adam Müller, we shall acquaint ourselves with what they thought about fruitfulness and the nature of a good; in connexion with List, we shall discuss protection and free trade; and so on. Furthermore, this critical and comparative method is the most effective one for the study of the history of doctrine, seeing that the writing of history lacks sap and vigour unless the historian acquires a characteristic outlook of his own. The notion that one who is perfectly "impartial" has also a standpoint, reminds one of an attempt to breathe in a vacuum. Essentially, this notion is a form of relativism. Of course, the various systems must be considered without prejudice. Each must be contemplated from its own angle, and must not be looked at through the spectacles of another system. But that towards which the great interconnexion of the systems points—therein is inherent the higher system which must supply the standpoint of the historiographer.

The advantage of such a method, the advantage of enlightening the student as to the various doctrines of a science which is at one and the same time highly abstract, and yet rooted in the concrete realities of life, is primarily this, that each doctrine is presented, not rigidly and imperiously, but standing out from amid its pros and cons, and, above all, in its genetical relations. Thereby the beginner is given a vivid glimpse of the far-reaching intellectual labours that were requisite for the establishment of concepts which, when present-day economics is studied systematically instead of historically, exhibit themselves only in a finished form. Light is also thrown on the great philosophical interconnexions without which no economic doctrine ever came into being. Finally, our method has the advantage of not committing the learner to any one particular system; but of opening up to him an understanding of all aspects of economic theory. In this way he is incited to return again and again to a study of the facts; to set out ever-anew from historical and social reality; and (most important of all) to grasp that this reality, live though it be, is still in the last analysis a reality of the mental world alone.

THE HISTORY OF ECONOMICS

CHAPTER ONE

ECONOMICS IN THE DAYS BEFORE THE MERCANTILE SYSTEM

NEITHER in classical antiquity nor yet in the Middle Ages did there arise any finished systems of politico-economic thought. In those epochs, when the mind was directed towards the heroic and the suprasensual, the economic sphere of activity was regarded with little esteem—as always in periods with an organised economy. Only when, as to-day, the individual is left so exclusively to his own devices, and only when the forces of free competition are stimulated to an extreme, is civilised life crudely dominated by economic considerations to an extent which seems self-evident to us to-day.

Even in those earlier ages, economic thought might well have been grounded on economic evolution. At all times economic life was multiform, and stood in need of assistance. It would be erroneous to picture the course of economic development as though mankind had passed on simply from a self-sufficient natural economy (the self-contained domestic economy) to the feudal economy and the medieval urban economy, and had at length "advanced" to a nation-wide capitalist economy. At all times there have been lesser economic corporations, such as peasant economies, that formed integral parts of larger, nation-wide or world-wide complexes. Thus in the primal days of man, during what is known as the Stone Age, intercourse for trading purposes went on throughout Europe; and there are proofs of the existence of foreign commerce during the Bronze Age, inasmuch as the constituents of bronze are not found naturally together. At the outset of

recorded history, in Babylon first of all, and subsequently in
Persia, Carthage, Egypt, Greece, and Rome, there was highly
developed capitalist trade, and there were branches of industry
carried on for export, with complicated systems of money,
credit, and bill-broking. Nor were there lacking in ancient
Greece and Rome what we should now call socialist movements.
Strikes occurred; socialist theories were promulgated; revolutions with a bolshevist complexion took place. Speaking
generally, the economy of ancient times was more purposively
organised than our own. Its nature is more easily comprehensible; and, because it is predominantly agricultural, it is
simpler.

Rodbertus and Karl Bücher (see the latter's *Entstehung der
Volkswirtschaft*, fourteenth edition, 1919) contend that the
ancient world did not, in the main, get beyond the system
of domestic economy. This view is erroneous; and it is unsound even as regards the imperial epoch, when the spread of
the latifundia (huge landed estates) undoubtedly resulted in a
reversion from a capitalist trading economy towards a "natural"
domestic economy. Bücher's doctrine of gradations—domestic
economy, urban economy, national economy—is false alike
historically and theoretically. It is the crudest Darwinism.
"National economy" has existed at all times.

But there were other reasons that militated against the rise
of economic science before the beginning of the modern
epoch, quite apart from the internal tranquillity of a more
purposively organised economy. In classical days, the scant
respect for labour was operative; and in the Middle Ages,
when labour was more highly esteemed, an ascetic trend was
dominant, for men's thoughts had turned away from earthly
things. Nevertheless, the beginnings of our science go back
to Plato and Aristotle.

Plato († 347 B.C.) and Aristotle († 322 B.C.) made notable
contributions to political science; but as far as economics is

concerned, mention need only be made of Aristotle's remarks on money, interest, and taxation.[1]

Aristotle sees the essential nature of money in this, that it intermediates in the exchange of utilities, thus functioning as medium of exchange. He regards it, however, as sterile; it brings forth no children (though τόκος means "interest" or "usury", as well as "the young of animals"); it cannot of itself produce any goods. Consequently, interest is reprehensible. This dictum exercised a powerful influence throughout the Middle Ages.—Regarding socialism in classical days, see below, p. 212; also pp. 63–4.

The economic thought of the Middle Ages was dominated by the teachings of Thomas Aquinas († 1274), who derived from Aristotle; and by the canon law (the Roman law of the *Corpus juris canonici*). Discussion chiefly centred round the notion of the "just price".

According to Thomas Aquinas, there are two kinds of justice: distributive justice, and compensatory justice or the justice of exchange. (Aristotle had already made this distinction in the fifth book of the *Nichomachean Ethics*.) In the matter of price, justice is to be found in the equality of reciprocal compensation in an exchange. What determines income is not the supply and demand of labour (as the subsequent mechanist economics teaches), but a normative outlook, the customary and average mutual adjustments between all the individuals that exercise economic functions, objective purposiveness. "Wherever a good is to be found, its essence consists in its due measure." Thus we get the idea of the income that is "suitable" or "proper" to a man's station. Interest on money is placed on the same footing as usury. "Pecunia pecuniam non parit" (money does not breed money). Money is a medium of exchange. Its use is its consumption. Consequently, for the use of lent money it is improper to demand any compensation in money, to expect anything beyond simple reimbursement. But Aquinas makes exceptions in the matter of tenancy,

---

[1] See Plato's *Republic* (various translations); Aristotle's *Politics* and *Nichomachean Ethics* (various translations of each). [Jowett's introduction to his translation of the *Republic* may be read with interest in this connexion.]

hire, and even credit for goods supplied.—In the later Middle Ages, it became usual to regard the following as justifiable grounds for demanding interest: lucrum cessans (missed opportunities of gain); damnum emergens (loss incurred by or injury accruing to the lender), this concession implying the recognition that, indirectly, money may be a productive good; risk; and delay in repayment.—The prohibition of interest or usury is fundamentally a measure falling within the domain of applied economics, being designed to hinder the development of capitalist forms of economy.

A century later, Nicole Oresme († 1382), a Frenchman whose name was Latinised as Oresmius, was an influential writer. Roscher terms him the leading ecobomist among the schoolmen. His views, like those of Aquinas, were based on Aristotle's, but he developed original outlooks upon matters of coinage and upon the debasement of the currency which was so common a practice in his day.

With the formulation of the teachings I have summarised, the Middle Ages had already made remarkable advances, but its ideas were grounded upon the purposively organised economy of the period and upon the ethico-religious conception of life then dominant. Hence the ensuing developments of economic science aimed either, as in the case of the mercantile system, at the supersession of the old urban-economic ties, or else, as in the case of liberalism from the time of Quesnay onwards, at the inauguration of a perfectly unhampered individualist trading economy. In doctrinal matters, earlier writers were ignored; innovation was the order of the day.

CHAPTER TWO

THE MERCANTILE SYSTEM

1. Leading Ideas of the Mercantile System

At the opening of the modern era, a new kind of economic practice and a number of novel and interdependent economic theories make their appearance in the form of what is known as mercantilism or the mercantile system. As List was the first to point out, the use of this name (introduced by Adam Smith) is not wholly warranted. The advocates of the new economic policy were quite as much concerned to further industrial developments as to promote the exchange of merchandise. Nor have we to do with anything that is strictly entitled to be called a "system", or with a circumscribed body of doctrines; the term "mercantile system" is loosely used to denote the aggregate of the principles actually applied by governments and men of business in the economic life of those days—though it is indisputable that these principles have an underlying general conformity. Mercantilism, therefore, was not deliberately thought out and artificially created by any individual; it was a creation of the time spirit, or a spontaneous growth of the time. Oncken aptly termed it "a system of sovereign welfare policy"; it was a system of political absolutism and centralisation in favour of the burgherdom and mobile capital, to the detriment of the nobility and the lords of the soil.—To throw light on the matter, let us first glance at the economic processes of this period of "early capitalism".

The economic organisation of the Middle Ages was disrupted mainly by those political changes which led in western Europe to the formation of large absolutist national States (France, Spain, Portugal, and England); and in Germany, later on, to the establishment of the territorial princedoms. As a result, the medieval economy, with its urban units, was replaced by larger units of a different kind, the unified national economic areas. Political concentration in these areas resulted in money and wealth becoming elements of political power in a way very different from of old. Bodin's dictum "Pecunia nervus rei publicae" (money is the nerve of the commonwealth) was in many respects new. Inasmuch as the State, which had been constitutional (in the feudalist sense), became absolute, a mercenary army replaced the feudal militia; and the centralisation of the administration established a salaried officialdom where feudal methods of self-government had prevailed. The result was that military and civil concerns, taxation, and the processes of State credit, tended more and more to be carried on upon a monetary basis instead of by the payments in kind of a natural economy, so that the monetary powers of a country acquired a political significance that was altogether novel.

These multiform changes were accompanied by the economic revolutions that followed the discovery of America (1492) and the opening of a sea route to the East Indies (1498). New possibilities of world trade came into being, giving fresh power to the peoples situated on western sea-fronts (the Spanish, the Portuguese, the Dutch, and the English), but weakening those cut off from the new commerce (decline of Germany). Trade, and the money standing behind trade, were thrust into the limelight as sources of wealth and political power.

The effects of these displacements of wealth were reinforced by a special process. Soon after the discovery of the New World, rivers of gold and silver began to pour from Spain across Europe, and the purchasing power of these metals fell enormously, with a consequent tremendous rise in prices (the "revolution in prices"). It is true, however, that the rise in prices began somewhere about 1510, whereas the great increase in the precious metals only began to make itself felt towards 1520, so there must have been a deeper cause at work in the economic evolution of those days. None the less, the superabundance of gold was an independent cause of a sudden rise in prices. The influx of gold played a great part in undermining the foundations of the old natural economy, for it favoured the diffusion of the means of credit and promoted the development of a capitalist economy.

All these circumstances tended to emphasise the importance of money, to stress the significance of commercial wealth as compared with the wealth that changed hands in kind during the processes of a natural economy. Thus whereas in the Middle Ages there had been a marked endeavour to check the growth of a monetary economy, the opinion now gathered headway that money, if not the only source of wealth, was certainly of decisive importance to the welfare of the nations. Two notable thoughts, therefore, began to dominate the minds of those who were turning their attention to political economy, two ideas which are still extremely influential to-day: a great esteem for money, and a great esteem for foreign trade (as the chief means for bringing money into the country). Implicit is a third notion: the fostering of industry, in so far as industry must be the precursor of commerce.—The "system" of practical measures which was deducible from these considerations may, when considered in constructive outline, be pictured as follows (making due allowance for extensive local variations, and for the fact that mercantilism cannot properly speaking be said to have originated as a purposively conceived and coherent doctrine).

The primary aim of the mercantilists, especially in the case of Italian and British writers, was to achieve a favourable balance of trade. By the term "balance of trade" is meant the counterpoise between imports and exports. When exports exceed imports, when the value of the goods sold to foreigners exceeds the value of the goods purchased from foreigners, the amount of money entering a country will exceed the amount of money issuing from it. Then the balance of trade is said to be favourable to the country in which money thus accumulates.—To achieve this favourable balance (which, as aforesaid, was the leading desire of the mercantilists), it is necessary to stimulate export trade, since only thereby is money brought into the country.

With that end in view, it is essential, on the one hand, to stimulate industries that create commodities for export (in those days spoken of collectively as "manufacture"), and, on the other hand, to check as far as possible the import of commodities. Both endeavours presuppose the fostering of home industry.

But if home industry is to be fostered, special attention must be paid to internal communications. It is necessary to abolish or to mitigate tolls, octrois, and the like, and to break down the barriers erected by the urban economy of the guilds. Furthermore, good roads must be built, canals must be dug, internal communication must be facilitated, home markets must be established.—Customs policy is, therefore, of supreme importance in the mercantile system. The champions of that system want to abolish export duties, and in case of need to stimulate exports by premiums; while they aim at reducing imports by a high import tariff or by actual prohibitions. Instances are Colbert's unified import tariff of 1664; the development towards such a tariff in England, especially after 1692; and, in Germany and Austria, sumptuary laws which were intended to restrict the use of articles of foreign origin. (A unified tariff on imports was rendered impossible in the case of Germany by the fragmented condition of that country, and in the case of Austria by the crownlands constitution). As corollaries to restriction of import, there had to be freedom for the import of raw materials needed by home industries, and prohibition of the export of such materials. Frederick the Great, for example, decreed corporal punishment for any one who should export wool.

The preexistent natural economy had to be further discouraged by the encouragement of manufactures through privileges and monopolies (whereby they were freed from the tyranny of the guilds), through exemption from taxation, and through other forms of support. In some cases, State factories were inaugurated, the State porcelain industry of Saxony being a vestige of one of these. Skilled foreign craftsmen were imported; industrial secrets were purchased; and so on.—On the other hand, by official supervision and thorough regulation of the whole process of production (supervision and regulation which extended into every detail concerning tools and methods alike), industry was to be kept up to the mark; and at the same time the consumer was to be protected by subjecting the process of sale to inspection. We see that in these matters the mercantilists clung to the traditions of the urban economy.—Another expedient of mercantilist policy was the foundation of colonies and trading companies.

Especially important was the (English) East India Company founded in the year 1600, and equipped in 1661 with the right to carry on war and make peace in non-Christian countries. Under Joseph II, Austria occupied the Nicobar Islands; and the Danubian Trading Company and the Austrian East India Company were founded.

Further, attempts were made to provide cheap labour power in order to strengthen large-scale industry. One means to this end was to promote the increase of population (a special desideratum in the depopulated Germany of those days); prohibitions on marriage were removed, premiums were paid to the fathers of large families (in France, for instance, a nobleman who had ten children was granted a pension of one thousand livres). Another means was to cheapen the necessaries of life, so that wages could be kept down. For this purpose, foodstuffs were freed from import duty, whilst high duties were imposed on exported grain—or the export of this staple was absolutely forbidden. (These measures, which were opposed

c

to the interests of agriculturists, were not openly advocated in mercantilist literature, but were often applied in practice— by Colbert, for example.)

·Finally the output of the precious metals was to be directly stimulated by encouraging silver-mining and gold-mining in the homeland, by State subsidies in certain instances. The attraction of wealthy foreigners into the country, prohibition of the export of the precious metals, and similar measures of minor importance, were to supplement and round off the expedients for increasing the national wealth.

A general survey of the items of mercantilist policy shows that the champions of the mercantile system took their stand upon a high estimate of the importance of money, but that they did not esteem money as an end in itself; they valued it as a means to the promotion of commerce and industry, they valued it on account of its productive effects. "Money begetteth trade", writes Thomas Mun, the mercantilist, "and trade encreaseth money." Another member of the same school, Charles Davenant, puts the idea tersely as follows: [Foreign] "trade brings in the stock; this stock, well and industriously managed, betters land, and brings more products of all kinds for exportation; the returns of which growth and product are to make a country gainers in the balance." [1] Colbert says the same thing from the outlook of the State financier: "If there be money in the country, the universal desire to turn it to advantage makes people set it in motion, and the public funds benefit thereby." [2]

It is essential to repeat, after giving the foregoing general outline, that the prevailing aspect of mercantilism varied greatly at different times and in different countries. In England, Holland, and Italy, the doctrine was predominantly commercial; in France, and still more in Germany, it was, rather,

---

[1] *Political and Commercial Works*, London, 1771, vol. ii, p. 221.
[2] *Mémoire au roi sur les finances*, 1670; *Lettres*, vii, 234.

industrial. These variations notwithstanding, and despite differences in the details of application, from the sixteenth to the eighteenth century all the leaders of European statecraft were guided by the principles adumbrated above. Enough to mention Charles V, Elizabeth Tudor, Cromwell, Louis XIV, Colbert, Peter the Great, Elector Frederick William, Frederick the Great, Leopold I, and Joseph II.

In England, though agriculture and manufacture were not neglected, mercantilism took a strongly commercial trend, which became exemplary. Cromwell's Navigation Law of 1651 decreed that no merchandise, either of Asia, Africa, or America, should be imported into England in any but English-built ships, belonging to English subjects, navigated by English commanders, with three-fourths of the crew English; seaborne commerce between England and other European countries was to be conducted, either in English bottoms, or else in ships belonging to the country with which trade was being carried on. These provisos ensured a practical monopoly of the seas for the English, and ruined the Dutch carrying trade. By the Methuen Treaty (1703), Portuguese ports were opened to British woollens, in return for special concessions to Portugal in the matter of the import of Portuguese wines into Great Britain.

In Germany and Austria, on the other hand, the need for promoting the increase of population in countries devastated by the Thirty Years War took the foreground. Nor could there be any question here of active endeavours to promote foreign trade. The main concern was to hinder imports from lands better equipped for manufacture, whose competition would prove destructive. Hence a demand for sumptuary laws is characteristic of mercantilist writing here.

In Italy we find, in conformity with the characteristics of the financial and commercial aristocracies of the urban republics in the peninsula, that authors of the mercantilist school are especially interested in the question of the balance of trade and in monetary problems.

In France, Colbert was the great and successful practical exponent of the mercantile system, so that it is sometimes known as "Colbertism". Jean Baptiste Colbert (b. 1619) became in 1661 superintendent and in 1666 controller-general of the finances. When he took office, French industry lagged behind that of England, and even that of Germany. The administration and the finances were in a sorry state. Ere long, however, internal customs dues had been in great part abolished; canals had been made; skilled workmen and entrepreneurs had been attracted from abroad; and, thanks to privileges, premiums, State subsidies, and other measures (above all, lucrative protective duties and the establishment of technical schools and academies), French economic life began to flourish abundantly, so that even England was outvied.

Observation 1. Since the day when Adam Smith, in need of an antithesis, pictured the mercantilists more than was warrantable as a unified school of thinkers, the notion of the mercantile system as a circumscribed body of doctrines has been repeatedly corrected; and at length (as shown above) Oncken declared that mercantilism was nothing more than a vague principle of applied economics. But F. K. Mann, in his "Critique of the Mercantile System" (this is the subtitle of *Der Marschall Vauban und die Volkswirtschaftslehre des Absolutismus*, Munich and Leipzig, 1914), empties the child out with the bath-water when he maintains that mercantilism did not really exist either as a theory or as a policy, and that the concept is an untenable one even as a historical hypothesis. This view simply ignores the foundations of mercantilism, which are at once psychological, historical, economic, and political (see Observation 2). Since these foundations actually existed, building upon them the "economists" of those days (endeavouring as they did to promote an advance from the medieval urban and natural economy to a unified national economy) conceived the notion of the balance of trade, attached excessive importance to money, studied the effects of customs tariffs, examined the sources of national wealth, and favoured various kinds of State regulation—and thus came to form an incontestable and durable though somewhat loosely organised unity. It is a unity which cannot be shuffled out of the world by that which Mann wants to put in its place, the idea of an "economic doctrine of absolutism".—Zielenziger, on the other hand, is right, though somewhat too general in his phrasing, when he describes mercantilism as "nationalism with political and economic centralisation as its guiding principle".[1] Sombart has aptly characterised mercantilism as "the political economy of early capitalism", discerning as its central feature the pro-

[1] *Die alten deutschen Kameralisten*, Jena, 1914, p. 46.

ductive activities of commerce. Commerce, says Sombart (1) "supplied the nations with the quantities of hard cash indispensable to the development of capitalism"; (2) "served to distribute to other countries the surplus produce of the land in any one country", thanks to which process the industrial potentialities of the soil were developed as well as the purely agricultural; and (3) "flooded the countries of western Europe with the products of lands across the sea, and with the articles which the countries of central and eastern Europe were willing to exchange for these exotics".[1]

Observation 2. As regards the social philosophy of the mercantile system, in its favouring of centralisation and the omnipotence of the State, it is in harmony with the individualist doctrine of natural right (see below, pp. 53 et seq.), and it also shares the rationalist and materialist leanings of the representatives of this trend. In so far as mercantilism would tolerate in the fullest possible measure the continued existence of corporations and guilds, and would everywhere initiate regulative measures on behalf of the common weal, the doctrine, on the other hand, appears to be one of liaison, to be a universalist system; it would seem to regard the national economy, not as an abstract sum-total of separate economic entities, but as a single politically organised aggregate. This is a matter for subsequent explanation (see below, pp. 59 et seq.).

2. LITERATURE OF MERCANTILISM

In France, the chief theoretical exponents of mercantilist doctrine were: Jean Bodin (*Six livres de la république*, 1577), the first explicit advocate of mercantilist measures; and Montchrétien (*Traité de l'économie politique*, 1615), the first writer to use the term "political economy".

In England a masterpiece of mercantilist literature is Thomas Mun's *England's Treasure by Foreign Trade*, written at various times from about 1622 to 1628, but not published till 1664, after Mun's death. The author recommends the export of bullion for use in foreign trade. His book, a small one, is especially well fitted to give the student an insight into the

[1] Werner Sombart, *Der moderne Kapitalismus*, second edition, Munich, 1917, vol. ii, part ii, p. 1042. See also pp. 938 et seq.

mercantilist mind. (Reprinted in 1895 by Macmillan, and in 1928 by the Economic History Society.)—Sombart drew attention to the importance of Davenant († 1714).—A notable book is *Compendious or Brief Examination of Certain Ordinary Complaints of Divers of our Countrymen in these our Days*, etc., "by W. S., Gentleman". [The authorship is uncertain. Absurdly enough, it was long supposed that "W. S." was William Shakespeare, who was only seventeen when the book was published in 1581. Then a more or less hypothetical William Stafford was put forward as begetter. There is considerable reason to suppose that the *Examination* was penned by John Hales, who was M.P. for Preston in 1548, and that its publication (like that of Mun's book) was held up for a generation.] The writer's interest centres on the great rise in prices to which allusion has already been made; he recognises its cause in the influx of the precious metals from the American mines; and, in general, he expounds comprehensively the principles of the earlier English mercantilists.—Other books deserving special mention are: Josiah Child, *Brief Observations concerning Trade and Interest of Money*, 1668; and James Steuart (1712–1780), *An Inquiry into the Principles of Political Economy*, 1767. Steuart was one of the most distinguished theoreticians and systematists of the mercantilist school, but wrote at a time when mercantilism was already being superseded by physiocratism and the doctrines of Adam Smith, so that his writings were regarded with scant respect in his day. He rejects the idea that wealth is identical with a hoard of the precious metals; in his doctrine of prices and in his theory of population, he is a forerunner of Malthus.

Among Italian mercantilists, I must name Serra and Montanari (both flourished about 1650), Belloni (*Dissertationi supra il commercio*, 1750), and Genovesi (*Lezioni di commercio ossia di economia civile*, 1765).

In Germany, mercantilism makes its appearance linked with what is known as "Kameralwissenschaft" (derived from "camera", a prince's treasury), as an amalgam of economic theory, financial policy, the science of government, and a modicum of technology; for the German mercantilists did not confine their interest to economics proper, but were also concerned with the study of the financial administration of the territorial princes, the management of industry, and the problems of mining. Among the earlier members of the school may be mentioned: Obrecht (professor in Strasburg towards 1600); Besold; and Kaspar Klock. A rigid type of mercantilism, though one modified by Aristotelian and scholastic ideas, was expounded by the younger cameralists: Seckendorff (*Der deutsche Fürstenstaat*, 1656); Joachim Becher (an especially noteworthy figure among the German mercantilists, author of *Politischer Diskurs von den eigentlichen Ursachen des Auf- und Abnehmens der Städter, Länder und Republiken*, 1668); W. von Hornigk (author of *Oesterreich über alles, wenn es nur will*, 1684, which Oncken believed to be a posthumous work of Becher's); Schröder (*Fürstliche Schatz- und Rentenkammer*, 1686); Justi (*Staatswirtschaft*, 1755); and Sonnenfels (*Grundsätze der Polizei, Handlung und Finanzwissenschaft*, 1763–1767). —Consult Axel Nielsen, *Die Entstehung der deutschen Kameralwissenschaft*, Jena 1911; Louise Sommer, *Die oesterreichischen Mercantilisten*, 2 vols., Vienna, 1920–1925; G. Jahn, "Mercantilismus", in *Handwörterbuch der Staatswissenschaften*, fourth edition.

3. A Critique of Mercantilist Doctrines, with an Introduction to Present-day Views on Money and on the Balance of Trade

Present-day economists hold conflicting views about mercantilism. Those who object on principle to State interference in economic matters (individualists and free-traders) are severely critical of the mercantile system; but those who hold that the State should actively promote economic development are, for practical purposes at least, closely akin to the mercantilists, seeing that to-day the problems that confronted the latter are again pressing for solution, and demand the adoption of measures resembling those to which they had recourse.

The leading doctrine of the mercantile system was that it was essential to establish a favourable balance of trade. Since this is primarily concerned with the significance of an inflow of money, let us first consider the theory of money.

a. Money. The mercantilists have often been accused of regarding money and wealth as equivalents. This charge is false, but they unquestionably formed a very high estimate of the economic importance of money and the precious metals, inclining to regard money as the "good of goods", which was natural enough at a time when a monetary and capitalist economy was in its early ascendant phase.

In a somewhat diluted form, this over-valuation of money persists to-day in the popular mind. To "make money" is, in ordinary parlance, synonymous with acquiring wealth; and political economy is often supposed to be mainly concerned with "making money". How far is this true? Contemporary science is not able to give a simple and straightforward answer to such a question; nor is it able to answer in any simple manner the more general questions that arise in connexion with the mercantilist doctrine of money. The answer cannot be deduced either from what is termed the metallist or from what is termed the chartalist theory of money. In the metallist view, the metallic nature of money as a commodity is the essential thing about it; whereas the chartalists insist especially upon the symbolic nature of money, this characteristic betokening either the nature of money as a State product or else some other relation of money to the whole body economic (see below, pp. 285 et seq.).

α. From the metallist standpoint, some such judgment as the following is passed upon the mercantilist conception of wealth. The essence of money is its function as medium of exchange. To make this clear, let us picture a circumscribed domestic economy A, which itself produces all the goods needed by the kinship. Still, it will often happen that the economic body A will be glad to exchange superfluous goods (an overplus of salt, for instance) for the superfluous goods (cattle or weapons, let us suppose) of the economic bodies B,

C, etc. But if, in the places where opportunities for such exchanges occur—at the "market", in a word—cattle and weapons are offered, but none of those with these things to dispose of happen at the moment to have any need of salt, the members of the economic body A will soon become aware of the advantages inherent in a mediate process of exchange; they will perceive the desirability of exchanging their salt for those commodities which enter most frequently into the process of exchange, for those which play leading roles in the market because any one who comes there is likely to want them. Such articles (cattle, for example, among nomads) are the most "marketable", and corporation A will, in the case we are considering, find it expedient to exchange its salt for cattle even though it has not itself any present use for cattle, seeing that cattle is most likely to be exchangeable in the near future for something that is actually wanted. This "acceptance of the most marketable commodities" (Smith, Ricardo, Karl Menger), even by those who do not need them for actual use, accounts for the origin and perhaps explains the fundamental nature of money, which is an intermediary in exchange, a means or medium of exchange. In the perennial competition for the right to perform this service, to function as this medium, the precious metals have—owing to their superior marketability, constancy and durability, divisibility, ponderability, and transportability—gained the victory over cattle, pearls, shells, hides, and all other commodities.

From such an outlook, the veneration of the mercantilists for money and the precious metals seems utterly wrong-headed. Money is but a commodity like any other; there can be no sense in hunting this commodity in especial, no reason for directing commercial policy mainly towards its acquisition. Besides, according to Ricardo and the latter-day economists who share his views, the only result of increasing the amount of money in the country would be to raise prices. If you double the quantity of money in circulation, you will halve the purchasing power of money; prices will rise accordingly; thereupon exports will decline and imports will increase; with the result that money will flow out of the country. If this reasoning be sound, there is an intrinsic contradiction in the plan for promoting an influx of money by means of a favourable balance of trade. (For further information regarding this "quantity theory of money", see below, pp. 288 et seq.)

β. What is known as the chartalist (sometimes unfortunately, because ambiguously, termed "nominalist") doctrine of money is less simple than the metallist doctrine (in this connexion, see the remarks below under Knapp, p. 286, and under Adam Müller, p. 158); but at any rate it conflicts with the quantity theory of money. According to the chartalists, the essence of money does not lie in its quality as a commodity; for they hold that cattle, for instance, when functioning as money have ceased to be cattle properly speaking, to become the sustainers of a specific function, that of betokening money, so that in them now their symbolic nature eclipses their qualities as commodities for use. Nor does the essence of money lie in its capacity for functioning as an instrument of exchange, but rather in its power of linking detached economic bodies, and enabling them to come to terms one with another (as to the views of various authors concerning this matter, see below, p. 285). Owing to this abstractly connective power of money (which is inherent in its relation to the economic community as a whole), money acquires "derivative functions" which are supplementary to its function as medium of exchange. These supplementary functions of money may be enumerated as follows: 1. as an article of general reference, that is to say as a measure of prices; 2. as a means of payment (payment is not always directly associated with exchange—for instance, the payment of taxes, or of the interest on capital); 3. as a means for the storing of value or capital (hoarding, etc.); 4. as a means for the transfer of capital, that is to say real goods, property (circulation). In general terms we may say that thanks to these functions money becomes the associater (organiser) and sustainer (representative) of goods of wealth. The assembling of money is, therefore, the indirect assembling of goods; and the transference of money is the indirect transference of goods.—Consequently, the chartalist schools can approve the mercantilist view that an influx of money signifies an increase in wealth. Nevertheless this outlook involves a danger of isolating money unduly, of detaching it from the economy at large, of misunderstanding its nature. Money can perform the function of representing property, only in so far as goods capable of being exchanged stand behind it to back it up. For, economically, money only has value in the same sort of way as that in which other intermediary and organising things have value; railways, for instance, or commercial treaties, which can respectively achieve something only in so far as there are commodities to be transported, or as there is business to be done between the two parties to the treaty. Money has no significance except as intermediary in the exchanges of commodities one for another. When exchangeable goods are wanting, as in war-time, during famine, or on the high seas, money becomes functionless.

Having grasped this fact, we are in a position to measure alike the weakness and the strength of mercantilism. Here is the weakness. For individuals, in private economic life, money is a commodity which can be exchanged for all other goods; it is "property" or "wealth" because for the individual who possesses it its potentialities of exchange make it the key to all storehouses. But in the economic life of a nation the accumulation of money has a different significance: here the matter of primary importance is that there should be on hand goods whose exchange can be effected by the money; failing this, the functioning of money as medium of exchange does not keep pace with the accumulation of money. Thus, in answer to the assertion that money is equivalent to wealth, it is necessary to insist that the primary constituent of wealth is not money, but goods and their production.—Here is the strength. The mercantilists did not fall into the crude error of regarding money, qua money, as wealth. They knew perfectly well (as Oncken has rightly pointed out in his *Geschichte der National-ökonomie*, vol. i, pp. 154 et seq.) that money is only wealth in virtue of its capacity for effecting transfers of property.

However, with this account of the representative function of money we have as yet said very little in defence of mercantilism. Cannot we find more cogent reasons for its support? Yes, we can find them in the stimulus to production which is given by an increase in money. Mercantilist statesmen and writers had good grounds for keeping before their eyes the growing need for money characteristic of the days in which they lived; they learned a lesson from their study of the quickening effects of an increase in the circulating medium—an increase that was, above all, essential to the transition from a more or less natural economy (that of the medieval towns, and of agriculture subject to the corvée) to a commencing capitalist and mercantile economy. The underlying purpose of the attempts to achieve a favourable balance of trade and thus to increase the amount of money in a country, was, both in theory and in practice, a determination to favour and protect national labour.

Observation 1. The mercantilists were neither metallists nor chartalists. They had no clearly formulated theory of money. True, they regarded money as concentrated wealth. But they did not contemplate money in the light of its nature as a commodity, or in the light of its function as medium of exchange. They looked on it as the sustainer of property; or, to express the matter in still more general terms, as the organiser of national economy, as capital of a higher grade. Herein they certainly transcended the metallism of the classical economists. (Regarding the concept of capital of a higher grade, see below, pp. 279 et seq.)

Observation 2. The above-mentioned functions of money are not granted equal recognition by all schools of economists. The function as means of payment, now regarded by Knapp as primary, and in earlier days thrust into the foreground by Knies and others, seems to me only a derivative form of the function as means of exchange.

Observation 3. As we have already learned, the classical economists, criticising the mercantilists, declared that money was but a commodity like any other—cooking utensils, for example. The contention is erroneous. Money is, beyond question, a "commodity" of a special kind; it is the commodity which forms the connecting link between all others, and is in this sense the leading or organising commodity. (See below, pp. 285 et seq.)

b. The Balance of Trade. The mercantilist view as to the balance of trade (balance of commodities) is intimately linked with the mercantilist doctrine of money. Before we begin our critical examination of the former, we must adjust its formulation by pointing out that the balance of trade, the balance between imports and exports, is not identical with the balance between the sums of money that cross the frontier in either direction—the so-called balance of payments.

For, in fact, this latter balance does not comprise only the discharge of the liabilities incurred for actual deliveries of goods. It includes, in addition: 1. the balance of payments for such services as are performed in the transport of foreign goods by water or by land ("England is the carrier of Europe"), or in the maintenance of travellers for the purposes of foreign trade—these services being in the nature of invisible deliveries of goods; 2. the balance of entrepreneurs' profits as between home and abroad; 3. the balance of the payment of interest as between home and abroad (on securities, notwithstanding debts, and so on); 4. the balance of the sendings of money and the movements of capital (such as the movements of capital in inter-State loans, or the taking over of foreign securities and loans); 5. to conclude, legacies, gifts, war indemnities, and similar once-for-all payments that pass from one country to another.—It is obvious, therefore, that the balance of payments can be regarded as a masked and enlarged balance of imports and exports, seeing that in the end "goods" are always paid for by "goods", exports by imports, and conversely; but some of these "goods" are invisible, i.e. are services.

Inasmuch as the balance of payments has quite another visage than the balance of concrete exports and imports, it is possible, nay it often actually happens, that the balance of payments may be "favourable" to a country while the balance of exports and imports is "unfavourable". Such was the position of affairs before the war in Britain, Germany, France, Belgium, and Austria-Hungary—the rich countries, in a word.

These wealthy lands are able to endure the persistence of an unfavourable balance between imports and exports because the payment of interest by foreign debtors, the sums received as profit on investments in foreign enterprises, and so on, enable them to go on paying for the excess of imports. For example, before the war, Germany alone used to receive in interest a sum which has been estimated at half a milliard of gold marks. Russia, on the other hand, being an agrarian country, and also the Balkan States and Argentina, had in pre-war days a "favourable" balance of trade, and so had the United States of America, for these countries had to devote the amounts realised by the sale of their harvests to the payment of interest to foreigners and to discharging liabilities incurred for services rendered by foreigners.

The foregoing considerations make it clear that a debit balance of trade, called by the mercantilists an "unfavourable" balance, may be unfavourable in one case and favourable in another.

The outlooks of modern science upon the theory of the balance of trade are three in number:

1. Those who adhere to the doctrines of what is known as the classical school contend that the idea of the balance of trade cannot be looked on as authoritative. The balance of trade, they say, is only the sum-total of all private balances. The general course of economic life as between nations is but the aggregate of the movements of a great number of individual economies, and not the expression of specific relations between one nation and another. Economically, therefore, it makes no difference whatever whether two persons who do business with one another belong to the same nation (residing, let us suppose, in London and in Manchester), or two different nations (a Londoner and a Parisian). If this standpoint be accepted, it is quite arbitrary to lump one group of balances together rather than another; there is no more reason for doing so in the case of London and Manchester, than in the case of London and Paris.—Thus to the adherents of the classical school the doctrine of the balance of trade seems devoid of a stable theoretical foundation.[1] As previously explained, they consider that the circulation of money regulates itself automatically in a way that confutes the doctrine of the balance of trade. If, thanks to a favourable trade balance, more money flows into a country, the quantity of money in that country increases, with the result that prices there rise, and become higher than prices in other countries (quantity theory of money), so that there is an increase of imports from the countries where prices are lower. For these reasons it is better for governments to refrain from interfering with the course

[1] Cf. Petritsch, *Theorie der günstigen und ungünstigen Handelsbilanz*, Graz, 1902; Terhalle, "Handelsbilanz", in *Handwörterbuch der Staatswissenschaften*, fourth edition.

of trade. (The "free-trade theory", see below, pp. 104–5
and 140–1.)

2. Those who belong to the historical school adopt an intermediate standpoint. They are not indifferent to the balance of
trade, but they consider that the mercantilists overrated its
importance, and applied the doctrine in too routinist a fashion.
Still, in the days when the mercantile system was dominant,
it had considerable practical utility, for only through having
a credit balance in the matter of foreign trade were those
countries that were striving to emerge from a natural economy
able to pay their debts abroad and to increase the amount of the
circulating medium at home. But to-day the wealthiest countries
have a debit balance in foreign trade (see above, p. 46).

3. Those, finally, who belong to the universalist schools
unreservedly accept the doctrine of the balance of trade.
From the outlook of his own universalist conception, the
author of the present work would insist that the balance of
trade and the balance of payments can by no means be regarded as "aggregates" of private balances. On the contrary,
the "private balances" (the term, be it noted, is a misleading
one) are only conceivable as parts of the balance of trade and
balance of payments. The independent whole of the nationally
organised economy has its own independent balance, the
balance of trade and payments, on which the individual
balances depend for their conditions of existence. It is therefore
correct to say that the total balance takes precedence of the
individual balance.[1]

Only by setting out from this proposition, is it possible to
do full justice to mercantilist thought, to recognise the large
measure of truth which the mercantile system contains. When
we do this we recognise that the above-described expansion of

---

[1] A more detailed discussion of the matter will be found in the author's
Tote und lebendige Wissenschaft, third edition, Jena, 1929, pp. 129 et seq.

the idea of the balance of trade (balance of commodities) to a balance of payments—which to-day is supposed to give mercantilism its quietus—is merely a rectification of a concept, and by no means suffices to "confute" the mercantile system. The problem is merely transferred to the balance of payments. The balance of trade must indeed be grounded upon the balance of payments; but only because the balance of payments is itself, in the last analysis, nothing else than an enlarged balance of commodities (and services). Even when the balance of payments is a credit balance, the balance of trade may show a debit, as we learned above on p. 46; yet there must be a concrete substratum for this credit balance of payments, a substratum having the nature of goods of some kind (e.g. capital invested abroad). That is the first great and lasting truth of the mercantilist doctrine of the balance of trade.— The second truth of the mercantilist doctrine of the balance of trade is this, that the economic agents, the persons doing business one with another, must not be regarded as individuals in any abstract sense, nor must their balances be conceived as abstract "private" balances; the persons and the balances must be looked upon as members of a national economic corporation which forms, to a degree, a unity or a totality.

If, as above shown, the balance of trade be something different from a sum-total of all private balances, and not merely something which has no existence until all these private balances have been added together, then it cannot be regarded as a matter of indifference whether the places whence the individual items of the account are drawn be situated at home or abroad. Nay, rather in the mutual interrelations of exchange among the various national economies endowed with independent actuality, there existed—before any particular balance was struck—determinative factors in virtue of which that balance became what it did become. Let the reader recall the incidents of the period of inflation, when, owing to the crashing of the currency, all private balances were undergoing rapid modification, and it was far from indifferent to a merchant in Berlin whether he incurred a debt in Hamburg or in London! In these cases it was manifest that a "private" balance was not really private, but was an intrinsic part of the general "national" or collective balance. The relatively independent national economy with its total balance comes first, logically; and the partial or separate balances come afterwards.

Of course we must not, for this reason, regard foreign trade as the true and original source of wellbeing for the national economy, though some of the mercantilists were inclined to do this; for foreign trade is itself, generally speaking, grounded on the home production of goods.

Consequently, all the difficulties of this chapter may be solved as follows. The "balance of trade" is a genuinely collective concept, but our direct concern is not with whether there is a credit or a debit balance in the case of payments, and still less whether there is a credit or a debit balance in the case of exports and imports. What matters is that which I may term the balance of productivity, that which forms the material substratum of and gives a meaning to the credits and the debits. The mere figures of the balance of trade signify nothing to us; they have to be translated into actual performances within the national economy, they must be reduced from quantities and magnitudes to meanings. Credits, for instance, due to a "clearance sale", as in Germany during the inflation crisis, are harmful; debits, on the other hand, incurred for productive purposes are beneficial. It follows that a balance of payments showing a debit even for decades in succession, need not be a sign of impoverishment. If the debts are incurred, not to pay for current consumption, but in order that the money may be invested in improving the land and in building factories, they will increase production and promote public welfare. Hence, it is not the coming in or the going out of quantities of goods that is important, but the "meaning" of these processes; the question whether the goods be fruitfully or unfruitfully articulated into the general structure of the national economy; this and the results upon that economy, the ultimate effects of the imports and exports, are what really matter.

One of the flaws in mercantilism was that its champions were often inclined to regard the mutual relations between the various national economies from the outlook of individualist economics (cutthroat competition), assuming that for the sake of its own enrichment each nation must strive to outwit and overreach its neighbours, and fancying that life on such terms would be an enduring possibility! This is not a tenable view. Just as every national economy is a whole dependent upon the fruitful mutuality of its parts, so the world economy is a super-whole dependent upon the fruitful mutuality of the national economies which constitute its parts. The essential characteristic of the world economy is not that one nation gains what another loses, but that both gain by mutuality.—In practice, however, this error was corrected, inasmuch as the favourable balance of trade had to be backed up by a most rigorous development of a nation's own economic energies. Thus mercantilism, notwithstanding all its defects, was a splendid conception of economic life as a truly integrated entity, a conception which led to the inauguration of many methods of State-aid in the economic field that are still models for to-day.

Associated with this unduly individualist attitude of the mercantilists in certain respects, was a tendency to appraise economic processes too much in accordance with their monetary form, instead of simply in accordance with their factual content, in accordance with their effective achievement.

c. *"Keeping Money in the Country."* This slogan, which was revived during the late war, is a corollary of the doctrine of the balance of trade. Thus Hörnigk, in *Oesterreich über alles, wenn es nur will*, writes: "It would be better to pay for any article two thalers that would remain in the country, than one only that would go abroad."—Let us illustrate this way of thinking by considering a State loan for railway construction. In such a case, "keeping money in the country" means: first, that the demand for funds is supplied out of the savings of persons resident in the country; next, that the productive and trading activities called into being by the expenditure of the money are also within the national boundaries, because all orders are placed in the homeland. But the important matter is the application of labour and capital at home, and not merely that "money is kept in the country". Still, even though, thanks to keeping money in the country, home labour is employed instead of foreign labour, we are not entitled to conclude without further enquiry that it might not have been more advantageous to the country if the orders had been placed abroad. Conditions may be such that capital and labour have been expended on producing things which might have been procured from abroad in exchange for domestic products obtained by an expenditure of one tenth of the amount of capital and labour. Only, therefore, when the production of the necessary articles at home does not cost more than their production abroad, or at least when the development of home productive forces and entrepreneurs' capital entails advantages that unquestionably outweigh the losses due to the comparative dearness of home production, can we say that it is an advantage "to have the money kept in the country", and therefore to employ home labour instead of foreign labour.

As to the connexion between the rate of exchange and the balance of payments, see below, pp. 291 et seq.

CHAPTER THREE

INDIVIDUALIST NATURAL RIGHT

WHILE the mercantile system was in course of development, in the domains of political science and philosophy an individualist conception of human social life was gathering force.

The general impression is that the Saxon Althusius (*Politica*, 1603) [1] and the Dutchman Hugo Grotius (*De jure belli et pacis*, 1625) were the founders of an individualist outlook in political science. But notions of the same sort are to be met with in the writings of the medieval nominalists and in the *Defensor pacis* (1324) penned jointly by Marsilius of Padua and John of Jandun. Marsilius advocates popular sovereignty in State and Church. Althusius develops the idea that the State is the outcome of a contract freely entered into by its members, although the "social nature" of mankind is an additional determining cause. Grotius sets out from the "inalienable and indestructible natural rights of the individual", deducing them, however, from the "originally social nature of man", so that in his opinion likewise the social principle collaborates in the foundation of natural right. He explains that the individual's "natural right" is a commandment of reason, in accordance wherewith necessity is automatically ascribable to an action in virtue of its harmony with the reasonable nature of man.

Natural right is a permanently valid and homogeneous right, inherent in human nature, formed by rational exercise, and recognisable by reason. From this outlook, reason becomes a power that generates right—the reason of the individual, of

---

[1] Cf. Otto von Giercke, *Johannes Althusius und die Entwicklung der naturrechtlichen Staatstheorien*, third edition, Breslau, 1913.

the abstract and atomically conceived individual. Natural right, therefore, is an individual right, a right that is equally unsocial and unhistorical. (The rationalism of natural right.)

But the natural right of more recent days is substantiated in a different way: either upon the individual alone (pure individualism); or else with the aid of social, that is to say universalist, elements (modified forms of individualism).[1]

The English philosopher Thomas Hobbes (whose chief work, *Leviathan*, was published in 1651), was the first to interpret the political life of human beings in a rigidly individualist fashion in accordance with the principle of natural right.[2] Hobbes recognises only the instinct of self-preservation. He starts with the assumption that in a state of nature all individuals are free and self-dependent; and that, as an outcome of this, they are perforce mutually hostile. Men are dominated by their dread of one another, and there is a war of all against all ("bellum omnium contra omnes"). To escape from that struggle for existence, they establish the State, join forces in an orderly association—and they do this, therefore, under the promptings of the instinct of self-preservation, and not, as Grotius opined, because the nature of mankind is social. By this step they renounce all their natural rights, and delegate them to an absolute ruler, under whose protection they place themselves. Thus the State, originating by a contract, comes into being as an absolutist construction, the renunciation of natural right being a primal element of the contract. But conceptually the State proceeds exclusively from the individual, who is self-dependent.

[1] I am not referring in the text to the concessions and reserves to be found in the writings of all the modern champions of natural right, whether on religious grounds, or on grounds of historical necessity. We are concerned only with the systematising features of the views put forward by each writer or school of writers.—Cf., for instance, Hobbes, *Leviathan*, chapter xiv.

[2] *Leviathan*, loc. cit.

These ideas of Hobbes were taken up by Spinoza (1632–1677). According to the latter, the original war of all against all does not lead to the establishment of an absolute authority. The citizens surrender their natural freedoms only in so far as is necessary for the existence of an orderly political life-in-common.—Thus whereas Hobbes considers that the authority of the State is vested in a single person, Spinoza ascribes it to all the members of the body politic, to the people at large. But both these writers look upon the State as the outcome of a struggle for power among individuals.

In Germany, Samuel Pufendorf (*De jure naturae et gentium*, 1672) endeavoured to find a middle course between Hobbes' purely individualist theory of natural right and Grotius' view which was partly social. The English philosopher John Locke (*On Civil Government*, 1689) put forward a milder version of the Hobbesian theory of a state of nature. He was the real founder of the theory of constitutional law. In the field of political economy, he laid stress on the importance of human labour in the creation of value, thus giving utterance to an idea which professional economists were to develop at a later date.

From Locke sprang the so-called philosophy of the Enlightenment, an arid rationalism (its watchword was the "rational shaping of human life"), which was by its very nature subjectivist, atomistic, mechanistic, and from the sociological standpoint individualistic. In England, there grew up from this root the teaching of Shaftesbury, whose leading notion was "common sense"; and in France, the sensualism and materialism of Diderot, Condillac, Helvetius, and others, which influenced the whole of Europe.

Closely connected with these theories of natural right and the social contract, is the development of the doctrine of sovereignty, to which Jean Bodin had earlier given precise formulation (as princely sovereignty) in his book *De la république* (1577). More and more this doctrine developed towards the idea of popular sovereignty, as we see beginning already in the work of Althusius. According to the exponents of the latter notion, the people is the one and only source of State authority, inasmuch as the contract whereby the State was formed issued from the general will of all the citizens, freely assembled. Hobbes, however, considered that the citizens, having come together of their own wills, then delegated authority to one supreme ruler. Montesquieu (*Esprit des lois*, 1748), with his doctrine of the partition of powers, enunciated a half-way theory, that of constitutionalism, which dominated political science for almost a century, and stood godfather to all the constitutions of Europe. According to this view, which still exerts considerable influence, the best form of State is that in which the legislative authority is in the hands of a freely elected assembly, parliament, while executive authority is committed to a monarch with responsible ministers, and judicial authority is entrusted to an independent body of judges.

In reality, however, the executive is also, to a predominant extent, the legislative authority, for most laws originate in the ministerial offices, and not in parliament at all. The demand for a partition of powers is a sign of decay, an indication of deficient unity and of an endeavour to mechanise political life.—It is an error to suppose that Montesquieu was an innovator. His immediate predecessor in formulating the doctrine of the partition of powers was John Locke. Moreover, the distinction between legislative, judicial, and executive powers is plainly indicated in Aristotle's *Politics* (B. vii, § 1), though Aristotle did not himself advocate the political severance of the three.

Jean Jacques Rousseau made a very powerful impression with his doctrine of the state of nature.

See *Du contrat social*, 1762, and *Emile, ou de l'éducation*, 1762. "Man is born free, but everywhere he is in chains." In a state of nature, human beings were good, free, and equal; civilisation has made them corrupt, unfree, and unequal. A return to a state of nature is essential. Since man is naturally good, we need merely remove misleading and vicious influences from his education, and he will spontaneously find his way back to the natural and to God. In *Emile*, Rousseau writes: "Wherever human beings are born, they can be made what I indicate."—Rousseau's conception of the State is that of the champions of natural right, but his individualism contains anti-individualist elements. Take, for instance, his idea of the general will ("volonté générale") as a counterpart to the will of all individuals ("volonté de tous"); and his idea of an obligatory State religion.—Rousseau is a vigorous and able writer, but his work bristles with contradictions. In some respects an ardent individualist, he nevertheless espouses the view that education is all-powerful, and coins the notion of "volonté générale". He must indeed be described as an a-logical, and in many ways an a-moral man. (He took his children to the foundling hospital!)—Rousseau's writings contributed in no small measure to the outbreak of the French revolution in 1789. The leading revolutionists, and Robespierre in especial, were his disciples. His influence upon European culture was likewise notable because, since he introduced into his teaching an irrational element (return to nature), he was an early apostle of a departure from the exclusive rationalism of the Enlightenment.

In the foregoing account of natural right, reference has only been made to the individualist and comparatively modern use of the term. But in earlier days "natural right" had a non-individualist significance, denoting "divine natural right", that is to say the divine ordering of right and the world ($\delta\ell\kappa\alpha\iota\sigma\nu$ $\phi\dot{\upsilon}\sigma\epsilon\iota$, lex naturalis = lex divina, jus divinum, divine right), as contrasted with the mutable and arbitrary right made manifest in the course of history ($\delta\ell\kappa\alpha\iota\sigma\nu$ $\vartheta\dot{\epsilon}\sigma\epsilon\iota$, the "established" or "conventional right" of the sophists). Heraclitus expresses this outlook clearly: "All human laws are nourished by a divine". Divine or super-individual natural right is expounded by Plato, Aristotle, the stoics, and Thomas Aquinas. According to Plato, the laws of this world are a direct efflux from the divine will; the divine law, the moral law inborn in man, is a part thereof; and positive right is no more than a deduction from this moral law. The "naturalness" of right signifies, in the case of divine natural right, its derivation from the objective laws of the world, from the objective social order, from objective morality and justice—in contradistinction to the derivation from absolute individuals in a state of nature (as in the teaching of the sophists, Grotius, and Hobbes).—When rigidly formulated, therefore, the antithesis between universalist natural right and individualist, may be expressed as follows: on the one hand, we have a social right, divine, super-individual right, as an order which is binding upon all, and assigns to all and sundry their suitable positions in the aggregate; and, on the other hand, an individual right, individualist natural right, as a reasonable right of the essentially independent individual.

CHAPTER FOUR

AN INTRODUCTION TO THE BASIC PROBLEM OF SOCIOLOGY — INDIVIDUALISM VERSUS UNIVERSALISM

THE individualist theory of natural right is something more than a theory of right; it is likewise a theory of the State and of social life in general. The main purport of any such theory of society must be to tell us upon what society is based. Is it based on the individual; or is it based on an objective spiritual reality, upon something which must be conceived as an aggregate of a peculiar kind on a higher plane than the individual and therefore super-individual?

From the former outlook, society would be regarded as the summation of independent individuals: as comparable to a concourse of atoms, to a heap of stones, in which every atom or stone remains independent, self-determined as it were, leading a separate existence; and in which the association of the parts has produced no more than a superficial and purely mechanical community. In that case, individuals form the real and primary being of society and the State. This conception is called "individualism", because it is one according to which society and the State are thought of exclusively in terms of the individual ;[1] and natural right is its chief type. But in every type of individualism, the individual is the main thing, not the community. Individualism has its own conception of right, apart from any assumption that there exists a society sui generis contraposed to the individual.—Individualism, which was already cultivated in antiquity by the

---

[1] Individualism is an analytical theory, not a political method, nor yet a philosophy, and it must therefore be distinguished from its politico-economical and philosophical consequences. The same remark applies to universalism.

sophists, and was fully developed in the form of natural right, seems at the first glance perfectly natural and self-evident. For society is in actual fact composed of individual human beings. None the less, we have to test the soundness of the doctrine. Close examination shows that it starts from false premises, is grounded upon erroneous notions both of the individual and of society. The individualist (regarding the individual as independent of society and as the founder of society) necessarily looks upon the individual as a self-determined, self-governing and separate atom; he thinks of the individual as mentally complete before entering into definite social ties; he conceives the individual to have an absolute existence, and to be capable of a self-centred life. In conformity with this outlook, society is imagined to be a purely mechanical aggregation of individuals; it is not looked upon as something which has a peculiar entity of its own, but is regarded as a mere summation—as, so to say, a sort of mutual assurance corporation formed by individuals. Both these premises are false. The individual is not mentally self-governing; and society is not a mere summation, is not a purely mechanical agglomeration, of such individuals.

The view that is the counterpart of individualism is known as universalism. Universalists contend that the mental or spiritual associative tie between individuals exists as an independent entity; that it is super-individual and primary, whereas the individual is derivative and secondary. In the history of the mind, universalism has played an even more important part than individualism. At first sight, perhaps, universalism may seem a little fantastic and extravagant, implying that the individual has no mental self-sufficiency. But, when we look into the matter more closely, we see that only from the universalist outlook can we really understand what the individual is, spiritually considered. According to universalist doctrine, the individual does not derive his intrinsic essence, his mental or spiritual being and nature, from himself qua individual; he is only able to form himself, is only able to build up his personality, when in close touch with others like unto himself; he can only create and sustain himself as a being endowed with mentality or spirituality, when he enjoys intimate and multiform communion with other beings similarly endowed. In every spiritual community, whether between mother and child, teacher and pupil, husband and wife, friend and friend, thinker and critic, there arise cognitions, feelings, and powers, which cannot be regarded as the outcome of a purely mechanical exchange, but are created by a reciprocal process of mental stimulation. Thus spiritual community is the true source of life for the individual, the air which the individual must breathe lest he perish.—Regarded in this light, "society" discloses itself to be a real entity, and we see that it is a living response from mind to mind, a spiritual association among the many, in and through which the individual for the first time achieves birth as a spiritual being, to attain his real selfhood as a reasoning and cultivated personality. "Society", consequently, ceases to be a mere agglomeration of absolutely independent individuals, a union in an outward sense only into which the components enter in a finished state; it is a spiritual entity sui generis, a necessary precondition of the life of the individual, and for this reason perforce an entirely ethical and not a merely "utilitarian" structure. Society stands on a higher plane than do individuals, inasmuch as it is the creative spiritual interlacement of individuals, the form under which individual life can alone come to full fruition. Individuals may no longer be looked upon as self-sufficing and independent entities; the energy of their being inheres in their spiritual interconnexion, in the whole, the universality, the collectivity. Hence the name universalism or collectivism.

To-day there is a mistaken inclination to deny the importance of this contrast between individualism and universalism.
As a matter of fact, it is of decisive importance, alike in matters
of theory and in those of practice, whether the economist has
an individualist or a universalist conception of society. For,
no matter whether we are concerned with metallism versus
chartalism, free trade versus protection, competition versus
cooperation, private bargaining versus collective bargaining,
the principle of every man for himself versus that of organised
work for the community, self-help versus social reform—these
and other fundamental antitheses are not "political" problems,
nor yet "philosophical" problems; and the answer to be given
in each case will depend in large measure whether the analytical
investigation is undertaken from an individualist or a universalist standpoint. According as we are individualists or
universalists, our general conception of economic life will
vary in one direction or the other, so will our method of enquiry,
even our formulation of the main notions of our science, and
(finally) our theoretical attitude towards differing types of
economic and social endeavour.

Since for individualism, the individual forms the only
substratum of the State, individual liberty is the political
principle of the doctrine.—The extreme form of individualism
is, therefore, anarchism, or the absence of any kind of ruling
power; a second fundamental form is what I will term Machia-
vellism (after Niccolo Machiavelli, 1469–1527), the doctrine
that the stronger individual should subjugate the weaker;
the third form is the theory of the social contract, or natural
right. Of this latter, there are three political varieties; enlightened absolutism, (constitutional) liberalism, and democracy:
and three economic varieties; the theory of free competition,
that of the freedom of industry, and that of free trade. (See
below under Quesnay, pp. 80 et seq.; Smith, pp. 103 et seq.;
and Ricardo, pp. 140 et seq.)

The political principle of universalism is justice, the allotting
to every one his due ("distributive justice"). The aim of uni-

versalism is to uphold the collectivity, but only because this is regarded as the sustainer of the individual, who cannot achieve a spiritual and moral existence except as a member of the collectivity. The varieties of universalism are: the theocratic conception of the State; the organic conception of the State (the view that the State is a more or less concrete entity, a super-individual organism); the feudalist conception of the State (cf. Adam Müller, below, pp. 158 et seq.); conservatism (the endeavour to maintain extant ties, authorities, and institutions); the national ideal, the so-called solidarism (cooperation); protection, social reform, land reform, and even mercantilism, in so far as they all aspire to realise a certain community of economic activity. Socialism, too, aims at a thoroughgoing community of economic activity, but is none the less only a hybrid form (see below, pp. 210 et seq., and pp. 230 et seq.).

To summarise, we can explain as follows the distinction between individualism and universalism. The basic problem is, whether the spirituality (or mentality) which is the essence of human beings is generated by the individual out of himself, or can only be generated thanks to contact with another spirituality (or mentality)—that of other human beings. The view that the individual can derive the whole of his spiritual and moral existence out of himself alone, and that he is therefore self-sufficing, self-governing, an absolute individual, is individualism; the view that the spiritual and moral essentiality of the individual can only be achieved by and through communion with another intelligence, is universalism. Individualism is based on the notion of the independence, the isolation, and the liberty of the individual; universalism, on that of spiritual communion, because this latter ensures the maximum spiritual productivity of the ego.

History of Universalism. Plato regarded the State as a super-empirical institution, as an actual incarnation of the moral ideal. It seemed to him that the idea of the good was realised, was made concrete, in the State, which was itself an organism of a higher kind. Individuals are only members of this organism, and justice assigns to them their positions in it and their functions.—In Aristotle's writings, likewise, and in those of the medieval schoolmen who followed in his footsteps, the universalist notion of the State holds sway.

In the modern age, however, the individualism of natural right was set up in opposition to the universalism of classical antiquity and the Middle Ages (see above, pp. 53 et seq.). But the individualist conception of the State proved practically unworkable as well as conceptually inadequate. When men guarantee one another nothing more than security, economic injuries are sustained owing to the unsatisfactory position of the propertyless members of society, while spiritual and moral damage ensues in consequence of the backward development of community life in its various forms. Individuals compete ruthlessly one with another; the prevailing tone of mind is materialistic; the cultural and spiritual life of society lacks energy and go.

It was inevitable that people should in due time become aware of the insufficiency of such an outlook upon society. Accordant with the German temperament, in especial, was the profounder, universalist view as to the nature of the community; and it was thanks to this that the revival of universalism was preeminently the work of Germans. It was German philosophy which first, in the writings of Fichte and his successors, reestablished the genuine universalist conception of the higher solidarity of the members of the State (a solidarity transcending any that could be based on a mere utilitarian purpose), and grounded it this time upon a more solid foundation than that of earlier days. Those err, therefore, who speak of a "rebirth of the ancient idea of the State". This new philosophy did not set out from the collectivity, the State, in order to contrapose it as great and durable to the individual as small and transitory. It set out from the individual, to discover that the very nature of man is such that he can only be conceived as a plurality! Spiritual community is the creative whole in which the individual finds the abiding place and the mould of his existence and his higher development.

There is a long road still to travel before it will be possible to say that this notion has struck deep roots in our culture, has permeated our national consciousness, and has finally overthrown the old individualist error, whereby the individual has been simultaneously flattered and impoverished. Nevertheless, the new universalism has become the foundation of modern German social reform.—Cf. in this connexion the sections on romanticism, social reform, and the dispute concerning method (pp. 154 et seq., 240 et seq., and 279 et seq., respectively). A more detailed account of the nature of individualism and universalism will be found in my *Gesellschaftslehre* (second edition, Leipzig, 1923); and concerning its importance in political economy in my address *Vom Geist der Volkswirtschaftslehre* (reprinted as appendix to my *Fundament der Volkswirtschaftslehre*, fourth edition, Jena, 1929). See also *Tote und lebendige Wissenschaft*, third edition, Jena, 1929.

CHAPTER FIVE

TRANSITION TO THE PHYSIOCRATIC SYSTEM

1. THE CRITICS OF MERCANTILISM; JOHN LAW

THE politico-economical ties that underlay the mercantile system were to an ever-increasing extent unloosed by the victorious advance of individualism in the field of political theory and of rationalism and empiricism in the field of philosophy. The economic trend that was the outcome of the aforesaid intellectual forces, worked in the same direction. The bourgeoisie, gaining strength, did all it could to liberate itself from the tutelage of the absolute State, and the landed interest had to take up arms in its own defence. Of outstanding importance in France, moreover, was the continual menace of a collapse of the State finances; and there was a widespread belief that the methods of State regulation characteristic of mercantilism were in great part responsible for these fiscal difficulties. Outspoken critics of mercantilism speedily appeared.

First of all, let me mention Boisguillebert (*Détail de la France*, 1712). Espousing the cause of the neglected agriculturists, he inveighed against Colbert's prohibition of the export of grain, which, by keeping down the price of that staple, was ruining agriculture; and against the mercantilist confusion of economic wealth with the possession of the precious metals. He emphasised the importance of the working as compared with the non-working classes.—Marshal Vauban, whose chief desire was to reform the theory and practice of direct taxation (*Projet d'une dîme royale*, 1707), moved along the same line. He advocated an enlightened absolutism, and demanded protection for the working classes, as the main pillars of social welfare.—Among the other critics of mercantilism may be named: Cantillon; Gournay, the liberal, who was for a long time erroneously believed to have been the originator of the physiocratic slogan "Laissez faire, laisser passer"; and the Marquis d'Argenson, the first literary

champion alike of "laissez faire" and of free trade. Goods were
to move across frontiers "as freely as air and water".—In
England, William Petty (1623–1687), John Locke (1632–
1704), Dudley North (1641–1690), and others, entered the
lists against mercantilism. According to Locke, human labour
is to be regarded as the principal source of wealth; according
to Petty, labour and the land.

When Louis XIV died, in the year 1715, the interest on the
national debt exceeded the current revenue, and France was
actually insolvent. Philip of Orleans, who became regent, lent
ear to the bold schemes of the Scottish adventurer and financier
John Law.[1]

John Law put forward a credit theory of money, to the effect
that land would be better money than the precious metals gold
and silver (which fluctuate in value); that land would be the
best, the most stable measure of value. Of course land could
not be put into circulation. Mortgage-notes should therefore
be issued upon land, which would in this way be mobilised.
The only money used for domestic circulation (not for purposes of foreign trade, where metallic money would still be
needed) was to be paper money upon the security of land.
Paper money of this kind would be better than silver, for
"land is what produces everything, silver is only the product"
(*op. cit.*, p. 100). "Land cannot lose any of its uses," but
"silver may lose the use of money it is now applied to, so
to be reduced to its value as a metal. It may likewise lose
a part of its uses as a metal, these uses being supplied by other
goods; so loses a part of its value as a metal" (*op. cit.*, p. 101).
Law goes on to argue that increase of credit is tantamount to
the increase of actual money, so that credit is independent,
new capital. Especially characteristic of this view of his as to
the nature of credit is his famous utterance, "C'est au souverain

---

[1] *Money and Trade Considered, with a Proposal for Supplying the Nation
with Money*, Edinburgh, 1705.

à donner le crédit, et non à le recevoir" (the ruler—or, to express it more generally, the debtor—should give credit, and should not receive it!).

In France the regent, Duke Philip of Orleans, regarded Law's plan as the last hope of extricating the country from its financial embarrassments. In May 1716, the Banque Générale was founded as a private bank of Law's, with power to issue notes, and it was successful for a time. In 1717, the bank became associated with the Mississippi company (Compagnie de la Louisiane ou d'Occident), and in 1718 its notes became the State currency. Paper money was issued in vast quantities, though not in conformity with Law's original plan of a mortgage bank. The notes were not secured upon land, for Law had now come to the view that the State could issue notes on the strength of its own credit. After a brief period of intoxication, there came a panic and a financial crash in the year 1720. In 1721, Law fled the country, and the State was declared bankrupt in 1722. Law died at Venice, in penury, seven years later.

2. Critique of John Law's Theory. The Theory of Credit

Law's theory has once more become of importance to-day. Shortly after the war, plans akin to his for the hypothecating of land as security for inflated paper money were widely recommended; and at length, in 1923, in circumstances which bore an outward resemblance to those that obtained in early eighteenth-century France, the German "Rentenmark" was issued, secured by compulsory mortgages on agriculture and industry. But Law's mortgage-money is seen at the first glance to be vitiated by the lack of fluidity of the pledges. It must, however, be admitted that Law does, in a sense, anticipate the "banking principle" (see below, p. 291) when he writes: "This paper money will not fall in value as silver money has fallen, or may fall. Goods or money fall in value, if they increase in quantity, or if the demand lessens. But the

Commission, giving out what sums are demanded, and taking back what sums are offered to be returned, this paper money will keep its value, and there will always be as much money as there is occasion, or employment, for, and no more" (*op. cit.*, p. 89). And again: "The paper money proposed being always equal in quantity to the demand, the people will be employed, the country improved, manufacture advanced" (*op. cit.*, p. 102). But prices will not rise. The money he proposes "will keep its value, and buy the same quantity of goods fifty years hence as now, unless the goods alter in their value" (*op. cit.*, p. 90).

The fallacy in Law's credit theory of money lies in the Scottish financier's supposition that credit can engender a second, independent capital, and thus create a new and supplementary value; his belief that money can be replaced by symbols of credit. That is not so, although there have been institutions that have seemed to lend colour to such a belief. The famous issue of assignats during the French revolution was in part based on a similar view. So was the theory of the nineteenth-century Scottish economist, Henry Dunning Macleod (1821–1902, author of *Dictionary of Political Economy*, London, 1859–1863), who likewise regarded circulating credit as capital, explaining capital itself as "power of circulation". Law and Macleod are at one in maintaining that debtors have the faculty of creating money by their credit papers.[1] Nor, indeed, is Knapp's modern "State theory of money" (see below, under "Theory of Money", pp. 285 et seq.) far removed from the opinion of those for whom credit is equivalent to real capital, for it ascribes to paper money no more than a formal (that is to say unsubstantiated) purchasing power. It is very important to clear up this matter thoroughly.

A loan is made, or credit is given, when B supplies A with

---

[1] The same view has recently been put forward by A. Hahn, *Volkswirtschaftliche Theorie des Bankkredits*, second edition, Tübingen, 1924.

money or goods for which A offers no equivalent, but only promises to furnish an equivalent later. The promise may be in writing, as in the form of a bill of exchange (an especially rigid pledge of indebtedness), with which B can pay his debt to C!

If what is supplied on credit is consumed, we speak of "consumptive credit"; but if it is utilised for production, as for engaging additional workpeople, it is termed "productive credit". In what follows, only the latter form of credit is considered.—Banks are the chief purveyors of credit in modern times; and when they give credit, it is not usually in the form of hard money, but by transfer of an outstanding debt.

It is essential to any credit that is to bear fruit that A should set to work with the moneys or goods that have been saved—not in his own, but in another's economy. Yet in this way there is established a new tie, a new community, between two economies that were previously unassociated, the economy that has saved the moneys or goods, and the economy that is going to turn them to account. Between the two there exists a simple reciprocity, in so far as the lending economy (the saver, or the producer who hands over certain goods to the borrower) is dependent on the borrowing economy (to use the surpluses effectively), and the borrowing economy is dependent on the lending economy (to obtain fresh capital). On the other hand, there is also a gradation, inasmuch as the lending economy takes precedence to this extent, that the borrowing economy has not itself been competent to provide out of its own resources the surpluses that are needed for the extension or the continuance of the enterprise. To the degree, therefore, to which credit becomes necessary, the dictum applies that credit takes precedence of capital owned by the actual user—financial capital of industrial capital.

A second main feature of credit is the existence of a

considerable interval of time between the borrowing and the repayment. By this means, A is enabled to operate with goods which he does not himself own, but for which he will only have to pay in the future. Thanks to this, his economy casts its shadow before, works towards the future. Nay more, this working towards the future may reproduce itself again and again. By means of successive endorsements, one bill of exchange will enable B to pay C, and C to pay D, with A's promise to pay, this meaning that the lien upon A is transferred by B to C and by C to D. Of course C, D, etc., in view of the fact that the bill does not become payable for some weeks or months, will deduct a certain charge for lost interest, this being known as discount. But that leaves unaffected the remarkable fact that B's business acquaintances can discharge their liabilities to one another by means of A's debts! A final intensification of this phenomenon may occur, when D is a bank, and buys the bill of C with banknotes, this meaning that D hands C further promises to pay, which continue to circulate as money. B's credit and that of the bank are now both at work, and continue to work (in the form of the bill of exchange and the banknotes); they are, so to say, materialised, and behave for a time like money. But is this credit really money? Can credit really become personally owned capital? That is the question we have to answer; and until it has been answered, neither the modern credit system nor yet the modern monetary system can be fully understood.

Let us try to get to the bottom of what happens when my friends pay their debts with mine. This means, really, that they pay their debts, not only with my promise to pay mine, but with my promise secured upon the capital that underlies it, the capital which has actually been transferred to me. When A repays what he has borrowed, all that happens is that the advanced goods and moneys come to light once more. My friends, therefore, do not strictly speaking pay their debts with credit in the sense of empty promises; they pay with promises substantiated by real values received, and by the new fruitfulness of a newly established economic community, whereby the lending economy is stimulated to form surpluses, and the borrowing economy to expend its own enterprise. Consequently, when a credit instrument becomes a part of the currency, this does not really mean that debts are paid with debts (fictitious values), but that they are paid in capital that has been deposited with the debtor, and is safeguarded by a newly established economic community.

Herein, then, we find the sound kernel of Law's teaching: that although credit is not new capital, it is real capital, pre-existent capital; and nevertheless this old capital is turned to useful account in a new way by its transference into another economy, this signifying the establishment of a new community between a saving economy and a producing economy, the former (the saving or lending economy) holding precedence over the latter (the productive or borrowing economy). In this transference of capital, and in the thereby created new economic community and economic expansion, inhere the new, the productive elements that credit introduces into the economic life of the community at large.

In contemporary economic life, savings and demands for credit accumulate for the most part in the hands of the banks, which are therefore in a position to "discount" bills of exchange (to buy them at a deduction for loss of interest) before they are due, or to allow overdrafts on the security of such bills. The temporary surplus of goods, and the powers of economic expansion inherent in the new community between lender and borrower, are what make it possible to await payment in this way, and to create new credit instruments.—Owing to the precedence taken by loan capital over the capital that actually belongs to the entrepreneur (a precedence which exists in so far as agriculture and industry are carried on with the aid of borrowed money), loan capital has a predominant power which is liable to be misused, and is often misused. From the very nature of the case, therefore, it is expedient that the use of credit should be controlled and modified in a way that will promote the general advantage. State intervention in the discount policy of the note-issuing banks, and public, cooperative, and corporative banking (banks for specific purposes), offer the most fruitful possibilities of this kind to-day.

In the history of economic doctrine, we must distinguish three main types of views regarding credit.

1. In the first group come the opinions of those who confounded a necessary precondition of credit with its true essence. Thus, some declared credit to be the "confidence" or a "frame of mind" of the creditor, or a "capacity" of the debtor. Cf. James Steuart (*Inquiry into the Principles of Political Economy*, 1767), J. B. Say, K. H. Rau (*Grundsätze der Volkswirtschafts-lehre*, eighth edition, 1868), Nebenius, Hildebrand, etc. Others have considered credit to be "a postponement of payment", as for example Mangoldt (*Volkswirtschaftslehre*, 1868).—But it is different if the "confidence" be merely the expression of the new economic community between lender and borrower!

2. Coming to the second group, we find that John Stuart Mill, criticising such views as those just epitomised, wrote accurately enough: "Credit" is "only permission to use the capital of another person"; and "Credit is but a transfer of capital from hand to hand" (*Principles of Political Economy*, book iii, chapter 11, § 1). Dietzel, and many other authorities, wrote in a like strain. Such a way of formulating the notion is not erroneous; but it is unduly mechanistic, and it ignores, not only the new and more fruitful community which credit establishes, but also the second act, the payment that is to be made at some future time. Nevertheless, this second act is of great importance, inasmuch as the demand for payment can enter into the monetary circulation vicariously, as if it were the actual payment.—Knies holds a kindred view (*Der Kredit*, i, 1, Berlin, 1876, pp. 7 et seq.), for he refers, not only to the transference of capital, but also to the time factor. Böhm-Bawerk writes in a similar strain.

3. To the third group belong Law and Macleod, who

do not regard credit as a transference of capital, but look upon the debt itself as a peculiar kind of immaterial capital, as an independent "additional" or "supplementary" capital.

The foregoing demonstration will have made it clear to the reader that not one of these groups gives a complete account of credit, but that all of them (and especially the second) supply important elements of a definition. Combining them, we discern the following characteristics in the notion of productive credit: 1. transference of money or real capital; 2. postponement of repayment by the borrower because of the deficiency of his own economic power; 3. enhanced utilisation of the borrowed capital by the borrowing economy as contrasted with the lending economy, this implying an increased productivity of the national economy and (in so far as the implication is fulfilled) the creation of new capital; 4. the establishment of an economic community between the lending economy and the borrowing; 5. precedence of the lending economy, because it is a saving economy and itself undergoes expansion through the instrumentality, as it were, of the borrowing economy; 6. the representation of the future payment by a promise to pay, which can enter into the monetary circulation. This currency, that is to say the therewith associated creation of money, is based upon the actually occurring economic expansion, not upon the debtor alone (Law), nor yet upon the creditor alone (Mill, metallism; the guaranteeing of the credit by goods alone; Smith's doctrine that money has been created by the division of labour, that is to say after the goods have been made); 7. the creditor's trust in the debtor, and the relevant legal regulations (the laws concerning credit and bills of exchange), are not "presuppositions" of credit, but something more than this, namely active formative factors in the economic process—they are "capital of a higher grade". (This notion cannot be fully elucidated here. See *Fundament der Volkswirtschaftslehre*, 1929, pp. 103 et seq.)

CHAPTER SIX

THE PHYSIOCRATS

1. AN EXPOSITION OF PHYSIOCRATIC DOCTRINE

ALTHOUGH the mercantile system was so abundantly criticised, a long time elapsed before the opposition to mercantilism crystallised into a coherent body of new doctrines. Such a new system of economic thought was first formulated by François Quesnay, the real founder of political economy as a systematised science, and also the originator of politico-economic individualism, to which he gave the descriptive name of physiocracy (the rule of nature).

François Quesnay (1694–1774) was the son of a lawyer who died when the boy was quite young. Brought up in the country, he did not learn to read till he was nearly twelve. At sixteen he was apprenticed to a surgeon. Removing to Paris, he carried on medical and scientific studies, and qualified as a master surgeon at the age of twenty-four. Having graduated as doctor of medicine in 1744, in 1749 he became body physician to Madame de Pompadour and Louis XV. His principal writings were the *Tableau économique*, 1758, and *Maximes générales*, 1758; but his first economic publications were the articles "Fermiers" and "Grains" in the *Encyclopédie* (1756 and 1757). A general edition of the *Oeuvres économiques et politiques* under the editorship of Oncken was published at Frankfort and Paris in 1888. By degrees a school advocating his views came into existence, the elder Mirabeau and Turgot being among the most notable adherents of the doctrine. Quesnay died in 1774, shortly after Turgot had become controller general and minister of finance. He thus lived to witness the victory of his school, and died before its collapse.

Quesnay's teaching is something over and above economics; it is part of a general philosophy. That is why it has greatness, unity, and boldness. Setting out from the materialist notions of his time, Quesnay wanted to have social and moral phenomena regarded as being no less "natural" than physical phenomena; and the laws governing the former equally with those governing the latter were to be conceived as mechanical laws of nature.

The natural right of human beings in the primal state before society came into existence was the right to property, that is the right to the free disposal of all the goods which the individual had made or appropriated by means of his own labour—this implying the right to a self-provided livelihood (existence). When, at a later stage, men, for the better safeguarding of their natural rights, entered into the social contract, it was essential that they should not forfeit the right which each of them had to earn his own livelihood. Inherent in this right is another natural right of the individual, the right to foster his own economic interest, to shape his own destiny as favourably to himself as possible. This pursuit of self-interest therefore leads to the establishment of a "natural order" in the economic association of human beings. That which seemed so uncongenial to persons still nourished on medieval traditions, the exclusion of all moral conceptions from the domain of political science (an exclusion which Machiavelli [1] was the first to advocate), was erected by Quesnay with certain reserves, and by his disciples more radically, into a finished system. Quesnay endeavoured to study the laws of the economic "natural order", which (in contradistinction to those of the "positive order", the actually extant historical order) were deducible by reason from the general plan of nature.—This doctrine concerning the "natural order" is fundamental in two ways. Inasmuch as therein the pursuit of self-interest is regarded as an economic postulate formulated in accordance with the theory of natural right, a system of

[1] Concerning Machiavelli's economic views, see Surányi-Unger, *Philosophie in der Volkswirtschaftslehre*, Jena, 1923, vol. i, pp. 198 et seq.

economic individualism is for the first time established. Secondly, the persons who, in the economic regulation of their lives, act consistently because they are guided by the motive of self-interest, resemble atoms with fixed properties; and the phenomena that result from their mutual contacts (in the market-place and elsewhere in society) are mechanically determined like those that result from the mutual contacts of the atoms. It follows that political economy, like the realm of material nature, is governed by purely mechanical laws, by natural laws.

To the question, what activity of the individual regulates the economic machinery, and upon what foundation the well-being of economic life depends, Quesnay answers: upon the natural economic activities, namely the agricultural; and consequently upon the exclusive foundation of the primal productive activity, above all upon the tilling of the soil, whereon the production of other goods and therewith the economy of the division of labour are upbuilded. "L'agriculture est la source de toutes les richesses de l'état" (agriculture is the source of all the wealth of the nation). Not money, trade, traffic, and industry are the true founts of public welfare, but the tilling of the soil. The former activities merely transform matter and move it from place to place; they are nowise creative. The husbandman renders them possible by nourishing those who engage in them, and he supplies the raw materials without which they cannot be undertaken. Commerce, industry, and transport are to be considered as forming a "dépendance de l'agriculture".

The physiocrats put the matter vividly, saying that the countryman gets hides, leather, and in the end his boots, from his oxen; wood, and in the end his tools, from the trees on his farm; and so on. But, they said, to avoid the squandering of materials and energy, it is better that he should not himself undertake these labours that ennoble and transform matter, but should have them done for him vicariously by specialists (the currier, the bootmaker, the joiner, etc.), whom he must support out of his agricultural surpluses. Things will be arranged as follows. A number of agriculturists will engage a man to make sabots out of their wood; another to tan and dress the hides of the oxen they slaughter; another to make boots out of the leather. This shows that the labour of the husbandman is the exclusive source of wealth, is "the motive force of the social machine", whereas industrial work merely transforms what is derived from that .source (Turgot). "In this circulation, . . . the initial impetus is given by the labour of the landworker" (Turgot). It is he who maintains and feeds the other sections of the community.

The only productive, the only creative labour is, then, labour on the land. It is true that work which transforms materials derived from the land, or moves them from one place to another, can enhance the value of these things; but the cost of the supplementary labour is defrayed by the agriculturist, who must feed the workers that perform it; and the increase in value thus produced is, therefore, accordant to the cost of the labour, is equal to the expense of maintaining the workers who do it—and is, consequently, once more covered and made good by labour on the land. The currier, the joiner, etc., who elaborate the raw materials derived from landwork, merely earn their own keep in the form of wages; they make nothing new. All they do, says Quesnay, is to "add", not to "create". The agriculturists' work is a work of creation; these industrial workers perform only a work of addition—of transformation or transport.

Thus the class of landworkers (consisting in those days chiefly of tenant farmers as contrasted with the territorial nobility) would appear to be the only "productive" class. The landowners, on the other hand, form a "proprietary" or "distributive" class; while the industrialists and craftsmen comprise a "sterile" class.

These three are considered to be the "active" classes of the population, whilst the wage-earners make up a fourth, a "passive" class. It has no economic activity of its own, since its members are not entrepreneurs, but receive fixed incomes (wages). This class, therefore, comes under consideration only as a class of consumers, and is especially commended to the care of the government.

Agriculture cannot continue to thrive unless grain realises high prices; for only then can agriculture provide a large "net product",[1] and thus become able to pay large incomes to the landowning class, the manufacturers, and the working class, and in this way to diffuse general prosperity. It is essential, therefore, to do away with all restrictions upon the export of grain.—Quesnay unhesitatingly rejected the mercantilist theory of the balance of trade. The demand for free trade was an inevitable corollary of his views (see below, pp. 84 et seq.).

The physiocratic system also gave a picture of the formation of value and of price. In certain connexions, Quesnay

[1] We think it better to translate this term, though English authorities incline to use the French original. Under the caption "Produit Net" in Palgrave's *Dictionary of Political Economy*, Ethel R. Faraday writes: "Quesnay uses the term 'produit net' as signifying the surplus of the raw produce of the earth left after defraying the cost of its production. He reasoned further that, since natural agents are the sole source of wealth, and since only one class in the State—the class of agriculturists engaged in obtaining raw produce—pays rent for the use of natural agents, therefore the 'produit net' is represented by this rent, which serves for the support of Quesnay's second or proprietary class, and the payment of his third or unproductive class of merchants, manufacturers, public officials, etc. On this theory it follows that the entire expenses of government are ultimately defrayed out of the rent received by the landlords; Quesnay was therefore quite consistent in proposing that all taxes should be repealed, and replaced by an 'impôt unique' laid directly on the rent of the land."—TRANSLATORS' NOTE.

emphasised the nature of value as utility. In connexion, however, with his doctrine of the net product, value and price were derivable from cost. The transformative labour of industry added to goods only so much value as this labour itself consumed in the way of the means of subsistence created by the labour of the agriculturist; only an amount of value, therefore, equivalent to its own cost.—It follows from this that the wages of labour are nothing other than the replacement of the labour power that has been expended, that wages are merely subsistence—a doctrine that was subsequently elaborated by Ricardo and the socialists (see below, "iron law of wages", pp. 138 et seq. and 148 et seq.).

For the physiocrats, money was not a commodity, but only a symbol.—Whereas the mercantilists were inclined to regard population as a cause of wealth, Quesnay held that increase of population was dependent on increase of wealth. Here he anticipated Malthus' theory of population.

The physiocrats agree with the mercantilists in the view that the essential of national wealth consists, not in the dead store of money and goods, but in the reproduction of goods. According to Quesnay, the surpluses of primary (i.e. agricultural) production move in a closed circuit when rendering possible the industrial processes that transform raw materials into finished products. The physiocratic conception of the circulation of goods is presented schematically in Quesnay's famous *Tableau économique*, which is reproduced (in English) on pp. 82–83.[1]

[1] Cf. Oncken, *Geschichte der Nationalökonomie*, Leipzig, 1902, vol. i, pp. 394 et seq. A facsimile of the Table as originally drafted by Quesnay was printed by the British Economic Association, London, 1894. Mirabeau reprinted the Table at the end of the third volume of his *Philosophie rurale*, Amsterdam, 1766. It will also be found in an English translation from the elder Mirabeau, *The Oeconomical Table*, London, 1766. I have added some notes of my own.—In the explanation that is given in the text, I follow Oncken, though I differ from him as concerns what he writes in his last paragraph on p. 395.

The sum standing at the top of the middle column is the annual net income of the landed proprietors, the amount of net product they receive as rent in the course of one year. According to the Table, this sum of £2,000 is distributed as follows. £1,000 go back to the farmers in virtue of the purchase of means of subsistence from them (the pointer to this division is given by the terms of lease customary in those days, for they provided that the rent of the farm was to be half the produce); and £1,000 go to trade and industry for purchases from that quarter.

The £1,000 that go to agriculture are utilised there "productively", giving rise to a raw product of £2,000. Half of this, namely the surplus ("surcroit") or net product, amounting to £1,000, goes back to the landowners, whilst of the remaining half a part (£500) is consumed by the agriculturists, and the other part goes to industry for the purchase of its products. Thus £500 go to the right, and, being there "sterile" expenditure (wages), is not doubled, but simply reproduced. Of the product, £500, the industrials use half (£250) to buy industrial products for consumption, and the other half (£250) to buy agricultural produce, and in this way £250 are sent travelling back to the left, the agricultural side. There, these £250 will again become productive, and will yield £500, of which £250 will once more go to the landowners (entered in the middle column), whilst the remaining £250 will be halved as before, a moiety of £125 going to industry. Of this sum one half, £62 10s., will go back to agriculture; and so on, until, by successive halvings, the amount becomes negligible.

The other £1,000, those which the landowners spend upon purchases from the industrials, take a course similar to that taken by the sums spent by the agriculturists on purchases from the industrials. One half, £500, goes back to agriculture, yields a net product of £500, and of this a sum of £250 goes

F

THE ECONOMIC TABLE

Things to be considered; 1, three different kinds of expense; 2, their origin; 3, their advances; 4, their distribution; 5, their effects; 6, their reproduction; 7, their relations one to another; 8, their relations to population; 9, to agriculture; 10, to manufacture; 11, to commerce; 12, to the total amount of national riches.

PRODUCTIVE EXPENSES	INCOME EXPENDITURE	BARREN EXPENSES
those of the husbandman	whose reflux upon the left and the right hand columns keeps the machinery of circulation going	those of manufacture, etc.
ANNUAL ADVANCES	ANNUAL INCOME	ANNUAL ADVANCES
for the production of an income of £2000	or landlord's share	for barren outlay on manufacture, etc.

£	s.	d.		£	s.	d.		£	s.	d.
2000	0	0	produce net	2000[a]	0	0				

←half goes this way   half goes this way→

| 1000[b] | 0 | 0 | reproduce net | 1000 | 0 | 0 | | 1000[c] | 0 | 0 |

half goes this way   half goes this way

| 500 | 0 | 0 | reproduce net | 500 | 0 | 0 | | 500 | 0 | 0 |

half goes this way   half goes this way

| 250 | 0 | 0 | reproduce net | 250 | 0 | 0 | | 250 | 0 | 0 |

half goes this way   half goes this way

| 125 | 0 | 0 | reproduce net | 125 | 0 | 0 | | 125 | 0 | 0 |

half goes this way   half goes this way

| 62 | 10 | 0 | reproduce net | 62 | 10 | 0 | | 62 | 10 | 0 |

half goes this way   half goes this way

| 31 | 5 | 0 | reproduce net | 31 | 5 | 0 | | 31 | 5 | 0 |

half goes this way   half goes this way

| 15 | 12 | 6 | reproduce net | 15 | 12 | 6 | | 15 | 12 | 6 |

£	s.	d.		£	s.	d.		£	s.	d.
15	12	6	reproduce net	15	12	6		15	12	6

half goes this way → | ← half goes this way

7	16	3	reproduce net	7	16	3		7	16	3

half goes this way → | ← half goes this way

3	18	1	reproduce net	3	18	1		3	18	1

half goes this way → | ← half goes this way

1	19	0	reproduce net	1	19	0		1	19	0

half goes this way → | ← half goes this way

0	19	6	reproduce net	0	19	6		0	19	6

half goes this way → | ← half goes this way

0	9	9	reproduce net	0	9	9		0	9	9

half goes this way → | ← half goes this way

*0	4	10	reproduce net	0	4	10		0	4	10

half goes this way → | ← half goes this way

*0	2	5	reproduce net	0	2	5		0	2	5

half goes this way → | ← half goes this way

*0	1	6	reproduce net	0	1	6		0	1	6

half goes this way → | ← half goes this way

*0	0	9	reproduce net	0	0	9		0	0	9

half goes this way → | ← half goes this way

*0	0	5	reproduce net	0	0	5		0	0	5

2000	0	0 = total		2000(d)	0	0		2000	0	0

* Approximate figures.

[Notes to table bottom of p. 84.

back to industry. Thereupon one half, £125, returns to agriculture; and so on, and so on, by successive halvings, till the
end.

"Ultimately", writes Oncken, "the £2,000 expended by the
landlords have run their course through the two other classes,
having on each side set the practitioners of various occupations
to work, and have step by step been reproduced by the productive class, until in the end the aggregate has been paid over to
the landlords as rent—for the same to start with afresh the
following year."

Applied Economics. From the suppositions of the physiocrats, the fundamentally important politico-economic deduction
may be drawn, that the individual should unrestrainedly act in
accordance with the dictates of his own economic self-interest.
Individual liberty, the free choice of occupation, freedom of
industry and consumption, freedom of movement from place
to place, and freedom of private property: these are the first
essentials. The famous motto of physiocracy, "Laissez faire
et laissez passer, le monde va de lui-même" (let do and let be,
the world goes of itself), was an obvious corollary from these

---

NOTES TO THE ECONOMIC TABLE

(*a*) These £2000, which in the course of a year are paid to the landowners,
are the true national income. The landowners distribute the sum as follows:
Half goes to the agriculturists (left) and half to the industrialists (right).

(*b*) Here is a point essential to the understanding of the table. These
£1000, like all the amounts entered in the left-hand column, are utilised
"productively" in agriculture. The sum is therefore doubled, to become
£2000. Of these £2000, one half (£1000) remains in the hands of the
agriculturist; the other half is paid as rent (net product) to the landlord, and
is entered in the middle column. Of the former half, the landlord expends
£500 on subsistence products for himself, and devotes £500 to the purchase
of industrial products (right-hand column).

(*c*) These £1000 are not doubled, but are merely reproduced. Half goes
back to agriculture, to be doubled there, and half remains in industry.

(*d*) With this sum of £2000, a new circulation, to be shown in a similar
table, will begin. It constitutes the aggregate national income produced by
the national economy; it goes to the landowners, and is by them distributed
to agriculture and industry respectively.

principles. The State should sedulously refrain from interference in the economic life of the nation.—Methodologically
considered, this signifies that self-interest is to be the basic
principle, the sole motive force, of economic activity.

This notion of "laissez faire" claims justification of two
kinds. In the first place, as has already been said, it claims a
philosophical justification in the doctrine of natural right.
The sacred, eternal rights of the individual must be treated
as inviolable. The second justification (also, in a sense, a
philosophical one) is based upon the view that the economic
happenings of social life are the expression of a rigid concatenation of causes and effects. Since economic laws cannot
run counter to the natural laws of social life, since they likewise are manifestations of the determinisms inherent in the
"natural laws" of the "ordre naturel", action in accordance
with the natural law which prescribes that a man should
obey the dictates of self-interest cannot fail to bring about
the most natural (and therefore the best) development of
economic life.

Physiocratic Doctrine of Taxation. Every one who receives
net product, should pay taxes. There should be no privileged
exemptions. Since land is the only source of wealth, it should
bear the whole burden of taxation; all the more, seeing that
the burden of taxation laid upon any other class is ultimately
shifted on to the landowning class. This train of reasoning led
to the demand for a land tax as a single direct tax (impôt unique
et direct). Indirect taxes are condemned as imposing hindrances upon intercourse and as pressing heavily upon the
common people.

2. VALUATION OF PHYSIOCRACY. AN INTRODUCTION TO THE
DOCTRINE OF FRUITFULNESS AND OF GOODS

a. Significance of the "Tableau". The *Tableau*, whose
conceptual significance in the history of economic science
has hitherto been underestimated, is to be regarded as the
first attempt to realise the idea of an "ordre naturel". But
in addition to giving a causally mechanical picture of the

economic life of society, it gave (though the author was hardly aware of the fact) an organic picture, in so far as it was based on the activities, not of economic individuals each seeking to further his own interests, but of economic subdivisions of society ("classes"). The three classes, as depicted by Quesnay, exhibit, so to say, systems of organs; and we have the idea of a kind of circulation within society analogous to the circulation of the blood. We are shown an unceasing movement; the economic organism is never at rest. There emerges the distinction between an immutable and a mutable, or as we should phrase it to-day between a "static" and a "dynamic" national economy.

If, to-day, one who is beginning the study of anatomy and physiology asks what is the structure of the human body, he is given a brief account of the osseous system, the muscular system, etc. Modern economics is still unable to answer a kindred question regarding the structure of society, for Quesnay's *Tableau* is incorrect, and subsequent economists have made the laws of prices the core of their theory, while paying little heed to the functional systems that form the connecting links between economic activities.—Cf. under this head, my own attempt to analyse economics into "partial aggregates" and "grades", *Tote und lebendige Wissenschaft*, and *Fundament der Volkswirtschaftslehre*, § 23.

Furthermore the *Tableau* made manifest (though once again its author was not fully aware of the fact) that the various branches of economic life are closely interrelated. As soon as the document had been published, it ceased to be a matter of indifference to which class the landlords turned when spending their incomes. If too much went to industry, or flowed across the national frontier, so that the primal productive activity lacked adequate stimulus, the effect upon the national income might be lastingly unfavourable, because too much of the landlords' expenditure was unproductive, and only the funds that went to agriculture could lead to the formation of "net product". Thus it was that the physiocrats came to regard the *Tableau* as a sort of "mariner's compass" that would give them precise information about the economic condition of a country; and they believed that the collection and tabulation of statistics would enable them to follow and appraise the course of economic development. That was what the elder Mirabeau had in mind when, in his funeral oration on Quesnay, he said there had been three great discoveries: writing, money, and the *Tableau économique*.—Finally, a very important feature of the *Tableau* was that it contemplated economic phenomena from the commodity outlook exclusively, regardless of money— a method I should like to-day to urge upon every beginner.

When forming his opinions on economic questions, the beginner should always keep his gaze fixed upon the real, tangible processes of economic life, upon the actual movements of goods or commodities; and should, to begin with, ignore the movements of money and prices, which are but intermediate links. He must learn to see through the veil of money. (The reader must not suppose me to imply that money is nothing but a veil. Money is "capital of a higher grade", that is to say the active organiser of economic life.) (See above, pp. 44 and 74; below p. 286.)

b. Exposition of the Main Teaching of the Physiocrats. The doctrines of Quesnay and his school are impressive. They supply a vivid picture of economic life, of its subordination to fixed laws, and of its interlacement with the social process as a whole. The entire development of the physiocratic system was, however, based on the presupposition that its doctrines were deducible from a particular philosophy, the rationalist and individualist philosophy of the Enlightenment. But we have seen that the apostles of that movement, believing as they did that social life was conformable to "natural" law, conceived the pursuit of self-interest to be the primary motive force of economic activity, and consequently expected that individual freedom to pursue self-interest would result in a harmonious development of economic life. The individualist view of economics, and the notion that economic activity is subordinated to the laws of a mechanical causation—these were the foundations on which the physiocrats established our science, the foundations that determined the characteristics of the subsequent edifice. In addition, the basing of economics on the motive of self-interest working like a mechanical force, led to the development of the deductive method which became thenceforward increasingly prominent. (See below, under Adam Smith and Ricardo, p. 114 and p. 146.)

Quesnay's fundamental notion that agriculture, as the primal productive activity, is alone fruitful, is indeed erroneous. Yet it still prevails in our own days, to work mischief under diversified forms in politics and economics. It is grounded, above all, upon a mistaken idea of the "net product" Let us analyse that notion.

The product or yield of agriculture is especially conspicuous. If, for instance, a farmer harvests ten times as much grain as he has sown, the "surplus" is obvious. But when a joiner shapes planks and nails them together to make a table, where, one may ask, is the surplus yield to be found? We answer: in utility. A table is different from planks, and more useful; a spear is something different from, something more than, the ashstaff and the iron spear-head out of which it has been made. If the spear proves a fruitful weapon of the chase, the hours spent in fashioning it are speedily outweighed by the time saved during the hunt. The hours thus gained during the whole lifetime of the spear constitute its net product. On the other hand, a tenfold yield of grain, this visible gross product, does not necessarily contain any net product at all, for the expenditure that has been needed to produce it may outbalance the return. From the outlook of economic theory, the net product, the surplus of yield over cost of production, is what matters; and we say, therefore, that an economic activity has not been successful unless it has resulted in a net product. Thus the main point is, not whether any particular labour creates new substance, but whether what is produced by the labour provides more utilities than the utilities expended in producing it. If this outlook be correct, we cannot term industrial labour sterile or fruitless if the requisite condition has been fulfilled. Take the making of a plough. Did the work of making it involve more in the way of sustenance for the maker, more renouncement in order to provide raw materials, etc., than is made good by the enhanced production consequent upon its use in agriculture? Should the balance incline one way, the making of the plough has been a sterile occupation; should the balance incline the other, it has been a fruitful one.

The remark applies equally to trade and commerce, of which Rau said about sixty years ago: "People may exchange goods as much as they please, but the amount of the goods is not increased thereby!" Marx said almost the same thing. At bottom, that is a physiocratic outlook. When considering the labour expended in bringing coffee, tropical fruits, etc., into our temperate climes (this involving, not freightage alone, but mercantile activity, search for markets), our real concern is with the question whether what is done produces more utilities than it consumes. Now, trade produces new utilities, when it conveys goods to a market where there is enhanced demand, as when it transports coffee from Pernambuco to London. So, too, with the liberal professions. In regard to the work of doctors, schoolmasters, barristers, solicitors, judges, legislators, etc.—work which promotes health, enlarges knowledge, helps to maintain law and order, improves the conditions of social labour, and the like—we, as economists, need only ask whether this work produces more utilities than it consumes. Those who contend that persons engaged in the liberal

professions are all supported upon goods supplied by agriculture
and industry, that trade merely shuffles from hand to hand
the goods derived from the same sources, and that consequently neither the liberal professions nor trade and commerce
are productive, completely overlook the fact that industry and
agriculture, in their turn, derive both goods of production and
goods for consumption from practitioners of the liberal or
intellectual professions: that the more obviously "productive"
persons thus obtain health, knowledge, artistic enjoyments,
security of life and property; things which serve, just as much
as do concrete utilities, to satisfy human wants, and which are
perpetually entering into all other processes of production as
fruitful elements, as elements tending to increase the yield.
Economists have often pointed out how contradictory it is
to describe the chemist's assistant who prepares a medicine
as a productive labourer, and the doctor who prescribes or
administers that medicine as unproductive; to describe as
productive the compositor who sets the type for a book and
the machinist who runs the printing press, whilst the imaginative writer who conceived what is printed and the engineer
from whose brain the machinery was born are looked upon
as unproductive.

Quesnay's economic outlook, according to which industrial
labour is merely transformative, not productive, is (as the
foregoing considerations show) purely technical, materialistic,
and is not truly scientific. Nor, indeed, is it wholly valid even
from a technical standpoint. For instance, chemical industry
creates new substances, just as agriculture does. The separation of nitrogen from the air is a creative act. Strictly examined,
moreover, what seems exclusively transformative labour,
creates new forces and enlists them in its service. A spear,
which works on the principle of the wedge, or a spade, which
works on the principle of the lever, is, considered merely
from the outlook of technique and energetics, something
essentially new, when compared with the raw materials out of
which either has been made. In this connexion, it is important
to realise that "goods" are, primarily, neither material nor

immaterial, but means of service. Bread is a means for relieving hunger; violin-playing is a means for satisfying the desire for music; and so on. This instrumentality, this purposive functioning, is the economic feature of a good; whether the good be material or immaterial is a question lying outside the scope of economics, and is nothing more than a technical quality.

A further objection to Quesnay's view, is that he overlooks the existence of a spiritual or mental primal productive activity in addition to a bodily one. Inventors, entrepreneurs, statesmen, artists, men of science, belong to this world in which primal productive activity is spiritual or mental: and if, in Turgot's phrase, agriculture be the "motive force" which "sets industry to work"; so they, these mental producers, are the "motive force" which "sets to work" the whole army of publishers, book printers, compositors, booksellers, actors, instrument makers, etc. To take Aristotle alone, during the two thousand years and more since he lived, he has been the spiritual progenitor of milliards of industrial working hours; and has indirectly "fed" a myriad of copyists, typesetters, publishers, papermakers, and commentators.

The physiocrats' chief argument (and it is one that still has a very powerful influence upon the minds of ordinary people) was that the agriculturist feeds the industrial worker and the trader. The statement is perfectly true, but it does not follow from this that all activities other than those of the agriculturist are sterile. Enough to rejoin that industry and commerce equip the husbandman with articles of consumption (clothing and shelter) and with articles of production (ploughs and agricultural implements of various kinds). The husbandman wants this equipment quite as urgently as the industrialist and the trader want food!—It must be admitted, however, that the need for food is the most vital of all our needs. Here is the truth at the core of Quesnay's theory of fruitfulness, that our wellbeing, our "economy", is built up in stages some of which are more vitally important than others. But that does not signify that the less vitally important branches of production are therefore less fruitful. When we are appraising the fruitfulness of any particular kind of labour, we have to ask ourselves, as a problem of wellbeing, how many of our wants we can satisfy; for within these limits of wellbeing or welfare all are, as a matter of principle, equally fruitful! (Here we have the concept of the equivalence of all the activities undertaken for the attainment of some particular state of achievement or aggregate utility.)—If we strive to attain ends which are out of touch with the economic potentialities of the time (if we should, say, secure at a moment's notice the appointment of one thousand additional teachers in the State schools), then, indeed, our labour will be unfruitful, for a superfluous amount of educational work will be undertaken, whereas other important wants, such as those for food and shelter, will be left unsatisfied. But our activity would be no less sterile if we were suddenly to increase a thousandfold the number of the cultivators of the soil, while the number of persons belonging to other sections of society remained unchanged! The safeguarding of the more important goods against the competition of those which, at the given instant, are less important, means no more and no less than that in economic life a due proportionality shall be maintained among all the branches of production; for when this is done, not one of the branches will be sterile.

c. The Idea of a Good. The foregoing considerations will have shown the importance of the idea of a good to the general body of economic thought. The definition of a good is vital to the decision whether a worker is or is not productive, i.e. whether his economic activity is one which produces goods. If most people are still inclined to say that the activities of teachers, university professors, doctors, statesmen and politicians, traders, and speculators, are unfruitful, and are only possible because agricultural and industrial workers provide their incomes, provide their "keep" (the incomes of the "unproductive workers" being regarded as "derivative"), this is due to the persistence of a way of thinking akin to that of the physiocrats. When those who hold such views think of "goods", they no longer, indeed, limit the term as did the physiocrats to the yield of the "primal productive activity" on the land, but they think only of concrete, material goods, and ignore the immaterial ones. In fact, however, just as industrial production is not "sterile", so the liberal professions and trade and commerce are by no means sterile, in so far as (in accordance with the principle discussed on pp. 89 et seq.) they achieve something that fulfils an aim. Consequently, we must regard as a good, everything—whether concrete object (a material good), an achievement (an ideal good), a relationship, or a right—that enters passively into the concatenation of economic activity, i.e. that is a functioning instrument for use in active procedures. A good is a passive instrument, and is therefore anything that can be introduced as a constructive element into the economic process. Every activity, then, which engenders a good, is economically fruitful, provided that it fulfils the formal conditions of fruitfulness, and especially those of "proportionality" and "utility". Fruitful, above all, is the brainwork performed in directive activities of every kind.

Historically considered, physiocracy represented a counterstroke on the part of neglected agriculture against industry as fostered by the mercantile system. Nevertheless, even in this one-sided attitude, it fulfilled a historical task. The champions of the mercantile system, joining forces with the territorial princes, had got the better of the feudal nobility; and mercantilism therefore (though founded to some extent upon the doctrine of natural right) had become absolutist and anti-individualist. In opposition to this trend, the physiocrats promoted individualism upon an economic and scientific foundation, at a time when that doctrine had long since become dominant in the intellectual world as a whole upon the philosophical basis of natural right.

During and after the war of 1914–1918, when there was a

great dearth of raw materials, there were good reasons why the physiocratic inclination to esteem agriculture and the production of raw materials very highly, should be in the ascendant once more.

3. THE PHYSIOCRATIC SCHOOL

A troop of devoted adherents soon collected round Quesnay, and they styled themselves "économistes". (The name "physiocrats" did not arise till later, and was invented by Dupont de Nemours, one of Quesnay's disciples.) To begin with, the government looked askance at the school; but it soon acquired great influence, and in a measure political power, for its most notable member, Turgot (author of *Réflexions sur la jormation et la distribution des richesses*, 1769–1770; English translation *Reflections on the Formation and Distribution of Wealth*, London, 1793; a new translation, 1898, edited by W. J. Ashley, in Macmillan's *Economic Classics*) was appointed controller-general of the finances in 1774. The eldest of Quesnay's pupils, who became the political chief of the physiocratic school, was the Marquis Victor de Mirabeau (generally known as Mirabeau the elder, or Mirabeau père, to distinguish him from his famous son, the Comte de Mirabeau), author of *Philosophie rurale*, 1763. He was much more uncompromising than Quesnay in his application of the laissez-faire principle, and desired a more radical and ruthless enforcement of the other principles of the system than did its founder. Quesnay always kept in touch with living reality, and perpetually emphasised the need for maintaining the experiential basis of his doctrines, so that for him the "ordre naturel" was never anything more than an ultimate ideal, to which the "ordre positif" could only be approximated by slow degrees.—Others who were quick to espouse physiocracy in the land of its birth were: Le Mercier de la Rivière (*L'ordre naturel*, 1767); Beaudeau; Dupont de Nemours; and the philosopher Condillac. A collection of their writings will be found in Daire's editions, *Oeuvres de Turgot*, Paris, 1844, and *Oeuvres des physiocrats*, Paris, 1846.

The physiocratic doctrine soon spread from France to foreign parts, but made little headway in England. It had immense influence in Germany, where Karl Friedrich, Margrave of

Baden, aided by Schlettwein, the most distinguished among
the German physiocrats, made an unsuccessful attempt to
put in practice the physiocratic principles of taxation.
Leopold I, Grand Duke of Tuscany (afterwards Emperor
Leopold II), endeavoured to introduce far-reaching physiocratic reforms, and especially the "land tax", in his duchy.
His brother, and predecessor on the imperial throne, Joseph II,
though a mercantilist, was contradictory enough to inaugurate
physiocratic experiments. His measures to improve the condition of the peasants (such as the abolition of serfdom in
1781–1782), and his reforms of taxation (the land tax of 1775),
were physiocratic in trend. Catharine the Great and most of
the other monarchs of that date who were tinctured with the
spirit of the Enlightenment, were likewise, to a degree, under
the spell of physiocracy.—Among the German physiocrats,
there should also be mentioned: Isaak Iselin (1728–1782), a
German-Swiss, secretary of State at Basle; Jakob Mauvillon
(1743–1794), German born, but son of a Frenchman settled
in Leipzig, the German translator of Turgot's *Réflexions*, and
the man through whose instrumentality the name "physiocracy"
gained general acceptance; and T. A. H. Schmalz (1760–1831),
a Hanoverian who has been called "the last of the physiocrats".
—The physiocratic doctrine found adherents also in Italy,
Poland, Sweden, and elsewhere.

After Quesnay's death (1774), dissensions broke out among
the French physiocrats, chiefly because of the unorthodoxy of
Condillac, who insisted that commerce and industry were
"fruitful" as well as agriculture. The disputes that ensued
paved the way for the collapse of physiocracy when Turgot
fell from power in 1776. The minister's dismissal was partly
due to his failure to reestablish upon a sound footing the
hopelessly disordered State finances. But there were contributory causes, for some of the things he had done and
others he had attempted (all in a rather high-handed and
doctrinaire fashion) had made him unpopular. He had proposed to abolish the corvées throughout the kingdom, and
to suppress the guilds; restrictions upon intranational trade
were to be done away with. In 1774 he had issued a decree
permitting free trade in corn within the country, but for-
bidding the export of grain. The harvest of 1775 was a poor
one, and the consequent rise in the price of bread had led
to corn-riots all over the country. These troubles had certainly

been instrumental in bringing about the controller-general's dismissal.

Immediately thereafter, the course of events was one which pushed physiocracy into the background. In politics, there came the great French revolution; and in the domain of economic science the doctrines of Adam Smith began to monopolise attention.

CHAPTER SEVEN

FULLY DEVELOPED INDIVIDUALISM, OR CLASSICAL POLITICAL ECONOMY

A. THE LABOUR OR INDUSTRIAL SYSTEM OF ADAM SMITH

SINCE England was the classical home of empiricism, and the first country in which modern large-scale industry developed, it was only to be expected that individualist political economy would strike deepest root and flourish most luxuriantly on British soil. Ere long the introduction of spinning machinery (Wyatt, 1738; Lewis Paul, 1741; Arkwright, 1769), the steam-engine (Watt, 1765 and 1770), and later of the power-loom (Cartwright, 1785; Jacquard, 1802), and similar transformations in the methods of industrial production, induced changes that led to an enormously accelerated growth of large-scale industry, and established that active, multifarious, and complicated life of a "free business economy" in which the numerous theoretical and practical problems of the individualist or capitalist epoch began to clamour for solution.

Adam Smith was the man who, upon these presuppositions, established a new system of economic doctrines.

Adam Smith was born in 1723 at Kirkcaldy in Fifeshire, Scotland. He studied theology, then philosophy, at Glasgow University, and at the age of twenty-eight, after six years at Oxford, returned to Glasgow as professor of logic. Next year, in 1752, he exchanged this chair for that of moral philosophy—which meant in those days that he lectured, not only on ethics, but also on political science, jurisprudence, and political economy. After his publication of the *Theory of the Moral Sentiments* in 1759, he was invited in 1763 to take the post of travelling tutor or companion to the young Duke of Buccleuch, and under these auspices he spent the years 1764 to 1766 in France. Here he became personally acquainted with the physiocrats, and this meeting exercised a great influence on him. For ten years after his return to his native land, Smith lived with his mother at Kirkcaldy, devoting himself almost exclusively to economic study and to writing his *Inquiry into the Nature and Causes of the Wealth of Nations*, which was published in 1776. He died in 1790. In accordance with his directions, all his unpublished manuscripts with the exception of a few selected essays were burned after his death.—In former days it was commonly assumed that Smith had derived his basic ideas of economics from the physiocrats, during his stay in Paris in the year 1766, and that his system was little more than a continuation of physiocracy. This idea is erroneous. It has been definitively disproved by the publication thirty years ago of the *Lectures on Justice, Police, Revenue, and Arms delivered in the University of Glasgow by Adam Smith, reported by a Student in* 1763, edited with an introduction and notes by Edward Cannan, Clarendon Press, 1896. This work makes it clear beyond dispute that the broad lines of Smith's doctrine were formulated before he went to Paris.

Adam Smith emerges from a mental and historical environment similar to that from which Quesnay sprang, that of the philosophy of the Enlightenment, of rationalist natural right, and of individualism. Of great importance is his relation to the philosopher Hume, with whom he was also on terms of close personal friendship. Before Smith, Hume had attacked mercantilist views on money and the mercantilist doctrine of the balance of trade; and had propounded a moral philosophy according to which sympathy is the leading moral principle. This was the doctrine which Smith espoused, and developed in his own *Theory of the Moral Sentiments*.

Smith declares that an action is moral when it has the approval of every unbiased onlooker. The approval depends on sympathy or fellow-feeling. This sympathy is conceived by Smith relativistically, as a subjective psychological manifestation; but at the same time he holds that the moral worth of an action is dependent upon its objective effect, that is to say, upon whether it is socially useful. (Social utilitarianism.) Nevertheless Smith is an individualist, for, like the physiocrats, he considers the individual's pursuit of self-interest to be the motive force of economic life. The apparent contradiction is resolved, for Smith, by his assumption that there exists in the world-order a natural teleology, thanks to which the individual serves and is useful to the community even when seeking his own ends. The same principle holds good for economic life. According to this author, its mechanism is such that individual self-seeking leads spontaneously to harmony and to what is best for all.

1. EXPOSITION OF THE SYSTEM

According to Adam Smith, the wealth of a nation does not depend either on the balance of trade, or on the quantity of money within its borders, or on exclusively agricultural labour. He opens his *Inquiry* with the words: "The annual labour of every nation is the fund which originally supplies it with all the necessaries and conveniencies of life which it annually consumes, and which consist always either in the immediate produce of labour, or in what is purchased with that produce from other nations." True, he makes an important reservation. Labour which is not devoted to the production of permanently useful things endowed with exchange-value, to the making of concrete objects, seems to Smith, as to the physiocrats, unproductive. Thus services of all kinds, and the work of the actor, the statesman, etc., are unproductive. The wealth of a nation is greater, according as a larger proportion of those who belong to it are engaged in useful labour, according as it contains a smaller proportion of idlers; and this, in turn, depends upon the amount of capital devoted to the employment of workers (the "wage-fund" or "wages-fund"),[1] but, above all, upon the

[1] This term does not appear in economic literature until after the death of Adam Smith, but the idea of it is implicit in the following passage from the eighth chapter, "Of the Wages of Labour" in Book I of the *Wealth of Nations*: "The demand for those who live by wages, it is evident, cannot increase but in proportion to the increase of the funds which are destined for the payment of wages" (Bohn's Standard Library edition, vol. i, pp. 69–70).—TRANSLATORS' NOTE.

fruitfulness of labour. The fruitfulness of labour is increased mainly by the division of labour. Consequently, the division of labour is the chief cause of enhanced prosperity; and Smith illustrates this thesis by the famous examples of pinmaking (*op. cit.*, vol. i, p. 6) and nailmaking (*op. cit.*, vol. i, p. 9). The further the division of labour is pushed, the more is production carried on with an eye to the market. Now, for the purposes of the market there must develop a general means of exchange or instrument of trade, namely, money. (Money, as explained above, p. 40, arises out of indirect exchange.) Commodities are exchanged in the market through the instrumentality of money as the medium of exchange, and there thus originates an exchange-value or price of goods as contrasted with their use-value. We see, then, that the division of labour is the starting point of the whole economic process and its development! It is the cause of the exchange of goods, for no one can live upon the produce of his own one-sided activity (and, besides, all men have a natural inclination to exchange things one for another). But exchange is effected in accordance with exchange-value (price); and the formation of exchange-value is therefore decisive: (*a*) for the distribution of the goods, since it settles the question who can buy them; and (*b*) for their production, inasmuch as this is guided by the expectation of the price to be realised.

Upon these considerations Adam Smith builds up his economic system; and so do all the individualist schools that follow in his footsteps. The laws that regulate the formation of exchange-value are held to be also the laws in accordance with which the wealth of nations comes into being; they are, in fact, the laws of political economy, the primary laws of economic motion.

By formulating this conception of the nature of political economy (one which, however, he failed to work out systematically), Smith made a notable step forward within the domain of individualist theory. He gave a new turn to economic thought. Whereas both the mercantilists and the physiocrats had made productive circulation the basis of their reasoning, now for the first time a study of the laws of exchange-value was undertaken. Thenceforward the theory of value and the theory of prices became the fulcrum of economic theory in general. For, since prices are the determinants of the production of goods, the laws of prices have the last word as to whether this or that or the other shall be produced; and since prices decide which among would-be purchasers have sufficient purchasing power, the laws of prices settle how goods shall be distributed. In a word, the laws of prices are also the laws of distribution. In the sequel, therefore, the theory of distribution is developed as a theory of particular prices (wages, landrent, etc.).

Smith, for this reason, establishes an elaborate theory of the formation of value and of price. Under primitive conditions, when there is still but little capital and when landrent has not yet come into existence, the value of goods is determined solely by the amount of labour that has been embodied in them. Things like water, which have the highest possible use-value, have no exchange-value; and, conversely, things with very little use-value, like diamonds, have a very high exchange-value. It follows that labour is the measure of the exchange-value of goods; it is their "natural price"! What matters is, not the utility of a good, but the amount of labour that has been expended in producing it. This theory of value is a labour-expenditure theory.—Contraposed to the natural price is the "market price." In accordance with the fluctuations of supply and demand, this market price swings like a pendulum to one side or the other of the natural labour-expenditure price. The various items out of which the actual or market price is made up, are the outcome of private property and the extant legal order, consisting of: (*a*) the direct costs of labour (wages); (*b*) the share payable to capital (capital [Smith here calls it "stock"] being the stored product of labour), or the profit of capital ["profits of stock"] (which, according to our latter-day notions, comprises interest plus entrepreneur's salary plus entrepreneur's profit); and (*c*) landrent, which may be regarded as interest paid for the use of land (equivalent to the difference between the price of the produce of the land, on the one hand, and, on the other, the expenditure of the farmer upon wages plus profit on his farming capital).

From this theory of prices is deduced a theory of distribution, or of the formation of income;[1] for, inasmuch as production is carried on with an eye to the market on the basis of the division of labour, the product is distributed in accordance with the laws of the formation of prices in the market. The distribution of wealth is effected in accordance with the constituents of every price; the worker receives the equivalent for his labour, and the capitalist and the landlord receive equivalents for the cooperation of capital and land. Thus "all the commodities which compose the whole annual produce of the labour of every country, taken complexly, must resolve itself into the same three parts, and be parcelled out among different inhabitants of the country, either as the wages of their labour, the profits of their stock, or the rent of their land. . . . Wages, profit, and rent, are the three original sources of all revenue as well as of all exchangeable value. All other revenue is ultimately derivable from some one or other of these."[2] (This theory that the income of persons who practise the liberal professions is

[1] Smith uses the term "revenue", but we have thought it better to translate *Einkommen* (the word used by Spann) by "income" as a general rule, unless when actually quoting Smith. The student should note, however, that though there is a tendency to restrict the term "revenue" to the total current income of a government, it remains in current use for income from any form of property.—TRANSLATORS' NOTE.

[2] *Wealth of Nations*, book i, chapter 6.—Bohn's edition, vol. i, pp. 52–53.

' derivative" is still widely held, but it is erroneous. See above, pp. 87 et seq., and below, p. 162).

From this, at a later date, was developed the theory of the "productive factors". Land, labour, and capital, have their specific share in production; they are the "factors of production".

Smith's theories as to the formation of the various branches of income—theories which concern the laws of motion or laws of development of the different parts of the national income; in a word, the laws of distribution—may be succinctly phrased as follows. Rates of wages are determined, like market prices in general, by supply and demand, thanks to whose operation they vary to one side or the other of a subsistence wage. The more capital there is in a country, the greater is the demand for labour (wages-fund), and the higher therefore are wages.—The profit of capital has the converse trend. The more capital abounds, the lower is its rate of profit; the more capitalists there are, the more do they incline to underbid one another. Consequently, the more labour there is in a country, and the richer it therefore is, the lower in general is the profit of capital.[1]

In the matter of landrent, a more complicated machinery is at work. Increase in the fruitfulness of labour (the division of labour) and the expansion of manufacture lead to a fall in the prices of the products of industry. To the extent to which this happens, the products of agriculture automatically become exchangeable for larger quantities of the products of industry; i.e. the former become dearer. This rise in agricultural prices is attended or followed by a rise in landrents.[2] Landrent also rises concurrently with an increase in capital; for, since more capital and labour are applied to land, and land is therefore used more effectively, the income from land necessarily increases.

Applied Economics.—"Self-love" is the source of all economic phenomena—which, indeed, in every instance, spring from the individual. Economic life develops best when it is left alone. The main business of the State is to keep order. Laissez faire,

---

[1] *Wealth of Nations*, book i, chapter 9.
[2] *Ibid.*, book i, chapter 11.

laissez passer. Economic activities, when left perfectly untrammelled, develop harmoniously, and enable free competition to do its work. Thanks to this competition the self-love of
every individual promotes the general advantage. Competition
forces every one to pursue his own economic aims with the
utmost vigour, to develop all his forces to the maximum, and
to produce as cheaply as possible. Every one keeps watch over
his neighbour, with consequent benefit to all sections of
society. Consumers are supplied with the best goods at the
lowest prices; entrepreneurs can devote their energies to their
tasks unhindered; and workers can seek employment wherever
wages are highest. In this way a condition of social harmony is
attained. At the same time it results that every one engages in
the occupation which comes most natural to him and is best
suited to his capacities. Division of labour takes place along the
lines that are most economical. In virtue of its own mechanism,
society can get the better of that egoistic principle which is
(primarily) hostile to society. Every one becomes enabled, by
the pursuit of his own advantage, to enter into his natural rights.

In accordance with these principles, it was essential to make a
clean sweep of feudalism with its ties and servitudes; of the
medieval urban economy with its guild restrictions and its
regulation of markets and prices; of the cleavage between town
and countryside; of mercantilist customs dues, monopolies,
and paternal control of production. The abolition of serfdom,
the inauguration of freedom of occupation and industry, freedom of movement from place to place, political autonomy here,
there, and everywhere—these were the inevitable corollaries of
the new doctrine.

A demand weighty with consequences, the demand for free
trade, formed a logical and essential part of the demand for
the abolition of all restrictions upon production, distribution,
and exchange. Smith's theory of free trade ran as follows. If

trade be freed from all restraints, through the working of competition it will come to pass in the long run that every country will produce those commodities which its natural facilities enable it to produce most cheaply. Thus there will arise a natural international division of labour, which will redound to the maximum benefit of each nation, for each will be able to buy all it wants in the world market at the lowest possible prices, while selling there to the greatest advantage those things which it is exceptionally fitted to produce. "It is the maxim of every prudent master of a family never to attempt to make at home, what it will cost him more to make than to buy."[1]

In respect of the possibilities of practically applying these free-trade theories, however, Smith was not an uncompromising free-trader, but a moderate. He agreed as to the expediency of excise duties as a source of revenue; as to the expediency of retaliatory duties imposed upon imports from countries whose policy was protectionist; and as to the expediency of duties for special purposes—for instance, where an industry essential to the safety of the country was in need of protection, or when an industry would decay if a protective tariff previously imposed were to be done away with. Smith, far from being a dogmatist, as those who subsequently opposed his doctrines declared, was reasonable and cautious in practical matters.

In rebuttal of the current opinion (which is based upon a confusion of Smith's own views with the modifications his teaching underwent at the hands of Ricardo and, later still, of the Manchester School of British free-traders in the eighteen-thirties—see below, p. 107), it is desirable to point out that Smith was by no means hostile to the landowning class. On the contrary, in accordance with the previously explained theory of distribution, he considered that the interest of the landowners, of those who lived by landrent, was "strictly and inseparably connected with the general interest" of society,[2] for their income increased proportionally to an increase in the general welfare. Of the capitalist class, on the other hand, he wrote that its interest had "not the same connexion with the general

---

[1] *Wealth of Nations*, book iv, chapter 2. (Bohn's edition, vol. i, pp. 456–457.)
[2] *Ibid.*, book i, chapter 11. (Bohn's edition, vol. i, p. 263.)

interest of society" as that of the landowners and the wage-earners. For, he said: "The rate of profit does not, like rent and wages, rise with the prosperity, and fall with the declension of the society. On the contrary, it is naturally low in rich, and high in poor countries, and it is always highest in the countries which are going fastest to ruin."[1]—Towards the workers, the wage-earners, Smith's attitude was friendly. "The interest of the second order, that of those who live by wages, is as strictly connected with the interest of the society as that of the first"[2] (the landowning class). In opposition to the mercantilists, he advocated high wages and freedom of combination; but he disapproved of State interference in the matter of wage contracts.

2. The General Acceptance of Smith's Ideas, and their Initial Elaboration by Others

It is true that Smith's teaching was not, historically regarded, an original or creative achievement, seeing that many of his leading ideas had been enunciated by earlier writers, and especially by the physiocrats. Locke, among others, had declared labour to be the measure of exchange-value. Nevertheless, in virtue of its intermediary position, of the way in which to some extent it reconciled and amalgamated physiocracy and mercantilism, and in virtue of its development of the notion of liberty and of the idea of a trading and business economy (which was still rejected by those who accepted the idea of economic circulation as expounded in Quesnay's *Tableau économique*), it had a revolutionary significance. Smith's economics were in conformity with the time spirit, an individualist spirit, which he made vocal. His *Inquiry*, translated into many tongues, and actually compared with the Bible, had a speedy and lasting influence on science, public life, and prac-

[1] *Loc. cit.* (Bohn's edition, vol. i, p. 264.)
[2] *Loc. cit.* (Bohn's edition, vol. i, p. 263.)

tical politics in all civilised lands, and especially in Germany, where Marwitz wrote: "Next to Napoleon, Adam Smith is now become the mightiest monarch in Europe."

Even though we agree that Smith had so powerful an influence, it would be a mistake to suppose that the individualist trend of the period following the publication of the *Wealth of Nations* was solely or mainly the outcome of his theories. An individualist conception of life had become general before Smith lived and wrote, and was inculcated as part of the higher culture.

Smith's influence on practical matters was less considerable in England than elsewhere, for the simple reason that under parliamentary government in that country most of the restraints imposed by feudalism on industrial development had already become things of the past. But the protection of native industry continued to be a part of British policy, and as late as 1833 a moderate protective tariff was adopted by parliament. Not until well on in the eighteen-thirties did the "Manchester School" of practical economists become dominant under the leadership of Cobden and Bright. This was a free-trade party founded upon the doctrines of Ricardo rather than upon those of Smith. Operating through the Anti-Corn-Law League, it carried on a vigorous agitation against the import duties on grain. In 1846 the Corn Laws were repealed, and in 1860 the last vestiges of the protective system disappeared, England thereupon becoming a free-trade country in which taxes were imposed for revenue purposes only. At this date British industry was so enormously in advance of the industry of other countries, that Britain could well afford to ignore her rivals.

In Germany, on the other hand, and above all in Prussia, Smith's teaching had very important practical consequences. For Prussia, Baron vom Stein had conceived, and in 1807 had begun, a primarily conservative and organically interconnected scheme of reforms. Hardenberg, modifying and liberalising these reforms, introduced during the years 1810 and 1811 a system of partial industrial freedom, liberated the peasantry, abolished many other feudal restraints, and gave the towns local self-government. Elsewhere in Germany, rural restraints were abolished during the early decades of the nineteenth century; and in other respects the practical workings of the new doctrine were considerable. In Austria, although serfdom had technically been abolished in 1781-1782 (under Emperor Joseph II), vestiges of the servile status lingered, to be finally done away with in 1848; the freedom of industry was not established till 1859; and in 1868 the still remaining rural restraints were annulled.—In 1869, the freedom of industry was declared in the Industrial Ordinance of the North German Federation.

There was little work left for Smith's teaching to do in France, for here the doctrine of natural right and physiocracy already held sway. The great revolution (1789) ruthlessly shattered the edifice that had weathered many centuries. On the "ever-memorable night" of August 4, 1789, with the approval of the nobility and the clergy, the National Assembly abolished at one stroke, without compensation, all feudal burdens and privileges. In 1791, when a republican government had been established, the guilds and their privileges were likewise swept away; but the protective system was maintained.— (Concerning the aspirations and endeavours of the fourth estate, and concerning Morelly, Mably, and Babeuf, see below, p. 213.)

Among the scientific expounders and advocates of Smith's teaching must be mentioned first of all the Frenchman, J. B. Say (1767-1832; *Traité d'économie politique*, Paris, 1803, English translation by C. H. Prinsep, *A Treatise on Political Economy*, London, 1821), "the godfather of Adam Smith's doctrines on the Continent," as Lorenz von Stein called him. Thanks to the brilliancy with which he championed the new ideas, he played a notable part in their diffusion. An especially important matter was that he systematised them, whereas Smith had merely put forward a loosely connected bundle of separate theses. Say developed them deductively from a rationalist cognition of natural right. (True, we cannot ascribe much scientific value to such an undertaking.) Say unconditionally recommended economic freedom, unfolding a theory of the harmony of the interests of all classes of the population and of all nations (contra-mercantilism), and also a theory of openings for trade ("théorie des débouchés"). According to this latter theory, every supply gives rise to a demand, for from the producer there always comes a demand for other goods. Consequently there can be no such thing as general overproduction. —Say was the originator of the still current classification of economics into the theory of production, the theory of distribution, and the theory of consumption.

In Germany, L. H. von Jakob (1759–1827; *Grundsätze der Nationalökonomie*, 1805) and Rau (1792–1870; *Lehrbuch der politischen Oekonomie*, 1826), both supporters of Smith, began to effect a separation between the theoretical and the practical aspects of our science, which now became subdivided into theoretical economics, practical or applied economics, and the science of finance. Among the early Smithians must also be counted Hufeland (*Neue Grundlegung der Staatswissenschafts-kunst*, vol. I, 1807, vol. II, 1813) and Lotz (*Revision der Grundbegriffe der Nationalwirtschaftslehre*, 1811 et seq.). Rau's textbook dominated German economic thought for half a century, and had an influence in foreign countries as well. Later there came to the front the most notable member of this series, F. B. W. von Hermann (*Staatswirtschaftliche Untersuchungen*, Munich, 1832).—It should be noted that the German Smithians have not, as a rule, accepted Smith's labour theory of value, but have tried to explain value as arising out of utility. (See below, p. 255.)

3. CRITIQUE OF ADAM SMITH'S TEACHING. INTRODUCTION TO THE THEORY OF METHOD

a. The System.—Smith's teaching brought into vogue an entirely different way of contemplating political economy. It did this, first of all, by freeing investigators' minds from the idea that the source of wealth is of a very simple nature. True, he regarded labour as the primary source of wealth, but the conditions under which labour had to operate were of vital importance, and especially the increase of its fruitfulness by the division of labour. This, in its turn, implied that production had not been carried on in accordance with the dictates of a natural economy, but for the market. As I have already pointed out, Smith regarded everything from the outlook upon exchange in the market; he conceived of economic phenomena as centering in exchange, in the processes of "trade", and his explanation of the motive force of economic life was exclusively derived from that conception.

It seems to me that Smith's chief contribution to economic doctrine was this neatly rounded and bold notion that economic life was a concatenation of processes of exchange. Herein lay such originality as he possessed. He gave the finishing touches to the idea of the "ordre naturel" (see above, p. 76), the harmonious encounter of numberless individual self-seeking economic activities. In his doctrine, exchange, the trading intercourse of the separate economic agents, became the central manifestation of economic life. His system was not a theory of production, but a theory of the formal laws of value and price, which, he considered, determined production just as much as distribution. Seeing that theory of economic life is still held by the leading schools, we must examine it more closely.

According to Smith, wealth primarily consists of the aggregate of the goods annually produced. This is a purely mechanical, and quasi-arithmetical, concept; one which pays no heed to the organic composition of wealth. Smith reckons as wealth nothing but material goods, nothing but concrete objects (an error into which many modern economists still fall), although services, capacities, forms of organisation, and mental or spiritual achievements come within the same category. Furthermore, he includes only those material goods which have exchange-value. According to this calculation, things which, though they have a use-value, have no price, cannot be deemed wealth.—Smith regards economic life solely from the outlook of turnover, exchange, the mechanism of the market. Although he never explicitly declares that such is his conception of economics, there can be no doubt as to the nature of his views, which may be formulated as follows. The wealth of a nation is dependent to a much greater extent upon the fruitfulness of labour than upon other things. The fruitfulness of labour is enormously increased by the division of labour, and this last presupposes the exchange of commodities in the market. Goods only acquire the characteristics of commodities through being brought to market and acquiring there an exchange-value. Commodities have the strange, abstract, but important quality of being the outcome of the division of labour, and of being therefore produced for exchange, for the acquirement of exchange-value. Furthermore, it is an essential prerequisite to the interchange of goods in the market that there should be a general medium of exchange, namely, money, thanks to which the commodities to be exchanged one for another are provided with a common denominator of value, with an exchange-value expressed in terms of money. Consequently it would seem that all labour which creates exchange-value, creates wealth.

Comparing Smith's views with Quesnay's, we derive from the *Wealth of Nations* a picture of the structure of economic life very different from that given in the *Tableau économique*. The essential feature of the latter (which was still in the main anti-individualistic) was its demonstration of an economic circulation, its insistence upon the interconnexion of economic processes. But what is fundamental for Smith is that the economic individuals, separated from each other by the division of labour, come into mutual contact in the market; and that value is generated by such mutual contacts. This means, according to Smith, that the production of goods is determined by the market, by exchange-value; and, further, that the formation of prices in the market determines the outflow of the aggregate product from the market to the buyers, whose income of goods ("real income") is thus constituted, and whose income of money was previously formed in like manner through the sale of labour power, capital ["stock"], and land [or the right to use land]. It is true that the elucidation of the essential nature of these different forms of income was left for Ricardo; but we owe to Smith the momentous, and still prevalent, individualist notion of economics, according to which the laws of the formation of value and those of the turnover of commodities in the market form the core of economic theory—the circulation of goods and the concatenation of economic functions and institutions being utterly ignored. Let us distinguish. We will speak of the "laws of value" as what they really are, the "laws of the calculation of value"; and, in contradistinction, we will speak of the laws of the articulation and concatenation of economic activities and functions as "economic laws". Well now, of Adam Smith and his school it may be said that by Smith and all his followers the "laws of the calculation of value" and "economic laws" were regarded as identical things.

Is Smith's view correct, and is it exhaustive?

The attempt to understand all economic processes from the outlook upon exchange-value cannot but result in missing their most important feature—actual achievements. Economic life consists of the actual achievements of the means used to attain certain ends. These achievements always form an articulated whole, and the object of economic science is to study the anatomy and physiology, as it were, of that whole. But this, which is the main task of economic theory, finds no place in the writings of Smith. Furthermore, he pays no heed to those goods which never come to the market for exchange; to demand (whose origin cannot really be explained simply in terms of exchange), as against supply; to production, as against marketing (exchange and trade); to the forces of production, as against finished wares; to the mental or spiritual, as against the material; to the organic harmony of the parts of economic life, as against the seeming independence of these parts. In fine, he ignores utility, use-value, the achievements of the means used to attain economic ends—ignores the very cause, meaning, and soul of all economic activity. How can the economic picture fail to be distorted and falsified when looked at exclusively from the standpoint of exchange? We are told to regard calculations of value and price as economically creative; whereas in verity production and achievement form the primary source of value. Beyond question this is the economics of a shopkeeper! (The matter is considered again on p. 138 and pp. 142 et seq.)

Among the later critics of Smith, two of the most notable were Adam Müller (see below, pp. 158 et seq.) and Friedrich List (see below, pp. 187 et seq.). Both of them made slashing and successful onslaughts upon his concepts of a good and of wealth, and upon his theory of value.—For a criticism of his idea of price, see my own *Tote und lebendige Wissenschaft*, third edition, Jena, 1929, pp. 63 et seq.—For a general criticism of Smith's system, see Seidler-Schmid, *Die System-gedanken der sogenannten klassischen Volkswirtschaftslehre* ("Deutsche Beiträge," vol. ii, Jena, 1926).

b. Particular Theories.—Smith's *Wealth of Nations* is likewise notable for the account it gives of certain particular economic processes (the division of labour, the accumulation of capital, distribution). Even though much of what he had to say on these matters has been superseded, his remarks have served as a platform for subsequent advances.

His contention that the value of things is the outcome of labour, was first elaborated by Ricardo, and was then seized upon by the socialists, who deduced from it that the worker, the wage-earner, did not receive in his wages the full value of his labour, and was therefore exploited. Thus it developed into Marx's famous "theory of surplus value" (see below, p. 219 and p. 226). According to Smith, the profit of capital, and landrent, are both the outcome of the established legal order of society; whereas in reality the main parts of these phenomena derive from the peculiar characteristics of capital or of land in relation to economic life as a whole (see below, p. 143).

Smith also became historically important because of the method of his research—although his successor Ricardo was in truth far more responsible for the method which is usually supposed to have been originated by Smith. In his writings, as in Quesnay's (more for Quesnay than for Smith, and more for their pupils than for themselves), the predominance of the deductive method—it would be better to say, an abstract conception of economics—is characteristic.

The deductive method is that in which particular conclusions are deduced from a general proposition, regarded as a general truth. The inductive method is that in which general propositions are established as truths by induction, that is, by the observation of numerous particular instances.

When we speak of the "abstract" conception of economics, we mean that economics is considered in isolation, apart from and contrasted with the other constituents of society and economic life—the State, politics, morality, religion, etc. It is abstracted, is isolated from these; whereas in actuality economic phenomena are inseparably linked with sociological, political, moral, and religious happenings. Thus by Smith and his followers economic activity is represented as being, by its essential nature, dependent upon economic self-love alone. (They admit, indeed, that error, uneconomic behaviour, and the like, interfere with unalloyed economic activity; but they exclude these disturbing factors from consideration.)

According to the present writer, the main defect of such a view is the severance of economics from the indivisible whole of society, and the assumption that there exists an undiluted instinct of "self-love" or "self-interest"—for this (conceived as a force working in isolation) is a mere figment.—The theory that individual self-loves are all harmonised through a simple concurrence in the market is likewise unsound. Always in the market, as in industry, there is a pre-existent framework, into which the individual has to fit himself. The material requirements of the framework, not the individual's subjective sentiments of self-interest, determine the nature of this process of adaptation. The objective reason for articulation replaces· subjective self-interest.

Cf. my article "Eigennütz" in the *Handwörterbuch der Staatswissenschaften*, fourth edition, Jena, 1925. See also below, pp. 150 and 282.

The abstract conception of economics certainly leaves a remarkably wide field of action for the deductive method, inasmuch as, once the effectiveness of individual motive, of economic "self-love" or "self-interest", has been postulated, all the processes of the formation of value, production, distribution, and consumption, become logically deducible a priori, in strict conformity with law. But it is obvious that even this method of investigation cannot dispense with continuous induction as well, so that it is wrong-headed to talk without qualification of the "deductive trend" of the classical economists (as people usually talk to-day). What is really distinctive of the classical economists is their conception of an economic science sedulously abstracted from all the other components of social life. It is important to make this clear, for the historical school of political economy which came to the front at a later day in Germany is distinguished from the classical school by its more extensive application of the inductive method, and by its historical and statistical outlook (but in these respects differs from the classical school rather in degree than on principle): whereas the historical school has completely abandoned, and on principle, the abstraction of economics from other social phenomena; and strives, instead, to demonstrate thoroughly empirical realities. It is upon this latter difference, too, that the still continuing controversy as to method ("Methodenstreit") mainly turns, and not upon any calculation of the relative proportions of induction and deduction in one method or another.

(In this connexion, see below under Ricardo, pp. 146 et seq.;
under Adam Müller, pp. 158 et seq. and pp. 166 et seq.; and
under List, pp. 199 et seq. See also pp. 281 et seq.)

Moreover, Smith himself made plentiful use of the inductive
method. Nor did he put forward his teaching as a "system",
but rather as an assemblage of detached theories.

Concerning the free-trade theory, see below, pp. 187 et seq.

B. FURTHER DEVELOPMENT OF INDIVIDUALIST ECONOMICS BY MALTHUS AND RICARDO

The diffusion of Smith's doctrine was attended with much
modification and elaboration. Attempts to develop his trend
involved, above all, an endeavour to explain the misery of
the working classes, and all the defects and disharmonies
that had become apparent in economic life during the rapid
development of the capitalist method of production in the days
that followed the publication of the *Wealth of Nations*. In view
of these phenomena, two contrasted attitudes were possible.
The observer could associate his condemnation of them with a
systematic criticism of the capitalist social order. In this way,
socialism arose. Or he could accept them with pessimistic
resignation, declaring them to be unavoidable consequences of
the working of natural laws. This was the course taken by
Malthus and Ricardo.

1. Exposition of Malthus' Theory of Population

Thomas Robert Malthus was born at the Rookery, near
Dorking, in 1766. He took orders as an Anglican clergyman,
and his experience of the condition of the English poor during
his work as a parson may well have contributed to the development of his view that the main cause of poverty was to be found
in the immoderate increase of population. In 1798 he published the first draft of his theory in the anonymous work,
entitled *An Essay on the Principle of Population as it affects the*

Future Improvement of Society, with remarks on the Speculations of Mr. Godwin, M. Condorcet, and other Writers. In 1799, he visited Norway, Sweden, and Russia, and later went to France. In 1803, he published an enlarged and revised edition of the *Essay*, this time giving his name on the title-page. The book had been enriched by the addition of much statistical and historical matter, and now attracted considerable attention. In 1804, he was appointed professor of history and economics in the East India Company's College at Haileybury. In 1820 appeared his *Principles of Political Economy considered with a View to their Practical Application*—a book conceived in the spirit of Smith and Ricardo. The *Essay on Population* was translated into nearly all European languages. Malthus died in 1834. A reprint of the seventh edition of the *Essay on Population* forms two volumes of Dent's Everyman Library.

Malthus begins his argument with an account of "the constant tendency in all animated life to increase beyond the nourishment prepared for it." In illustration, he quotes Benjamin Franklin. "It is observed by Dr. Franklin that there is no bound to the prolific nature of plants or animals but what is made by their crowding and interfering with each other's means of subsistence. Were the face of the earth, he says, vacant of other plants, it might be gradually sowed and overspread with one kind only, as for instance with fennel: and were it empty of other inhabitants, it might in a few ages be replenished from one nation only, as for instance with Englishmen."[1]

It follows from this that population has a constant tendency to increase beyond the means of subsistence. Studying the increase of population in the American settlements, where there was an ample supply of fertile and previously untilled land, and where there were few natural checks to the growth of numbers, he came to the conclusion that during about one hundred and fifty years the population had doubled itself every twenty-five years. The natural increase of population therefore

Everyman edition, vol. i, p. 67.

took place like the increase in the series of numbers 1, 2, 4, 8, 16, 32, 64, 128, 256. In short, population, when its growth is unhindered, tends to increase in geometrical progression.

It is impossible, on the other hand, that the produce of the soil can be increased in such a ratio. Under favourable conditions, we may suppose that by improving the land already cultivated, and (in a country already settled) by bringing comparatively infertile and hitherto neglected areas under cultivation, it would be possible to increase very considerably the yield from the land. But the increase in twenty-five-year periods (those in which the population can double) could not be expected to proceed more rapidly than is represented by the series of numbers 1, 2, 3, 4, 5, 6, 7, 8, 9. "It may be fairly pronounced . . . that, considering the present average state of the earth, the means of subsistence, under circumstances the most favourable to human industry, could not possibly be made to increase faster than in an arithmetical ratio."[1]—To sum up, whereas population can increase in geometrical progression, the means of subsistence can increase only in arithmetical progression.

Population, therefore, is necessarily limited by the means of subsistence. As an outcome of the tension inherent in the contrast between these two possibilities of increase (increase of population by geometrical progression and increase of means of subsistence by arithmetical progression) there is a tendency for population to increase beyond the means of subsistence, with the result that population increases in any country when the means of subsistence increase—whether in consequence of more intensive culture, the import of foodstuffs, or changes in the distribution of the national wealth (thanks to social reforms, etc.). The continuous and forcible limitation of increase by the

[1] Everyman edition, vol. i, p. 10.

insufficiency of the means of subsistence makes itself felt in the form of checks. These checks are of two kinds, positive and preventive. The positive checks to population are those which act by destroying excess of population already produced; the most conspicuous of them being war, pestilence, and famine, but they "include every cause, whether arising from vice or misery, which in any degree contributes to shorten the natural duration of human life".[1] Preventive checks are those which take the form of deliberate measures, rationally conceived, in order to prevent an excess of population over the means of subsistence coming into being: abstinence from marriage, abstinence from the begetting of children, the postponement of marriage, moral restraint. "By moral restraint I . . . mean a restraint from marriage from prudential motives, with a conduct strictly moral during the period of the restraint."[2]

Applied Economics.—Malthus infers from his law of population that governments should, on the one hand, remove all hindrances to the cultivation of the soil, and, on the other, favour preventive checks, and especially the postponement of marriage. The following passage has attracted especial attention: "A man born into a world already possessed, if he cannot get subsistence from his parents on whom he has a just demand, and if the society do not want his labour, has no claim of *right* to the smallest portion of food, and in fact has no business to be where he is. At nature's mighty feast, there is no vacant cover for him. She tells him to begone, and will quickly execute her own orders, if he does not work upon the compassion of some of her guests."[3] Malthus therefore recommends the reduction of poor relief to a minimum. Money devoted to the support of the indigent or destitute is taken from the other classes of society, and especially from the stratum of the working class that is only a little less needy—for this poor relief

---

[1] Everyman edition, vol. i, pp. 13–14.   [2] *Ibid.*, vol. i, p. 14.
[3] This passage is not in the anonymous first draft of the *Essay* (1798). It appears on p. 531 of the one-volume quarto edition of 1803, and was withdrawn from subsequent editions.

increases demand, and thus raises the price of the necessaries of life. No harm is done, perhaps, if I feed a poor neighbour out of the produce of my own potato-patch, for I am then merely providing for him out of my own superfluity. "But if I . . . give him money, supposing the produce of the country to remain the same, I give him a title to a larger share of that produce than formerly, which share he cannot receive without diminishing the shares of others."[1] Malthus' main demand, therefore, is for "moral restraint". He writes: "It is clearly the duty of each individual not to marry till he has a prospect of supporting his children; but it is at the same time to be wished that he should retain undiminished his desire of marriage, in order that he may exert himself to realise this prospect, and be stimulated to make provision for the support of greater numbers."[2] Later, as an inference from this, it was proposed to put legal difficulties in the way of marriage. The poor who had no prospect of being able to support a family, were to be forbidden to marry.[3]

The Malthusian doctrine attracted widespread attention, and was accepted almost without qualification by scientists. It also made a strong impression on governments, and its effects were seen in the increased stringency of the marriage laws. Down to the close of the war of 1914–1918, vestiges of this persisted in Bavaria and some of the oldtime Austrian crownlands (Tyrol and Carniola), where marriage could not be entered into without the assent of the commune.

As to further consequences of Malthus' teaching in the domain of applied economics, it is worth noting that Malthus did not (as Ricardo did later—see below, p. 143, the Ricardian theory of landrent, whose fundamentals had already been enunciated by Malthus[4]) base upon the inevitable tendency of landrent to increase, an inclination to regard landowners with hostility. On the contrary, he favoured a protective tariff in conformity with the wishes of the landed interest.[5]

---

[1] Everyman edition, vol. ii, p. 39.   [2] *Ibid.*, vol. ii, p. 159.

[3] This proposal did not emanate from Malthus himself. Indeed, he expressly repudiated it. "I have been accused of proposing a law to prohibit the poor from marrying. This is not true." (Everyman edition, vol. ii, p. 64.)—TRANSLATORS' NOTE.

[4] *An Inquiry into the Nature and Progress of Rent*, 1815.

[5] *Observations on the Effects of the Corn Laws*, 1814. *The Grounds of an Opinion upon the Policy of Restricting the Importation of Foreign Corn*, 1815.

2. VALUATION OF MALTHUS' TEACHING. INTRODUCTION TO
THE SO-CALLED LAW OF DIMINISHING RETURNS FROM
LAND

a. Friends and Adversaries.—Malthus had had forerunners.
Plato, Aristotle, Botero, Montesquieu, Quesnay, Mirabeau,
Benjamin Franklin, James Steuart, Ortes, Arthur Young,
Townsend, and others, had recognised more or less distinctly,
the existence of a disharmony between the growth of popula-
tion and the possible increase of the means of subsistence.
Within a few years of Malthus' death, Darwin read the *Essay on
Population*, and received therefrom the impetus to the formula-
tion of his doctrine (an erroneous one, indeed) of the struggle
for existence.[1]

Among the adversaries of Malthus must be mentioned first
of all the socialists; then List, Carey, Dühring, Spencer, and
others. Recently, Franz Oppenheimer, by making a fierce attack
on Malthus,[2] has fanned the embers of the controversy that
formerly raged over the doctrines of the author of the *Essay*;
but most contemporary German economic experts (for instance,
Adolf Wagner, Dietzel, Bortkiewitsch, and Budge) have rallied
to the defence of Malthus. Still, a number of authorities (above
all, Julius Wolf, and later Mombert, Brentano, Pohle, Herkner,
and Diehl) have agreed with Oppenheimer that the Malthusian
law of population no longer applies to the modern world.[3]—

[1] For a criticism of the Darwinian theory, consult Uexküll, *Bausteine zu
einer biologischen Weltanschauung*, Bruckmann, Munich, 1913. [This book
has not been translated, but a later work by the same author, *Theoretical
Biology*, translated by J. L. Mackinnon, Kegan Paul, London, 1926, is
available in English.]

[2] *Das Bevölkerungsgesetz des Robert Malthus und die neuere Nationalökonomie*, Berlin, 1901.

[3] Julius Wolf, *Ein neuer Gegner des Malthus*, "Zeitschrift für Sozialwissenschaft," vol. iv, 1901; *Der Gebürtenrückgang, die Rationalisierung des Gesch-
lechtslebens*, Jena, 1912; *Die Volkswirtschaft der Gegenwart und Zukunft*,
Leipzig, 1912.—Mombert, *Studien zur Bevölkerungsbewegung in Deutschland*,
Karlsruhe, 1907.

Latter-day supporters of the Malthusian doctrine of population are inclined to jettison the two progressions (on which Malthus himself laid little stress). In my opinion they are wrong to discard the view that population tends to increase in geometrical progression. There may be various opinions as to the time-cycle, but as to the geometrical progression I do not see how there can be any dispute. No doubt Malthus' cycle of twenty-five years for the doubling was too short; but spin out the period as you please, and a time will come when the population will have doubled. Now the doubled population will be ready to double itself once more in the same term of years, unless there should be a decline in the energy of increase. It follows that the increase tends to occur by a series of successive doublings, that is to say, in geometrical progression.

An objector might contend that the returns from land will also double themselves after a time. If they have increased in proportion with the series 1, 2, 3, 4, they have doubled themselves twice. But here we are on a different footing from that of the increase of population. In accordance with our suppositions, population retains throughout its increase an undiminished capacity for expansion. When a population of 4 has increased to 8, these 8 have unimpaired energy for an increase to 16; and so on. Cultivated land, on the other hand, has, in accordance with our suppositions, a steadily diminishing capacity for an increase in the returns.

b. Law of Diminishing Returns from Land.[1]—The actual fact is that an increase in the yield of land is uncertain and irregular. The principle of the matter is embodied in the "law of diminishing returns", according to which, in the cultivation of land, assuming that the technique remains unchanged, each successive increment of capital and labour applied to it beyond a certain amount (the optimum expenditure upon this particular

[1] As to the theory of diminishing returns, see my article *Gleichwichtigkeit gegen Grenznutzen*, "Jahrbücher für Nationalökonomie," vol. cxxiii.

area with this particular technique) produces a smaller increment of yield. Accordingly, beyond the optimum expenditure,
further increments of capital and labour no longer produce
equal increments of yield, but progressively diminishing ones.
To put the matter in more general terms, the conditions remaining in other respects unchanged, increments of expenditure
prove successively less profitable. If, for instance, the expenditure of 1,000 units of additional capital produces an additional
yield of 500, the expenditure of a second 1,000 will bring a
yield of only 300, that of a third 1,000 an additional yield of no
more than 200, and so on.

This view was, in substance, already put forward by Turgot
and by James Anderson,[1] and later by Edward West.[2] It is
wrongly coupled to Ricardo's name in conjunction with the
theory of landrent, and also to the name of William Nassau
Senior (1790–1864). See below, p. 136. The law still finds
general acceptance among economists to-day, though there
have always been some authorities to contest its validity.

The inevitability of a diminishing return after the optimum
has been surpassed, is, indeed, logically deducible. The chain
of reasoning may be summarised as follows. In industry, the
demand for a double yield is satisfied by setting to work with
two workers, two machines, and two units of raw material,
where previously only one unit of each was utilised. But in
work upon the land it is a fundamental fact that the surface of
the area under cultivation is a primary datum, and cannot be
increased, and that the necessary amounts of light, air, warmth,
moisture, and nutrients, are likewise primary data which, if
capable of increase at all, can be increased only within strict

---

[1] *An Inquiry into the Nature of the Corn Laws, etc.*, 1777. Anderson
likewise enunciated the theory of landrent which subsequently became
associated with the name of Ricardo (see below, p. 136), but deduced from
it politico-canonical conclusions differing from those deduced by Ricardo.

[2] *Essay on the Application of Capital to Land*, published anonymously,
London, 1815.

limits. Consequently, in agricultural production, a number of the factors of production are incapable of intensification or can be intensified only to a moderate degree. The only factor that can here be intensified as much as we please is the expenditure on capital and labour. But if some of the factors of production are incapable of intensification, it is impossible that intensification of the other factors should bring about an increase in the yield proportional to the increased expenditure. Additional increments of expenditure will necessarily lead to no more than progressively diminishing increments of yield.

A concrete instance will help to make this clear. Let us suppose that with a particular technique and a specific expenditure of capital, the optimum cultivation of a certain area of land can be effected with two ploughings and the application of x manure. In that case, four ploughings and the application of $2 x$ manure, would certainly increase the yield, but would not double it, since by hypothesis the optimum application of labour and manure has already been reached. The reason why the new yield must perforce be less than double the old, is that all the other factors of production are fixed, and cannot be doubled like the labour and the manure. Obviously, the law of diminishing returns will apply wherever some of the factors of production are immutable—even in industry, though here up to a point a law of increasing returns prevails because the overhead charges are proportionally smaller when a larger sum is devoted to production. The law of diminishing returns applies when an increase in raw materials and labour means that inferior raw material and inferior (or more expensive) labour must be employed, or when for any reason one or more of the factors of production are fixed in quantity or intensity. If in industry, for example, a doubling of the output cannot be achieved by the employment of two workers and the use of two machines in place of one, it will be necessary (by working longer hours, or by speeding-up the machinery, or what not) to effect a one-sided intensification of the mutable factors of production. But this is thriftless expenditure, inasmuch as it causes only an absolute increase in output, not a relative one. For the speeding-up, etc., do not bring about the optimum use of the factors of production. That we assume to have been attained before the attempt was made to increase output.

We must not overlook the fact that there is a law of increasing returns as well as one of diminishing returns and that the former comes into operation: (1) wherever the optimum has not yet been attained, whether in industry or agriculture (and, for practical purposes, wherever there is a dearth of capital, for in that case increments of capital give increasing returns until the optimum is reached); (2) wherever a new and better technique comes into operation, or when new aims are being cultivated (e.g. the temperance movement).

The law of diminishing returns from land is valid only so long as agricultural technique remains unchanged. It is suspended by technical advances, thanks to which there will be increasing returns for additional expenditure until the optimum expenditure for the new conditions is reached. Thenceforward, of course, increments of expenditure will be less and less fruitful! But owing to these jumps taken by the curve of output, it is impossible to express returns in terms of an arithmetical progression showing a steady diminution in the increments of output brought about by increments of expenditure on agricultural production.

One limitation is imposed on the laws of increasing and diminishing returns by this, that a change in technique necessarily occurs when an increment of expenditure is applied to some only instead of to all of the factors of production. When one of these factors is modified, there must follow a change (however small) in the working of the other factors. For this reason, the abstract notion of diminishing returns ceases to be applicable in the following circumstances: (1) When the application of supplementary means brings about notable changes in the articulation of functions. For instance, an increase (not a change) in supervision in a factory may bring about a disproportionately large improvement in general functioning (this is equivalent to an increase in "higher-grade capital"). (2) When the additional means can be utilised for the attainment of new and more important ends. Suppose, for example, that a new water-supply is installed—water laid on for general purposes, for cleaning in the grand style, where hitherto there has only been a limited amount of well water procurable in buckets for drinking and cooking. If this has, as it presumably will have, a beneficial effect on the public health, the resulting improvement in the general welfare and the consequent saving of health and of lives will be an increasing and not a diminishing return— although no new technique will have been established. (See below, p. 264.)—No doubt, it is possible to regard these as being still instances of the "attainment of the optimum", but only in the sense that the one-sided increase of a particular means may make it possible to surpass an optimum previously attained, and may do this by a change in the articulation of functions, without the introduction of any new technique! The law of diminishing returns, the principle that increments of expenditure do not result in proportional increments of output, does not come into operation until the absolute optimum has been attained. Between the respective optima, there is a stage in which the irregular progression of the increments or decrements becomes manifest—in contradistinction to the spurious regularity which the mechanically conceived laws of diminishing and increasing returns would lead us to expect. The inevitable inference is that the laws of diminishing and increasing returns are not mechanical laws, are not "laws of nature", but merely descriptions of the manner in which, within the given articulate structure of means, an increase of means achieves its purpose.

   c. *Objections to the Malthusian Doctrine.*—Some of the objections put forward by socialists are utterly invalid—for instance, the contention that the human power of reproducing the species declines concomitantly with an advance in human evolution. (Carey said the same thing, see below, pp. 204 et seq.; so did the English philosopher Herbert Spencer.) Other socialist objections miss the point—for instance, the contention that for the present there is an abundance of untilled land.

The last-mentioned argument against Malthus is a favourite one, but it really contains an implicit admission of his thesis, for people do not trouble to bring new land under cultivation until the old land is overcrowded. The difficulties of breaking up and settling virgin soil are so tremendous[1] that no one would attempt to overcome them unless through pressure of population (above all, when it enforces emigration). A further hindrance to the settlement of new land arises out of the cruelties, the combats, and the perils that are attendant on the process of driving out the indigenous population of the country that has to be settled.—In the domain of theory, therefore, the assertion that there is still plenty of room in the world is no answer to Malthus. As far as practice is concerned, it has little or no bearing on the question, for a nation cannot afford to allow its agriculturists to be ruined by the unrestricted importation of agricultural produce from newly settled lands. When, in any country, the growth of population has by degrees led to the bringing of less and ever less fertile land under cultivation, and thereupon new and economical methods of transport threaten to flood the country with foodstuffs that have been more cheaply produced on more fertile and recently settled land in other parts of the world, to allow unrestricted import would, generally speaking, ruin the agriculturists of the home country. That was the position in Germany, Austria-Hungary, and indeed in most of the countries of Europe, when towards the middle eighteen-seventies the development of steamship traffic brought cheap transatlantic grain into the European market—at a time when Germany, owing to growth of population, had become a grain-importing land. Unless a nation, under such conditions, is to take to extensive culture (with the inevitable result of losing most of its peasantry), it must bear

[1] A vivid picture of these difficulties will be found in the short story *Pioneers* by the Finnish novelist Juhani Aho in the volume *Squire Hellman and other Stories*, translated by R. Nisbet Bain, Fisher Unwin's Pseudonym Library, 1893.

part, at least, of the consequences of increasing population in the form of a protective tariff.

Among the socialists, Karl Marx has formulated objections that seem weightier than most, but they rest upon an inversion of the Malthusian argument. He says that the superfluous workers who make up what he terms the industrial reserve army are not the outcome of overpopulation but of the increasing use of labour-saving machinery. On this theory, it is the chaotic nature of the capitalist system that must be blamed for the continuous increase in unemployment. Thus what appears to be overpopulation is really a defect of distribution, not an outcome of the error of excessive breeding.—A corollary to this train of thought is the conception of a varying "capacity" for population in various kinds of economic order (for Marx considers that the "industrial reserve army" could immediately be turned to a good use by a socialised community). What seems to be a surplus population is, therefore, not an absolute, but a relative surplus population. (See below, p. 222.)—The idea of relative overpopulation is found already in the writings of List. (See below, p. 195.)

The notion that overpopulation is merely relative, is not a valid objection to Malthus' law of population. Malthus himself entertained it (though he did not use the same terminology); and pointed out that in varying stages of economic development and in varying economic orders there were different capacities for population. Indeed, the idea is indispensable if we wish to explain why a country populated by hunters and herdsmen is able to nourish and sustain fewer people than one inhabited by husbandmen and industrial workers. It is upon such advances as that from hunting and fishing to herdsmanship, from herdsmanship to agriculture, and from agriculture to industry, that the possibility of an absolute increase in population mainly depends. All that Malthus said was that every society, progressive societies included, is necessarily overpopulated. This applies even to a stagnating society like that of contemporary France, where the difficulty of supporting a large family acts preeminently by preventing the growth of population. Besides Marx's objection is shortsighted. Let us admit, for the sake of argument, that a communist organisation of society would temporarily absorb the extant surplus population. The next question we have to answer is whether overpopulation would then recur, or not. Marx makes no attempt to answer it. On the other hand, both Plato and Aristotle, in their schemes for ideal commonwealths, foresaw that population would increase faster than the means of subsistence, and they therefore made provision for emigrant settlements.

Another objection, voiced by Oppenheimer in the before-mentioned book, in a kindred form by Carey and Bastiat (concerning these two, see below, pp. 203 et seq.), by Henry George (1839–1897) in his famous book *Progress and Poverty* (1879), and by Eugen Dühring, is that the law of diminishing returns is sound as far as it goes, but that without fail the inadequacies of agricultural production are more than made good ("overcompensated") by technical improvements in industry and agriculture. Increase of population, therefore, say these writers, can never be a cause of poverty, but must always lead to increasing prosperity. The advances in agricultural technique alone suffice to invalidate the law of diminishing returns; and their effect is enormously reinforced by progress along other lines. Increasing density of population makes cheap transport possible (canals and railways); it also leads to the establishment of great markets, and this in turn facilitates the growth of large-scale industry and an extended application of the territorial division of labour. These multifarious and immense enhancements of fruitfulness do much more than counterbalance the diminishing fruitfulness of successive increments of expenditure in agricultural production. Such is the reasoning of Oppenheimer, Carey, George, and Dühring. Carey declared that the more people there were, the greater was their power "to make effective demands upon the treasury of nature". He did not admit the validity of the law of diminishing returns.

Is Carey's optimism justified? Is his reasoning logically correct? We shall return to these questions in due course.

d. The Latter-day Fall in the Birthrate.—Before the war, numerous experts, equipped with huge arrays of statistics, were calling attention to the steady decline in the birthrate which had been going on for about four decades in almost all civilised countries, and especially in France. In Germany, Julius Wolf was the first, followed by Mombert, to draw attention to the matter in conjunction with an arraignment of Malthus. In France, before this, Bertillon and others, and in Belgium Smissen,[1] had done the same thing. The decline in the birthrate is an incontestable fact. As regards Germany[2] and France,[3] it has been definitely proved that the decline has been associated with a lowering of the average age at which marriage takes places, this indicating that there must be a diminishing fertility of married couples, due to the artificial prevention of conception. Other causes, such as the decline in infant mortality (which must automatically reduce the birthrate) exercise a contributory influence, but are not the main factors.

e. Summary.—In the foregoing, Malthus' teaching has been expounded, and the arguments levelled against it have been adduced. It seems to me, however, that there is more to be said about this contentious topic. We should distinguish between: (1) the general tendency of population to increase; (2) the question whether an increase of population is likely, of

[1] Edouard van der Smissen, *La population*, Brussels, 1893.

[2] Cf. Mombert, *Studien zur Bevölkerungsbewegung in Deutschland*, Karlsruhe, 1907.

[3] Cf. for the present century, Bertillon, *La dépopulation de la France*, Paris, 1911; and for an earlier period, Goldstein, *Bevölkerungsprobleme in Frankreich*, 1900.

itself, to promote the general welfare, or to increase and aggravate poverty; and (3) the cultural and national aspects of the problem. I shall consider the matter briefly under these three heads:

1. Of the general tendency of population to increase, it must first of all be said that this tendency is not a purely biological or bodily manifestation, as Malthus opined, and his adversaries no less. Associated with the biological cause is a mental or spiritual one, and it is the latter which is ultimately decisive. Young and vigorous nations make the fullest possible use of their biological capacity for increase, for they are animated by the will to live, by a desire to enjoy a full measure of their simple and temperate existence. They are also strong enough to bear the consequences of overpopulation, to accept privations, and to carry on unceasing struggles. Weary, outworn nations and civilisations are endowed with an equal biological capacity for increase, but on the spiritual plane they lack vitality, and have lost much of their will to live (or at any rate to live simply), have become disinclined to endure privations and engage in struggles. Hence there ensues an artificial restriction of births, with moral decay, and, ultimately, extinction. (Consider the fate of the ancient Greeks and Romans!)

Rightly understood, however, the decline of the birthrate cannot be said to invalidate the formal accuracy of the Malthusian doctrine. What has happened is that since Malthus' day certain preventive checks (the artificial prevention of conception, and a reduction in mortality) have become far more significant than they were when Malthus wrote. Nowadays it is these preventive checks, rather than positive checks, which hinder population from pressing too hard upon the means of subsistence.

2. Now let us turn to consider the economic question, whether an increase of population tends, by itself, to promote welfare or to increase poverty. Carey and his followers took the former

view; but when we examine their arguments closely we see that these writers were inclined to lump the beneficial effects of technical advances with those of an increase of population pure and simple.

It is an indisputable fact that every new consumer is also potentially a new worker; but only in exceptional circumstances do we find the fruitfulness of his work to be increased by the mere fact that he comes as a supplementary hand, and we therefore cannot agree that on principle increase of population will promote the general welfare. The primary result of the arrival of a fresh consumer is to intensify poverty: for, first of all, his demands for agricultural produce can only be satisfied (under the assumed conditions) by the expenditure of an amount of labour disproportionate to the return; and, secondly, the cost of his education and of his equipment with the requisite productive capital is considerable. In pre-war Germany, with a yearly increase of population (excess of births over deaths) amounting in round figures to 800,000, an annual expenditure of one and a half milliards of marks was needed for fresh housing accommodation alone.—Economic advances are, therefore, essential if the increase in poverty due to the new arrival is to be counterbalanced, or (better still) outweighed. Now, the crucial fact we have to remember is that these economic advances do not occur automatically as necessary accompaniments of the increase of population, but have to be wrestled for under stress of overpopulation. Furthermore, the possibilities in this direction are restricted, whereas the tendency of population to increase has no time-limit. After a certain density of population has been reached, a further increase in density will no longer promote such an expansion of markets as might amplify the division of labour and thus cheapen production. On the contrary, strong counterposing forces come into operation, in industrial as well as in agricultural production: raw materials become scarce and costly; the crowding together of the population forces up urban groundrents, and makes house-room very expensive; the transport of food to the towns becomes dearer because the margin of cultivation has been pushed farther and farther away—beyond question the necessaries of life cost more in great towns than in small.—While we have to agree, then, that, in many places, there occurs, after a time, a compensation for pressure of population (and, indeed, that without such a compensation the historical fact that an absolute growth of population has been accompanied by an increase in general prosperity would be inexplicable); none the less we have to recognise that in its very nature this compensation is secondary, is a late effect of the pressure of population, and that there is never any guarantee that the process of compensation will continue. We must not be led to entertain any illusions because in our own time there has been progress by leaps and bounds, for that progress has been unexampled in history. The law of increasing returns and the law of diminishing returns have both been at work!

In this matter, once again, it is a mental or spiritual cause that must have the last word—the will to overcome difficulties, and the power to enforce that will. Such a will and such a power are not present to the same degree at all times in all civilisations and among all peoples.

3. This brings us to the national aspect of the question. Mechanically contemplated, an increase of population is a cause of impoverishment. But under stress of this impoverishment, under the pressure of overpopulation, there ensues a struggle to achieve technical and organisational progress. "Under the pressure of"—this implies the working of cultural, national, and ethical factors. A nation must have sufficient energy, first to create this pressure, and then to get the better of it. A healthy expansion in numbers, a healthy pressure of

population on the means of subsistence, is necessary for a nation—if it is to remain young, if it is to advance, if it is not to fall sick or become weary. This expansion in numbers is at one and the same time a factor of impoverishment and a fountain of youth; it has a shady and a sunny side.

Taking it all in all, Malthus' doctrine is sound at the core. Nevertheless, though it is the most accordant with historical fact and the least individualistic among all the teachings of the classical school of economists, it is conceived too mechanically, as was to be expected of any product of the individualistic age in which he flourished. Malthus could see and his modern disciples can see nothing but the night side, the negative aspect, of the movement of population. In its mechanical and negative formulation, the Malthusian theory of population leads to an artificial restriction of births and to national extinction; but understood universalistically, it is a doctrine of life.

f. Poverty and Pauperism.—Only to outward seeming is the problem of poverty and pauperism solved by the Malthusian idea of the failure of the growth of the means of subsistence to keep pace with the growth of population. If, in any community, a number of persons are superfluous, we still have to ask: "Who are thrust down into the abyss of poverty?" The question will press for solution even in a socialist State, for this likewise will have its poor, will have in it persons who are permanently incapable of performing or are unwilling to perform the average economic tasks. Recent investigations have shown that in great measure the poor are afflicted with infirmity of will, or are in some other respect of below-average economic capacity.

3. Exposition of Ricardo's Teaching

Adam Smith's economic teaching was rounded off by Ricardo, a man of great perspicacity. Developing the abstract and individualist trends of Smith's *Wealth of Nations*, he became one of the most influential economists of the nineteenth century.

David Ricardo (1772–1823) was born in London. His father, born in Holland, was of Portuguese Jewish stock. The father made a moderate fortune on the London Stock Exchange, and the son was educated, partly in London and partly in Holland, for a mercantile career. David Ricardo thus gained an extensive knowledge of the business world, and in that world won for himself both wealth and respect. After a time he devoted himself mainly to study, at first to mathematics and chemistry, and then (after reading Adam Smith's *Wealth of Nations*) to economics. His chief work, *On the Principles of Political Economy and Taxation*, was published in 1817.

a. Theory of Value.—Ricardo's continuation of Smith's teaching begins with an explanation of value. Whereas Smith had taught that in a natural economy, and in that alone, labour was determinative of the exchange-value of goods (use-value being excluded as common to all goods), and that in later stages of economic development wages, profit, and landrent became the determinants of value—Ricardo declared that during all these economic phases the quantity of simple labour that had been requisite for the production of a commodity determined its exchange-value or price—determined it in the case of commodities multipliable at will, commodities that had a scarcity value (the first introduction of this concept into the theory of value; but for Ricardo scarcity plays an insignificant part in the creation of value, as compared with labour, which is the essential factor).—Carrying out this idea logically, he regards landrent, not as a price-forming factor, but as the consequence instead of the cause of the formation of price; he considers wages to represent the cost of maintaining the worker, as equivalent to the cost of reproducing the labour; and he resolves capital likewise, as stored labour, into a labour-cost element, the labour-cost being proportional to the amount of capital that is used up. On the other hand, he does not resolve profit into labour-cost, for profit is left as a residue (the "residual theory"). The "market prices" of commodities coincide with their labour value, which is their "natural price": not a precise coincidence, indeed, for prices fluctuate under the varying influences of supply and demand; but market prices tend always to approximate to natural prices, seeing that capital invariably inclines to flow into those branches of production whose products, owing to a shortage of supply, command exceptionally high prices. This is the law of the gravitation of prices towards least cost, when commodities are multipliable at will, under the regime of free competition.—But Ricardo's contention that, under free competition, "in one and the same country profits are, generally speaking, always on the same level",[1] involves a difficulty in the application of the before-mentioned propositions of the Ricardian theory of value. (This is a matter to which we shall return on p. 142.) Another fruitful constituent of the Ricardian theory of value is the notion that the sum of wages and profits forms a constant magnitude. For, since exchange-value is objectively determined by the quantity of labour, it must always remain the same. Consequently, if wages should rise, this rise cannot affect the exchange-value of the commodities (seeing that the amount of labour put into them remains the same); so it must reduce the profit. Conversely, if profit rises, wages must fall. This idea is perpetually recurring in Ricardo's writings.

b. Theory of Landrent.—According to Ricardo, the same laws of the formation of exchange value apply to agricultural production. He therefore refuses to regard this as an utterly distinct type of production, as do the physiocrats. Moreover, whereas Adam Smith had declared landrent to be an additional constituent of the price of the produce of the soil, Ricardo held

[1] *Principles*, chapter vi (1817 edition, p. 157).

that landrent only comes into existence through the operation of the laws of prices, thanks to the monopoly position of the landowning class.

This basic idea of the Ricardian theory of rent (Ricardo here used the general term "rent" with a specific application to the rent of land, or landrent) had been already formulated by Turgot, by James Anderson (1739–1808) in *An Inquiry into the Nature of the Corn Laws*, Edinburgh, 1777, by West (1815), and, in especial, by Malthus. Anderson considered that the system of paying landrents was beneficial, leading to the improvement ("melioration") of the rented land. (See above, pp. 123 et seq.)—[Of course Ricardo gave the theory a turn peculiar to himself.]

The Ricardian theory of landrent may be summarised as follows:

In a newly settled country, where there is a superfluity of unoccupied land, the settlers bring only the best land ("land of the first quality") under cultivation. The price of the products of the soil, like that of all products multipliable at will, is determined by the cost of production. Ere long, however, owing to the growth of population, there arises an increased demand for foodstuffs, with the result that prices rise to a point at which it pays to bring land of the second quality under cultivation; or else to make additional expenditure upon the already cultivated land of the first quality (expenditure which, under the operation of the law of diminishing returns, will be less lucrative than is the original, optimum, expenditure). The owners of land of the first quality have now a monopoly position as against the owners of land of the second quality. Assuming the application of equal amounts of capital and labour to equal areas of firstrate and secondrate land, the difference between the yield of the firstrate and that of the secondrate area is a rent provided by the land of the first quality. Furthermore, the primary, more lucrative expenditure upon the land yields a rent as against the latter, supplementary expenditure, which is less lucrative in accordance with the working of the law of diminishing returns. In the further course of development, land of the third quality is brought under cultivation, then land of the fourth quality, and so on; and all the while new rents are being formed, and simultaneously the old rents increase. All the different qualities of land pay rent, except for the very last quality of land fit for cultivation in existing circumstances ("land on the margin of cultivation"). When all the cultivable land in a country has been occupied, there may arise an absolute rent, a rent of land of the worst quality; but there cannot be a rent of the last increment of capital expended on the land.

Deducible from this Ricardian theory of rent, is the general law of prices, according to which the prices of commodities that are not multipliable at will are determined by the cost of the most expensive method of production which it still pays to use ("law of rent-prices").

Just as there are rents brought into existence by differences in the quality of cultivable land, so there are rents brought into existence by differences in the situation of cultivable land. (See below, under Thünen, pp. 172 et seq.)

c. Theory of Wages and of Distribution.—Wages are likewise subject to the laws governing the formation of prices. According to Ricardo, labour is a commodity multipliable at will; and its natural price (wages) is therefore determined by the cost of producing the labour, which is the cost of producing the necessaries of life requisite for the maintenance of the worker and for enabling him to reproduce his kind. The market price of labour, like that of other commodities, tends always to approximate to the natural price. For, whenever wages rise so that the worker is enabled to marry earlier or to bring up more children, the working population increases more rapidly than before, and thereupon wages are forced down to the natural price of labour, because the supply of labour is in excess of the demand. If, on the other hand, wages fall below the cost of subsistence, there are fewer marriages, and there is an increase in infant and child mortality, and even the numbers of the adult workers are directly reduced by their enhanced privations. In due course, therefore, the supply of labour will be less than the demand, and wages will rise to the natural price of labour. At a later date, Lassalle called this the "iron law of wages". By that teaching, the pessimist inferences from the individualist conception of the economic order (inferences already drawn by Malthus) are reached by another route. The whole circle has been rounded, and the theory of economic harmony proclaimed by Quesnay and Adam Smith has been given its quietus.

Ricardo's theory of wages has given rise to a wages-fund theory, according to which the demand for workers at any time is a fixed magnitude, determined by whatever amount of the national property is devoted to the payment of wages. This amount is the "wages-fund". Only by an increase in the wages fund can the demand for labour increase so as to bring about a rise in wages.

d. The Movement of Distribution.—By regarding wages as representing the cost of production of labour, Ricardo secured the foundation on which was upbuilded his doctrine of distribution and of the internal movement on which he believed distribution to depend. His views on this matter have been summarised by Karl Diehl as follows: "The national income is distributed in three main channels, namely, wages, the profit of capital (interest plus entrepreneur's profit), and land-rent. Wages are really (though not nominally) constant, being determined by the cost of the worker's necessary subsistence. The price of the means of subsistence is, in its turn, mainly dependent on the price of grain; and the price of grain depends on the cost of producing it from land upon the margin of cultivation. In the 'natural' course of economic events, more and more land is continually being brought under cultivation to supply the necessary quantities of food, and for that reason an increasing proportion of the national income must go to rent; this reduces profit, since all that remains of the national income when wages have been paid is divided between profit and rent. The 'natural' tendency in any country, therefore, is towards an increase in rents, and a reduction in profit, while (real) wages remain constant."

Ricardo also formulated his own theory of money and banking, the so-called "quantity theory of money". (See below, pp. 288 et seq.)

e. *Applied Economics.*—Ricardo was an uncompromising free-trader, for in this as in other respects he was more radical than Adam Smith in carrying the principles of individualism and laissez-faire to their logical conclusion.

This radicalism was afterwards erroneously ascribed to Smith as well as to Ricardo, and indeed was ascribed to the whole "school of classical economists", which was thus represented as championing mobile capital, unqualified free trade, and ruthless individualism. But the "Manchesterism" of Cobden and Bright (see above, p. 107) was grounded much more on Ricardo than on Smith. The general classification which would include Smith among the typical forerunners of the Manchester School casts its net much too wide, as Oncken has rightly insisted.[1]

The Free-Trade Doctrine. As a corollary to Ricardo's view of the movement of distribution, we have a new theory of free trade. The aggregate of profit plus wages is perforce a constant; hence profit can only be increased by a lowering of (real)

[1] Cf. Oncken, *Was sagt die Nationalökonomie als Wissenschaft über die Bedeutung hoher und niedriger Getreidepreise?* Berlin, 1901; and compare with this the exaggerations of Held, *Zwei Bücher zur sozialen Geschichte Englands,* 1881.

wages; but wages cannot be permanently reduced except by a reduction in the price of the necessaries of life upon which the wages are spent; and a reduction of this kind can most easily be effected through having recourse to the best land in foreign countries. "If, instead of growing our own corn, or manufacturing the clothing and other necessaries of the labourer, we discover a new market from which we can supply ourselves with these commodities at a cheaper price, wages will fall and profits rise."[1]

"Free trade" as understood by Smith means, to have commodities as cheap as possible. "Free trade" as understood by Ricardo means, to have commodities as cheap as possible, in conjunction with the abandonment of the cultivation of the poorest land in the home country, with a consequent decline in real wages and a rise in the profit of capital. These are the different conceptions, though the fact is usually overlooked.— In practice Ricardo's attitude towards the landed interest was a moderate one; for he was not altogether blind to the dangers entailed upon agriculture by a policy of unrestricted free trade.

In respect of the social valuation of the various economic classes, Ricardo's standpoint was opposed to Smith's: for Ricardo considered a high profit on capital to be accordant with the general interest of the community; whereas Smith declared that in wealthy countries the profit of capital was low, and in poor countries high, so that the interests of the capitalists did not wholly accord with the demands of economic progress, whilst the interests of the landowners and the wage-earners did! (See above, pp. 105–6.) Conversely, Ricardo deduced from his theory of landrent a theory of distribution, to the effect that landrent increased at the expense of the capitalists and the wage-earners, this indicating, as far as applied economics was concerned, an attitude hostile to the landed interest but friendly to the capitalist interest.

[1] Ricardo, *Principles*, chapter vi (1817 edition, p. 154).

4. VALUATION OF RICARDO

a. Theory of Value and of Prices. Ricardo's teaching, like Smith's, rests upon the notion that economic phenomena are, at bottom, nothing but processes of exchange. According to both these authorities, the circulation and distribution of goods is explicable through knowing how prices are formed. Upon the formation of prices depends what is produced, who buys the products, and whither they flow.

Consequently the criticisms of Smith formulated on p. 109, apply with equal force to Ricardo. The latter's whole teaching has his theory of value as its fulcrum. Now, Ricardo held the labour theory of value, and from the outlook of contemporary science we are entitled to say without circumlocution that that theory is erroneous.

The difficulties in which the Ricardian theory of value is involved (the same difficulties with which, later, the Marxian theory of value had to wrestle) arise out of the different ways in which capital is used in the various branches of enterprise, and out of the conception of profit.

Since Ricardo holds that under a regime of free competition all profits are at the same level, it follows that those branches of industry which involve the locking-up of large quantities of capital for a considerable time (such as in machine making), and which have therefore a long "production period", sell their products for prices in excess of the labour-value; for were it otherwise they could not make profits equal to those of their competitors who have a rapid turnover of capital (e.g. money invested in domestic industry). This surplus over and above the labour-value is termed by Ricardo "compensation for time". Conversely, enterprises in which there is a very rapid turnover of capital sell their products at prices below the labour-value.

In enunciating his theory of landrent, Ricardo refers to scarcity as a factor of value, in addition to the factor of labour, though this conflicts with the unity of his explanation.

Ricardo's theories of value and wages became in due course the foundations for the theories of Rodbertus and Marx, and in especial for Marx's theory of "surplus value". We already find in Ricardo's writings the idea that profit is a sort of residuum after wages have been paid and the capital used up has been replaced; and this residuum is what Marx speaks of as "surplus value". (See below, pp. 226 et seq.)

Ricardo's two laws of prices, concerning the tendency of prices to gravitate towards the highest or lowest costs, are in the theoretical field untenable, but are none the less often useful in practice as rule-of-thumb guides. In actual fact there is not a gravitation of prices towards the lowest costs, for the reason that there are no commodities permanently multipliable at will. Nor is there any levelling of prices, either actual or ideal. The notion of the gravitation of prices towards the highest costs is more consonant with reality, inasmuch as, even in the case of what are regarded as commodities multipliable at will, the prices have to accommodate themselves in accordance with the most expensive of manufacturers, traders, machines, raw materials, wage-earners, etc., among all those actually in operation upon any branch of production. For that reason "rents" come into being everywhere.

b. Ricardo's Theory of Landrent reconsidered. To-day this theory is almost universally accepted, but wrongly so. For, first of all, land has not the exceptional position Ricardo assigned to it. A worker endowed with exceptional skill, a machine more effective than the usual run of machines (new inventions!), and a commodity with qualities that especially fit it for consumption, have privileged positions likewise. In one sense or another, each part of an articulated whole is unique, and for this reason monopolist conditions arise everywhere in labour and capital. Secondly, the idea of "rent" introduced by Ricardo, the notion of a claim that can be enforced upon the product of other's labour ("differential" rents are, we are told, paid by the consumer), is unsound. Fundamentally, the special allowance that is assigned to distinguished service or function is not deducted from the yield of others' labour; it is the outcome of the fact that in the absence of the distinguished service or function (better land, better work, patented inventions, etc.) what is actually done could not be done at all, or could be done only to less effect. Leadership is essential to the performances of the led.—The whole idea of rent has to be reconsidered; the matter has to be understood from the outlook of the aggregate yield of what is the extant higher integration. If, for instance, Iceland, as a country supplying raw materials to a world economy that is on the up grade, draws a larger rent from that world economy than does Bulgaria, this does not mean that Iceland is "exploiting" Bulgaria.[1]—Furthermore, the higher the price of grain which makes a profit (a "rent") possible, becomes a factor in the improvement of the land, that is to say in the development of the most important of the essentials to production, and it is therefore a mistake to look upon it as a "gift" to agriculture at the expense of the community at large. In the case of all the means of production alike, the capital requisite for their development and for their maintenance in good condition must be placed at their disposal. (See below, under List, pp. 190 et seq.)

Especially to be deplored is the economic inference drawn by Ricardo from his theory of landrent, the inference that a hostile attitude towards the landed interest was warrantable.

c. *The Laws of Distribution.* The Ricardian labour theory of value is of such a nature that under its auspices exchange-value and economic substantiality coincide, and so in like manner do the law of the calculation of value and economic law, for according to that theory labour is at one and the same time the substance of economic life and the essential factor of the formation of value. Along this line of argument Ricardo

---

[1] Cf. my article *Gleichwichtigkeit gegen Grenznutzen*, "Jahrbücher für Nationalökonomie," vol. cxxiii (1895), p. 329.

like Smith, proceeding by way of the laws of value and of price, arrived forthwith at the so-called "laws of distribution"; and thence he passed on to a causal and mechanical explanation of all economic activities in terms of natural law. Notably he was enabled to explain in this way the seamy side of capitalist development, to account for the evils of capitalism as necessary evils, as the inevitable accompaniments of the process of distribution. Wages could not fail to be pressed down to the level of subsistence; profits must in course of time decrease more and more; and the rent of land, on the other hand, was predestined to rise and rise and rise again. But even though (as I have already shown on p. 142) Ricardo's theory of value is untenable; even though the proposition on which his law of distribution is based (the contention that the sum of wages and profit is a constant) is incorrect, seeing that, according to latter-day opinion, wages and profit can rise together when the fruitfulness of labour increases—none the less in Ricardo's doctrine there was formulated for the first time a clear and consistent body of economic theory constructed out of stable concepts. For a hundred years this doctrine was supreme, and is still supreme to-day wherever individualist views are dominant.

Moreover, in Ricardo's theses concerning distribution and the resultant economic developments, Malthus' theory of population was (likewise for the first time) turned to practical account. In Ricardo's *Principles*, the increase of population is disclosed as a primal economic force, working itself out, on the one hand, in the iron law of wages, and, on the other, in the inevitable augmentation of landrent. Therewith, at the same time, Ricardo introduces a novel outlook into economic science —that of evolution. Thenceforward economics presents itself, no longer as a general process of circulation which goes on forever after the same manner (the picture given in the *Tableau*), for economic life is portrayed as subject to a determinate evolution thanks to the continued activity of the laws of prices. Nevertheless the Smithian and Ricardian theory of distribution is invalidated by certain fundamental errors of principle. These are identical with the ones which flaw the teaching of the latter-day Ricardians, such as the marginal-utility school and the school of the Swedish economist Gustav Cassel.

From the outlook of those who adopt the organic conception of political economy, the basic defects of Ricardo's theory of distribution are: first, that he always thinks of the distribution of individual goods that have come to the market in a completely finished state, whereas in reality all goods (or, to speak more accurately, their achievements) are only in a state of becoming when they enter the market, and goods only arrive at the state of being finished goods (finished achievements) through getting into touch with one another, through reciprocity; and, secondly, that he conceives distribution to be a consequence of prices, when in reality distribution is a consequence of the articulation of functions, and prices are only the expression of this articulation. Price does not precede distribution, for distribution precedes price. (Cf. my own book *Tote und lebendige Wissenschaft*, third edition, 1929, pp. 77 et seq.)

The doctrine of the "three factors of production" is likewise erroneous. (See below, p. 148 and pp. 278 et seq.)

d. The Problem of Method. From the methodological standpoint, it may be said that the main characteristics of Ricardo are his distinctively abstract conception of economics and his use of the deductive method. The individual's self-love (the individual's pursuit of his own economic interest—free competition and private property being included in this notion, as axiomatic), and persistent overpopulation, are the postulates, and the only ones, with which he works. He thus regards the "economic agent" as isolated, as self-sufficient, as, so to say, an atomised individual. His teaching, therefore, like that of

Smith, becomes individualistic and abstractly isolative, which means that it becomes unsociological and unhistorical. At the same time it is, under another aspect, the completion of the individualist conception. In it, everything is put on a quantitative footing ("cost"—substantiality!), everything is mechanised and atomised; unqualified self-seeking dictates the behaviour of the individual who comes to exchange his wares in the market, and these wares are themselves nothing but congealed labour, objectified value. Therewith Quesnay's "ordre naturel" (the economic order that is conceived as developing in a predetermined way under the working of natural laws) is drawn with the outlines filled in. The result is that Ricardo's weaknesses are more glaring than those of Smith. Ricardo neglects demand as compared with supply, production and productive energy as compared with exchange; and he wrenches economics out of its setting in actual life, in the nation, in the State, and in popular culture. (See above, pp. 113 et seq.)

Elsewhere I have shown at considerable length that the laws of prices are not in reality laws of mechanical causation, but laws of the significant interconnexions of the activities concerned (analogous to the logical interconnexions of premises and conclusions); that consequently they are not primary factors of economics, but merely expressions of the articulations of economic instruments; and that it follows from these considerations that the whole idea of the "ordre naturel" is erroneous. There is sound economics and there is unsound economics, but there is no such thing as mechanically determined economics. (Cf. *Tote und lebendige Wissenschaft*, Jena, 1929.)

e. Theory of Wages. The abstract method of procedure involves two main dangers. The first danger is that the erroneous supposition of an atomised isolation of the persons engaged in economic activity may lead to mistaken inferences. The second is that the investigator, having discovered the laws of economic activity, may ignore the need for revising and adjusting them in the light of universal historical life. In the matter of the iron law of wages, more especially, Ricardo fell into both these pitfalls.

Ricardo considered that the restriction of the wage-earner's means of livelihood was an outcome of the working of the "natural laws of prices"; and to this extent, therefore, he regarded the restriction to a low standard as inevitable. Alike theoretically and historically, such a view is untenable. For, first of all, Ricardo overlooked the possibility of increasing the productivity of labour—a possibility to which Thünen drew attention. When technical or organisational advances are made, or when there is a very large increase in the capitalisation of enterprise, this means, above all, that the output of labour will increase, that the national income will expand, and that therewith there will be an augmentation of the productivity of those higher economic aggregates out of whose yield the share of the wage-earners is derived. Thus only can we account for the way in which increasing prosperity so often accompanies an increase in population; and thus only for the high wages of the United States worker (as member of a lucrative national economy) in contrast with the low wages of a German worker (as member of a comparatively poor national economy). (See above, pp. 132 et seq.) Again, hardly even do we find that in practice labour is multipliable at will, for in most partial labour markets it is rather a scarce commodity, so that supplementary amounts of it may only be obtainable at increasing prices. I say "partial labour markets" because it is into such that what we generalise as the labour market is in fact subdivided: into markets for men's labour, women's labour, and child labour, respectively; markets for unskilled, skilled, and highly skilled labour; the market of those who offer personal services, that of those competent to become officials or other salaried employees, and that of those qualified to practise the liberal professions. These various partial markets in any country will not be equally "overstocked", and are seldom in any way comparable one to another. Thirdly, Ricardo overlooked the fact that a rise in wages necessarily has an influence on production, and that within certain limits it augments the efficiency of the worker, rationalises the enterprise in which he is employed, and thus increases the fund out of which his wages are paid. It is the extant articulation of the instruments of any particular national economy (especially the relation between capital and labour), and the efficiency of these instruments, on which will depend the amount of capital saved—the amount out of which the worker receives as wages his average share of the aggregate income of the world economy and the national economy. Wages, and incomes of every kind, are not derived exclusively from the activity of individuals; they come also from the general output of the world economy and the national economy. Fourthly, neither the need for a minimum subsistence, nor yet the worker's standard of life, determines wages; but, conversely, wages determine what is regarded as a minimum subsistence, and what can be maintained as a standard of life.[1]—In practice we find additional and important limiting factors at work, thanks to which it becomes impossible to regard labour as being a simple commodity like any other. When the workers organise themselves in trade unions (collective bargaining, strikes, boycotts) they are able to modify the movement of prices [for labour] to their own advantage, and in this way they can often raise their standard of life considerably. Still more is it possible for the State, by means of labour-protection laws (the graduated taxation of incomes, a tax-free minimum of subsistence, and the like), to make sure that the wage-earners shall receive a larger share of the national income. (Cf. below under Thünen, p. 183.) Ricardo himself stressed the point that wages were based, not upon the physiological minimum found necessary to subsistence, but upon the traditional standard of life (though this admission conflicted with his fundamental theory that prices represented the cost of reproduction).

Turning to actual economic history, it is plain that in all the countries where large-scale industry prevails there has been a gradual but steady improvement in the condition of the working class. Cf. W. J. Ashley, *The Progress of the German Working Class in the last Quarter of a Century*, Longmans, London, 1904.

---

[1] This has been demonstrated by Zwiedineck-Südenhorst, "Lohntheorie und Lohnpolitik", *Handwörterbuch der Staatswissenchaften* (Reversal of the Iron Law of Wages). See also below, p. 183.

Ricardo, by formulating what Lassalle afterwards called the iron law of wages, and by inaugurating the idea that profit was a "residuum", laid the theoretical foundation for the pessimistic outlook on capitalist evolution, and also for the notion of the conflict of interests between capital and labour. By alleging a law in accordance with which, as economic evolution proceeds, the rent of land must rise and the rent of capital must fall, he also brought to the front the idea of a conflict of interests between mobile capital and landed property. Thus his writings contain the germs of the doctrines of Karl Marx.

The mechanical resolution of economic activities into quantitatively determined processes of exchange, the postulation of the "economic individual" as a self-sufficing and self-governing person who guides his actions by self-love alone, the detachment of economics from its living interconnexions with society and the ideal world—taking them all in all, they are characteristic of Ricardo and his kind. We have here great perspicacity and marked powers of abstraction; but we have pure intellectualism, and in the last resort this always signifies a loss of breadth and of depth.

5. A Succinct General Criticism of Smith's and Ricardo's Teaching

If we examine the broad lines of Smith's and Ricardo's teaching, we see that certain systematic notions emerge as of fundamental importance, and that there are certain primary defects.

1. For Smith, Ricardo, and their followers, economics was, in the main, the science of the "commerce" between economic individuals; it was a theory of commerce or trade, and that was what made it big with destiny in the history of political economy.

2. Big with destiny, because this outlook meant that the concept of production was ignored; that the theory of value and the theory of prices became the groundwork of the new economic edifice; and that the laws of value and the laws of economics were treated as coincident. (See above, p. 110 and p. 144.) 3. But the Smith and Ricardo theory of value and prices is erroneous for it sets out from the quantity of labour instead of from the purposive economic functions and the validity of these. The truth is, not that labour creates value, but that labour is itself value in so far as it is a means to an end. "Value", therefore, is not a quantity but a grade—the grade of achievements in the edifice of means to an end. 4. More especially, Ricardo's theory of wages and his idea of profit as a residual magnitude (residual rent) are erroneous. The former does not allow for the productivity of labour, or for the circumstance that, in general, distribution follows the articulation of function; and the latter notion is only deducible from the erroneous labour theory of value. 5. Furthermore, the notion of differential rent in the landrent theory is theoretically unsound. It is essential to set out from the aggregate output of the economic totality, not from an isolated plot of land, for neither this nor an isolated functioning of labour can furnish an output. (See above, p. 144.) Nor is "rent" a deduction from the yield of others' labour. 6. Most disastrous of all has been the effect of the doctrine of self-love, or the pursuit of self-interest, for it was this which rendered possible the formulation of the doctrine of price, as a doctrine of the gathering together of economic agents in the market, and the explanation of economic happenings as the (unpurposed) outcome of the interaction of forces in the market. In actual fact, what makes the individual's activity an economic activity (i.e. makes it an articulated part of the economic aggregate), is not self-love as a purely subjective and individual "force"

but the objective reason or purpose for articulation into an always pre-existent whole. In order to make an actively economic subjective self-love must be transformed into an objective reason for articulation. 7. From this it follows that we must repudiate the isolative and deductive method of Smith and Ricardo, and must disallow the alleged moral neutrality of economic activity. Speaking more generally, we must repudiate the notion of the "homo oeconomicus". For to be "articulated" into an organic whole must always imply something very different from acting upon purely subjective and profit-seeking motives; it must imply action in accordance with the presuppositions of the extant economic aggregate, and participation in the life of an economico-social, and therefore moral, whole. 8. Unsound, finally, is the quantitative and mechanical method which was the outcome of Smith's and Ricardo's general attitude. For if the essence of economic activity consists, not in quantities of labour or quantities of goods, but in the purposive articulation of functions in the extant aggregate of the economic body (or the functioning economic organism), then there is no more place in economics for "laws of mechanical causation" than there is place for mechanical causation to intrude among the laws of logical thought (which are likewise purposive and not mechanical). Economics has, indeed, an inner and unambiguous determinism; but that determinism is not mechanically causal. The "laws" of supply and demand, therefore, like the "laws of prices" are neither natural nor primary laws, being solely the expression of purposive, articulate, functional interrelations. Supply and demand, in especial, and also the processes of the market, are derivative phenomena—like fever, which is only symptomatic, and not primary.

Untenable, to conclude, is the applied economics deduced from the doctrines of Smith and Ricardo—the demand for perfect freedom of economic action, for free competition, and free trade. Since there are no natural laws of economics, it follows: first, that applied economics may purposively sway and transform the articulation and the calculated design of the economic aggregate; and, secondly, that economic freedom and free competition among individuals cannot be the right foundation for applied economics, seeing that the primary reality of economics is not vested in the individual. Rather we have to recognise that the economic aggregate must always be our first care, inasmuch as the primary reality of economics is vested in the aggregates. Consequently it is essential that there should be ties between the aggregates and individuals, so that customs dues, preferential taxes, freightage rates, and, above all, concrete interconnexions between the various departments of economic activity, will always remain indispensable factors of applied economics. The course of historical evolution has shown how unwarrantable was Ricardo's enmity towards immobile capital on the ground that the rent of land tended towards perpetual increase. During the hundred years since he wrote, agriculture has earned comparatively little, whereas the earnings of trade, commerce, and large-scale industry have been enormous.

CHAPTER EIGHT

POLITICAL ECONOMY IN GERMANY

THE economics of Malthus and Ricardo ended with a justification of the seamy side of capitalism by demonstrating that the defects of the capitalist order were inevitable. Socialist thinkers, on the other hand, drew from the existence of these evils the inference that a communistic society must be established. But in Germany another trend became manifest. Here economists turned away from an atomist and mechanist view towards an organic conception of society, a conception which was rooted in philosophy and bore fruit in the romanticist movement. A universalist social and economic idea was contraposed to an individualist one. The hour for this mental revolution struck in 1794, when Fichte published his *Ueber den Begriff der Wissenschaftslehre* (translated as *The Science of Knowledge*, Philadelphia, 1868, London, 1889), which gave a decisive impetus to romanticism. This impetus was reinforced when two years later the same philosopher, in the *Grundlage des Naturrechts* (translated as *The Science of Rights*, Philadelphia, 1868, London, 1889) for the first time superseded individualist natural right.

A. THE ROMANTICISTS

> He only who, with his eyes, plumbs the depths beneath him, becomes fully aware of the giddy height on which he stands; and he only who cognises the imperishable, is able to forget the perishable.

By the growth of the romanticist movement, the centre of gravity of the philosophical and sociological development of Europe was transferred to Germany.

The decisive part of this revolution occurred in the domain of philosophy. One of the greatest among the historic achievements of the German spirit was that in the post-Kantian philosophy the old individualism based upon the idea of natural right was discarded, and was replaced by a universalist, an organic conception of the State. This process has often been described as "the rebirth of the Greco-Roman idea of the State", but the term is not wholly applicable. The new universalist idea of the State and the community was conceived independently of the classical philosophy, and was based on very different presuppositions from those of Greco-Roman philosophy, for it had its birth in the overthrow of empiricism effected by the Kantian philosophy. As I said just now, it was Fichte, in his *Science of Rights*, who broke away from natural right, inasmuch as he rejected the notion of the absolute, self-sufficing individual, and substituted for it that of the creative community, the living relationship between the ego and the tu. Kant had been content to insist upon man's power of moral self-determination, and in ethical and political science had remained (despite his confutation of the empiricism and rationalism of the Anglo-French Enlightenment) entangled in individualism. Fichte left moral self-determination intact; but human beings, epistemologically considered, had become for him no longer individuals; they were members of an aggregate, parts of an organism established upon the principle of spiritual reciprocity. "If there are to be human beings at all, there must be a plurality of them", wrote Fichte. "So soon as we fully define the concept of the human being, we are impelled to pass beyond the thought of the individual, and to postulate the existence of a second, for thus only can we explain the first." [1]—Schelling, Hegel, Baader, Schleiermacher, Krause, and others, developing this conception of the State,

---

[1] Fichte, *Grundlage des Naturrechts*, 1796, p. 47.

applied it to ethical and political science. A historical outlook on jurisprudence (that of Savigny and Puchta), based on the same groundwork, and contraposed to the abstract idea of the social contract founded on individualist natural right (see above, pp. 53 et seq.), soon became dominant.

1. THE NATURE OF ROMANTICISM AND THE ROMANTIC SCHOOL

The new philosophy needed a new cultural consciousness, and the expression of this consciousness was romanticism. Thus, from the first, romanticism was something more than an artistic or aesthetic trend; it was also a cultural movement.

Certainly it began in the main as an artistic and literary trend, associated with the names and writings of August Wilhelm and Friedrich von Schlegel, Novalis, Tieck, Brentano, Achim von Arnim, E. T. A. Hoffmann, and Eichendorff. But, from its very nature, it inevitably extended ere long into every aspect of life and into the domains of most of the sciences. Historism in all its branches, Germanistics, and linguistic science, owed their existence to it. Its essence, however, was bound up with its philosophical character, for romanticist art and science were, wittingly or unwittingly, but wholly, dominated by the relation to the suprasensual, the divine, and the infinite. Primarily, indeed, romanticism was philosophy rather than art. It was the outcome of the all-pervading sense that existence was an enigma; of the painful consciousness that the world is full of inadequacy, evil, and death; but also of the yearning to find appeasement in the contemplation of the titanic and perdurable elements of the universe, in the longing to open the doors of the heart to these mighty influences. Thus romanticism was a strenuous oscillation between the poles of despair and pious self-surrender. Though people often say that quixotism, nebulousness, and subjectivity, were the salient features of romanticist poesy, this view is false. Its leading traits were the before-mentioned philosophically grounded conviction (or, rather, feeling) that existence was incomprehensible, and an internal conflict between scepticism and mysticism: thence was derived, as a secondary characteristic, its visionary, confused, and incoherent quixotism; and thence, likewise, came the formlessness of romanticist literature, thence sprang the subjectivity of writers whose being was in a state of incessant oscillation between the ego and the world.

Only as a philosophy and as a cultural movement did romanticist art exert an influence upon all fields of life and knowledge. Regarded by the romanticists as a part of a universe, man (his struggle with subjectivity notwithstanding) was no longer looked upon as individualistic, as isolated; he had now become a member of the cosmic commonwealth. Thus, too, in the State and in society he was no longer contemplated as subjective and self-governing, but as a member of a living and organised social aggregate. The scepticism and mysticism of the ego must be extended to the community; State and society had to be absorbed into the cosmic continuum, and it was in this wise that they became the objects of romanticist scrutiny.

Romanticism was the first counter-movement directed against the Enlightenment, humanism, and the Renaissance. In it the German spirit was striving to return to its former self, to the self which had come into being in the Middle Ages. Hence romanticism may be aptly termed neo-Gothicism.

Certain recent attempts to dismiss romanticism as nothing more than obscure sentimentalism are too trivial and absurd to be worth considering.

Since the days of Roscher, it has been usual to speak of

three writers as the chief representatives of the romanticist trend in political science. These were: Adam Müller; Friedrich Gentz (born at Breslau, 1764, died in Vienna, 1832); and Carl Ludwig von Haller (born in Berne, 1768, died at Solothurn in 1854). Haller's most important work was *Restauration der Staatswissenschaft oder Theorie des natürlich-geselligen Zustandes*, 6 vols., 1816–1834. Though Müller, Gentz, and Haller were lumped together by Roscher as forming a "romantic school", there is no theoretical unity between them, but merely a political unity—and even this latter can be admitted only with reservations. In especial, Haller's "patrimonial theory of the State", according to which the medieval State was a sum-total of private contracts, was thoroughly unromanticist, and at bottom it was individualist.— Gentz, moreover, was not a theoretician at all, but only a practical politician of the same type as Metternich.—The sole writers on political theory to set out at that date from romanticist premises were Adam Müller, Franz von Baader, Görres, and Novalis.[1]

2. ADAM MÜLLER

Adam Müller was born in Berlin in the year 1779, studied theology there, and subsequently studied jurisprudence and political science in Göttingen. A Protestant by birth, in 1805, while in Vienna, he was received into the Catholic Church. From 1806 to 1809 he lived in Dresden, being associated with Kleist in the editorship of "Phoebus". Next, he spent two years in Berlin, returning in 1811 to Vienna, and there entering into close relations with Friedrich Schlegel, Zacharias Werner, and Clemens Hofbauer. Then (still on the move), in 1813, having entered the Austrian State service, he became rural commissary in Tyrol; in 1816, Austrian consul in Leipzig; and in 1827, councillor in the State chancellery in Vienna. He died in 1829. He was a friend of Gentz and a confidant of Metternich.— His main ideas were already enunciated in his first published work, *Die Lehre vom Gegensatz*, Berlin, 1804. His most important books were: *Elemente der Staatskunst*, Berlin, 1809

[1] Cf. Novalis' admirable little work, *Europa oder die Christenheit*, and his *Fragmente*. Among other editions may be mentioned that of Baxa, *Staat und Gesellschaft im Spiegel der deutschen Romantik*, Jena, 1924.

(new edition in 1922, edited by Baxa, who also discovered, and gave to the world in 1926, *Handschriftliche Zusätze*); *Versuche einer neuen Theorie des Geldes mit besonderer Rücksicht auf Grossbritannien*, 1816 (new edition, edited by Lieser, in 1921); *Vermischte Schriften*, Vienna, 1812, second edition, 1817 (Baxa's edition, *Ausgewählte Abhandlungen*, Jena, 1921).—In Adam Müller's later writings, we discern an inclination to break away from the romanticist pantheism which characterises his earlier ones, for, in the end, he moved to a rigidly Catholic standpoint. See, for instance, *Von der Notwendigkeit einer theologischen Grundlage der gesamten Staatswissenschaften und der Staatswirtschaft insbesondere*, Leipzig, 1819; *Die innere Staatshaushaltung*, 1820. They were reprinted in *Adam Müller's gesammelte Schriften*, Franz, Munich, 1839.—A very important source of information concerning romanticist political science is *Staat und Gesellschaft im Spiegel der deutschen Romantik*, edited by Baxa, Jena, 1924, in the collection "Herdflamme". Here the scattered literature of the topic is brought together for the first time. See also Baxa, *Einführung in die romantische Staatswissenschaft*, Jena, 1923.

a. Theory of State and Society. Adam Müller applied the newly acquired philosophical notion of community to economics, politics, and sociology. In his view, the State was "the aggregate of human affairs, their interconnexion to form a living whole";[1] it was something absolutely vitalised and spiritual, "the realm of all ideas, for ever in motion";[2] it was a moral community, which became unified through the surrender of its parts to the world, through love for mankind. Thanks to this mediate relationship to the world (God), the State acquired a cosmic, a religious stamp, and likewise universal validity; for thenceforward there was no longer, strictly speaking, any happiness for the individual considered as a being apart; happiness could only be found in self-surrender; and man could not attain his true self in any other way than through his relationship to the cosmos.

[1] *Elemente* (Baxa's reprint), i, 66.   [2] *Elemente*, i. 63.

Philosophically, the affiliations of this notion of the State must be traced back to Fichte and Schelling; but in the matter of practical application it had a remoter source. Medieval Germany was the ideal State, with its feudal rights, its personal and spiritual (not commercial) ties between the members of the body politic. In Adam Müller's opinion, the best embodiment of this feudalist spirit was still to be found in English political life, for this had not come under the harrow of the rationalist Roman law. Müller had a great veneration for Edmund Burke (1729–1797), whose famous anti-Jacobin polemic, *Reflections on the Revolution in France*, had been translated into German by Gentz.

Adam Müller was a fierce and vigorous critic of the theory of natural right and of Smith's individualist conception of economics, the "doctrine of the radical decomposition, dissolution, and dismemberment of the State" and of political economy! The notion of absolute private property (a notion common to Roman law and to the champions of the doctrine of natural right), and Smith's idea of pure income, "the privatising of all occupations", in place of family and corporative right, seemed to him on all fours, and equally disastrous.[1] His criticism of Smith was simultaneously a criticism of the capitalist system. He also attacked Montesquieu's theory of the partition of powers in political life. (See above, p. 56.) Above all, in his opinion, landed property was not private property, but property held in trust for the community.

b. Economic Teachings. To the individualist conception of economic life (an isolating conception based upon the notion of self-love), Müller contraposes, with the utmost emphasis, the idea of the interconnexion and unification of all social elements. At the same time he pays due heed to their historical setting (the historical method). He speaks of the "mysterious reciprocity of all the relationships of life". For him the prerequisite of all scientific thought concerning social questions

[1] *Elemente*, ii, 121.

was that it should permeate every aspect of community life; the economic, the political, the religious, and the moral. It is here that the specifically romanticist outlook becomes manifest, the outlook of one who contemplates everything from the philosophical viewpoint already indicated. Just as little as the unity of the State can permit a severance of private right from State right, just so little ought there to be a conflict between life and art, or between life and religion. Life has to be unified spiritually and philosophically; but it has to be unified no less in its economic and political activities. Here we find a sociological conception associated with a historico-universalist one; we see that Müller directs his gaze towards social life as a whole—in contradistinction to Smith, who abstracts economics, to contemplate it in isolation.

The spirit of this mutual interpenetration was described by Müller in the following words: "The soundness of our ancestors' view of the essence of political life (a view that was not distorted by any intrusive theory) is shown by this, that, despite all the subdivision of urban industry, they did everything they could to ensure its vigorous unification. The arts and the sciences became severed one from another, but only in so far as they respectively entered into the close corporations of the guilds. The more the functions of an urban handicraft were assigned to a number of different hands, the more energetically did the master re-collect the scattered threads into a whole; but he himself, the master, stood once more as a journeyman, as an individual worker, within the body of the guild; the individual guild, again, entered into a sort of marriage with the corporation of urban industry; urban industry, too, strove to achieve a mutual interpenetration with rural production, represented by the nobility and landed gentry; and even though the supreme relationship of economic mutuality in the State was never wholly and perfectly achieved, we nevertheless find all economic functions tending in this one particular direction."[1]

[1] *Versuche einer neuen Theorie des Geldes*, 1816; Lieser's reprint, Jena, 1922, p. 37.

L

Adam Müller objected to the glorification of competition as a creative energy in economic life, setting up against it the vitalising energy of the personal interdependence of all the members of the community, as in the patriarchal family, in the craft guild, and on a landed estate. He strongly condemned the cleavage between capital and labour which was showing itself as the outcome of the new individualist evolution (capitalism), and was tending to range wage-earning workers and "revenue-receivers" (capitalists) against one another as two reciprocally hostile classes.[1] To him we owe the first outspoken criticism of capitalism—a criticism far more effective than that voiced some decades later by Karl Marx. Müller wrote: "The spirit reacts unceasingly against the division and mechanisation of labour, which Adam Smith prized so highly; the spirit wants to preserve man's personality."[2] "There is no separate occupation in bourgeois society . . for whose sake . . . a man should forget his own self."[3]—He describes the "freedom of industry" as "a general, unregulated activity . . . in which one wave of diligence swallows up another, instead of there being steady work."[4] All the same, Adam Müller did not repudiate the capitalistic factor in commerce, industry, and even agriculture; he would only approve it, however, as one factor among many, as (for example) a supplementary factor to national work performed as a kind of public service in undertakings that were not "free" but were "bound" in the feudalist sense, or in guilds and similar corporations. (Cf. *Innere Staatshaushaltung.*)—He was strongly opposed to a purely mechanical idea of wealth (which Smith had regarded as consisting of the aggregate of all material goods); and was opposed, more especially, to Smith's whole idea as to the

[1] *Gesammelte Schriften*, 1839, vol. i, pp. 275 and 279.   [2] *Elemente*, i, 57.
[3] *Versuche*, 1816, p. 107. See also my article "Klasse und Stand" in *Handwörterbuch der Staatswissenschaften*, fourth edition, 1922, vol. v, p. 692.   [4] *Gesammelte Schriften*, 1839, vol. i, p. 298.

nature of goods. Wealth, said Müller, consisted not merely of things, but also of their usefulness. Material objects were not the only goods; their "civil character", and the forces of their utilisation (spiritual goods), had to be included in the concept as well. Consequently the greatest wealth was to be found, not where there was the largest quantity of concrete property; but where there were the strongest forces to retain it, and the most considerable feelings to esteem it.[1]—Müller's theory of productivity was in conformity with this outlook. Whereas Smith had regarded as productive that work only which was devoted to the making of concrete things, Adam Müller included under the head of production the "ideally productive" achievements of the statesman and the artist. "Ideal production, . . . the most splendid of a nation's assets, . . . was according to Smith valueless when it was a question of estimating the total wealth of a nation. The words of the statesman, which would perhaps bring millions in actual money into existence; the words of the priest or those of the artist, which might ennoble the heart or enlarge the imaginative faculty of the nation—these counted for nothing. I fancy I hear the objection, . . . that you can only reckon up things that can be handled, measured, and weighed. . . . I answer that the national existence in its widest possible scope is the true wealth of a nation."[2] Profoundly significant are his utterances concerning the fruitfulness of the labour of the State: "An individual productive force can only produce in so far as it has itself been produced by a higher productive force. If the State ceases to produce, . . . then, automatically, all the less productive forces cease to operate."[3] The "product of all products", or the "intensification" of them all, is the economic community, the

[1] From Müller's *Adam Smith*, 1808, reprinted in *Gesammelte Schriften*, 1839, i, p. 113.
[2] *Gesammelte Schriften*, i, 112–114.   [3] *Elemente*, vol. ii, 256–257.

national economy.—In respect of the theory of value and prices, he rejects Smith's mechanistic labour theory of value, and formulates in opposition to it a theory which may be called the organic-use theory of value. Over and above the individual use-value of goods, we must recognise a public or "sociability" value (that is to say the conformity of individual use-values). "If we say of a thing that it is useful, we mean that it has a value in relation to civil society." [1] Value can only be ascertained when a thing is in its place in the totality of the economic and political body of the community. "The value of a thing is its meaning in the State and its contribution towards the rejuvenation of the State." [2] Social utility is also a guide for him in his theory of money. All economic things, all commodities and services, have a monetary quality in so far as commodities and services are paid for with commodities and services.

Money, says Müller, is not (as Smith opines) a particular commodity, is not "the acceptance of the most marketable commodity" (see above, p. 41). "Money is a quality inherent in all the individuals of civil society, a quality in virtue of which they . . . can enter into ties with all the other individuals of that society, and then disrupt those ties once more." The monetary characteristic is personal and concrete "universal validity", "convertibility", "public value". Money, "wherever it appears and in whatever form, whether as paper money or as metallic, is only money in so far as it is not private property but is the common property of as many persons as possible, and, indeed, of all. For . . . only at the moment of exchange, or of the circulation of the substances of money, are these latter really money"; and at this moment they have become feod, that is to say feudal, public, no longer private property.[3]

That which (to the exclusion of other things) we are wont to call "money", metallic money, has to a fuller extent than has anything else this faculty of forming ties and dissolving

---

[1] *Elemente*, ii, 192.   [2] *Versuche*, Lieser's reprint, 1921, p. 59.
[3] *Ibid.*, p. 31.

them—but does not possess it exclusively.[1] Metallic money is not the only, though it is the most effective, expression of the "national value" of the "national force". A reciprocal interaction of metallic money and paper money provides the safest monetary system. The view "that State paper is a mere substitute for metallic money,. . . and that it is unmeaning unless it has a reference to the metal", puts the cart before the horse. "The metals are the representatives, the urgent need of interconnexion, which binds the individual organs of mankind together antecedently to all division of labour; . . . that which the process of minting first gives to the metals and makes them money, that which in due course and through the further development of civil life secures expression in State paper—is the main thing." [2] Money in this widest sense of the term did not in the first instance arise (as Smith supposed) out of the practice of exchange, for it is one of the primary needs of economic life. This was a fundamental and brilliant discovery made by Adam Müller, and it has been confirmed by the recent history of money.[3] Just as the State is the living expression, and the law the juridical expression, so money is the economic expression of that inner spiritual unity of the many which is conformable to the nature of man. (See below, pp. 285 et seq.)

Müller rejects free trade. It is not suitable until "the State has within its own borders acquired those ties which renounce only indubitable superfluity . . . but no important vital energy".[4] Here the self-government idea of the mercantilists and the cameralists has recurred.

According to Adam Müller, the general structure of economic life is as follows: There are four primary factors of production; land, labour, concrete capital, and spiritual capital. Land represents the permanent factor; labour represents mobility (development); capital, in which the past is slumbering, unites both, in that it sometimes quickens production, sometimes inhibits it. These four factors correspond to the four elements

---

[1] *Elemente*, vol. ii, pp. 192 et seq. *Gesammelte Schriften*, vol. i, pp. 84 et seq.

[2] *Versuche*, Lieser's edition, pp. 139 et seq.

[3] Laum, *Heiliges Geld*, Tübingen, 1924; Pran Nath, *Tausch und Geld in Altindien*, Vienna, 1924. See also my own references to the matter in the "Jahrbucher für Nationalökonomie und Statistik", vol. cxxiii, Jena, 1925.

[4] *Gesammelte Schriften*, i, 353.

of the family: youth (the forward aspiration); age (inhibition); virility (production); femininity (conservation)—and also to the four fundamental ideas of the national State, which the four different estates of the realm serve: teachers, soldiers, producers of necessaries, and traders, who by their contrasts must create the harmony of the whole. Furthermore the productive nature is conformable to the feminine principle of conservation, and leads us to the territorial nobility and gentry (landed proprietorship, conservation); labour is conformable to the virile principle, and leads us to the estate of burghers; concrete capital leads us, by way of the element of youth that concrete capital embodies, to the trading or mercantile estate; and spiritual capital leads us, by way of the element of age it embodies, to the estate of teachers and clergy. The most efficient and the liveliest reciprocal interaction, and the most successful coordination into an organic whole, arise when these various elements of the population are duly balanced.—Non-economic social phenomena also came within the range of Adam Müller's investigations. He declared, for instance, that war was not exclusively a phenomenon of consumption, for it was also the creator of powerful and vivifying energies within the State. He regarded the institution of hereditary nobility as an important instrument for linking one generation with another, seeing that society too must have an organic nexus in time. Indeed, speaking generally, Müller regarded duration as one of the most important problems of sociology.

Neither the law of diminishing returns nor the other doctrines of Ricardo and Malthus had any influence upon Adam Müller's thought—at least I can detect no trace of such an influence in his writings. With sure insight, however, he anticipated Thünen in distinguishing between the two main types of agriculture, the intensive and the extensive, the former being "mercantile", and carried on with an eye to a market near at hand, whereas the latter was "national" and comparatively self-dependent. He also recognised a third category, horticulture, which he spoke of as "energetic agriculture". (*Agronomische Briefe*, republished in *Ausgewählte Abhandlungen*, Jena, 1921, pp. 71 et seq., et passim.)

c. Valuation. Adam Müller's imperishable service lies in the fact that, as a pioneer in modern days and at a time when individualism was rampant, he worked out for himself a universalist conception of economics; and that he contraposed to the teachings of Quesnay and Smith, sound doctrines and eternal verities that were simultaneously the fruit of a brilliant intelligence and an ardent intuition. In respect of the notions of wealth, productivity, and money, he was the first to get beyond the mechanistic, quantitative, and materialist outlook of his contemporaries. Moreover, he elucidated the nature and working of a paper currency in a way which went to the very heart of the matter, and thus formulated a theory of money which still remains the profoundest ever conceived, despite all the developments of latter-day economic science.—In face of Adam Müller's wealth of ideas, Marx's purely dialectical acuteness, and even Ricardo's analytical power, pale their fires. What attracts him, what he especially studies and elucidates in every economic enigma, is the basic phenomenon of reciprocity—this attitude contrasting strongly with the misleading tendency to isolate and to abstract which was characteristic of the individualist classical economists.

Unfortunately Adam Müller never made any notable advance beyond the splendid beginning he achieved in his early and principal work, *Elemente der Staatskunst*. The wandering life he led was, no doubt, partly responsible for this. Roscher writes: "Had Müller, who was thirty years old when the *Elemente* was published, subsequently developed in a normal fashion, had he devoted himself to making his knowledge more thorough and more practical, to rendering his notions clearer and more consistent, he would unquestionably have become one of the greatest economists of all time." [1]

Adam Müller actually was the greatest political economist of his own day. If his position in the history of our science

---

[1] *Die romantische Schule der Nationalökonomie in Deutschland*, "Tübinger Zeitschrift für die gesamten Staatswissenschaften", 1870, p. 91.

does not correspond to his intellectual importance, this is because his thoughts were not adequately clarified and systematised before being given to the world. As far as particular applications were concerned, his writings were confused, and often unworthy of the greatness of the fundamental principles that inspired them. A failure to carry things to an end was his foible. When he came to write his later books, his analytical powers had declined, and his ardour had cooled. None the less, there is still a wealth of unutilised treasure in his economic writings. It is easier to blame Adam Müller for his lack of precision than to do justice to the man's sterling worth. For the latter, we must realise how much insight and moral energy were needed in order to run counter to Smith's individualism. Even in our own day, Müller continues to be undervalued. He may have lacked sturdiness of character, but there flowered in him the supremest culture of his time. As economist, he possessed unrivalled discernment, and was able to detect the innermost vibrations of the social consciousness. Nevertheless, as yet few people seem to be aware that almost all the main ideas developed in his polemic against Smith have become parts of the general heritage of science.[1]

Nor has it been generally recognised to how great an extent List (see below, pp. 199 et seq.) and subsequently the historical

[1] Since the first edition of this book was published, a considerable literature relating to Adam Müller has come into existence. Cf. Friedrich Lenz, *Agrarlehre und Agrarpolitik der deutschen Romantik*, Berlin, 1912; Tokary-Tokarzewsky-Karaszewicz, *Adam H. Müller von Nittersdorf als Oekonom, Literat, Philosoph und Kunstkritiker*, Gerold, Vienna, 1913 (useful as introduction to the study of Müller's writings); Bruno Moll, *Logik des Geldes*, Munich 1916, second edition, 1922; Baxa, *Einführung in die romantische Staatswissenschaft*, Jena, 1923. As regards romanticism in relation to historiography, see Below's *Die deutsche Geschichtschreibung*, second edition, Munich, 1924; in relation to mythology, see Bäumler's preface to Bachofen, *Der Mythus vom Orient und Occident*, Munich, 1926. (But I must protest against the distinction between a Heidelberg romanticist circle and a Jena circle, as made by Bäumler in his otherwise excellent preface—Görres versus Schlegel). For an introduction to the artistic side of romanticism, see R. J. Obenauer, *Hölderlin und Novalis*, Jena, 1925.

school of political economy (see below, pp. 240 et seq.) drew upon Adam Müller for their inspiration. However, Roscher's great esteem for him, and Hildebrand's highly appreciative account of him,[1] suffice to show that the founders of the earlier historical school were greatly indebted to Müller.

Considered as a whole, romanticist economics did not undergo any considerable evolution, and failed to exercise notable influence. It remained ineffective chiefly because, in the field of applied economics, Adam Müller, Gentz, and Haller in especial, inclined towards an extremist and reactionary absolutism. In this they were swimming against the current of events, and Müller was penalised by neglect—to the great detriment of our science. The political program of these economists was based on the unqualified rejection of all liberal reforms, the liberation of the serfs seeming to them no less undesirable than the freedom of industry. They wanted a simple return to medieval conditions. Here sound views and unsound ones were huddled together pell-mell. In 1811, Müller penned a memorial to Hardenberg, in which, while condemning the reforms of Stein and Hardenberg, he urged the reestablishment of the provincial constitution and the convocation of a Landtag.—Furthermore, in Austria, Gentz and Müller were the political henchmen of Metternich, the ultra-conservative. But whereas Haller, guided by a distorted view of the Middle Ages, wished to resolve the State into isolated patrimonial relationships of dependence and dominion, Adam Müller had in mind a retrogression that was to be a reformation, "a step back which was at the same time to be a step forward". He wrote: "The elements of all political life . . . are to be found in the Middle Ages. The union of these elements . . . was incomplete, because it was effected federatively rather than organically."[2] Indubitably, words of wisdom! It is necessary to insist that this romantic "school" can only be regarded as having been an entity in the field of practical endeavour, for on the theoretical plane we can hardly say that these thinkers formed a school. Gentz was a man of unmetaphysical, unimaginative disposition; Haller was really

[1] *Die Nationalökonomie der Gegenwart und Zukunft*, 1848, p. 35.
[2] *Elemente*, ii, 134.

of little moment, and he too (as already said) was essentially unimaginative.—On the other hand, the following writers had a true kinship with Adam Müller: Novalis (pen-name of Friedrich von Hardenberg, 1772–1801); Johann Josef von Görres [1] (1776–1848); Fichte (1762–1814), in his *Der geschlossene Handelsstaat* (see below, p. 216); Felix Theodor von Bernhardi (1802–1885, see below, p. 202); and Franz von Baader (1765–1841).

3. FRANZ VON BAADER

Until recently, no one was aware that among the romanticists there was, in addition to Adam Müller, another economist of first-class importance. It was left for Johannes Sauter to prove by his edition of *Baaders Schriften zur Gesellschaftsphilosophie* [2] that, upon a philosophical and sociological foundation, Baader established an economic doctrine which, though it was never systematised, ranks with that of Adam Müller. Independently of Müller, Baader, taking his stand upon a genuinely organic conception of economic life, refuted the atomistic and individualist economics of Adam Smith.[3]

As early as 1809, Baader wrote as follows in condemnation of Smith's mechanist conception of the division of labour: "However much economists have copied one another in writing about the division of productive labour, not a single one of them has traced its genesis in the idea of an organism; . . . and in like manner when describing the division of production, they have ignored the necessarily concomitant and contraposed consolidation of consumption; and just as little has it been clear to them that this division of production is not to be considered a separation or isolation of production, but rather . . . an association or articulation of production.[4]

[1] *Sämtliche Werke und Briefe*, edited by Schellberg, 1927 et seq.

[2] Jena, 1925, in the collection "Herdflamme". Sauter has thus revived the memory of the most utterly forgotten of all the romanticists. He has been the first to attempt a comprehensive presentation of Baader's philosophy, sociology, and economics, which have hitherto been ignored by specialists.

[3] Cf. Sauter, *Baaders Schriften*, etc., pp. 790–838.   [4] *Ibid.*, p. 792.

Baader's principal economic work was the treatise *Ueber das dermalige Missverhältnis der Vermögenslosen oder Proletairs zu den Vermögen besitzenden Klassen der Sozietät* (1835),[1] which contains a much more effective criticism of capitalism than Marx's. Sauter summarises its upshot as comprised in the following recommendations: (1) suitable renovation of the estates of the realm and the corporations; (2) enfranchisement and representation of the fourth estate (by compulsory enrolment of proletarians in trade unions with priests as leaders and the "right of advocacy"); (3) a modernised association of a monetary economy with a natural economy; (4) abolition of the unconditional freedom of industry at home, and of the unconditional freedom of foreign commerce.[2]

If the romantic school of sociology and economics decayed and fell into oblivion, this was only in part because these writers failed to elaborate their ideas properly. The main reason was that the trend of the time was unfavourable. The individualist notion, and Marxism (its reduction to absurdity), had first to gain the victory, live out their life, and display their true visage to mankind. Not until then could a movement in the precisely opposite direction begin and gather strength. To-day we are in the midst of this historical process, and it is one which imposes a decisive responsibility upon our generation.

B. HEINRICH VON THÜNEN

The two investigators from whom the comparative independence of German economics really dates are Thünen and List. Although neither of these writers had a consciously thought out philosophical foundation for his teaching, they both of them turned away from the individualist conception of the State, and they were both dominated by an organic and universalist view.

[1] Reprinted in Sauter's edition, pp. 319 et seq. See also pp. 838 et seq.

[2] *Ibid.*, p. 851. Sauter also adduces good reasons for believing that Marx drew from Baader without acknowledgment.

a. EXPOSITION

Johann Heinrich von Thünen, born in 1783, was the son of an Oldenburg squire. Although for a short time he was at the University of Göttingen, he owed his scientific training, and his knowledge of the philosophy of German idealism, chiefly to self-tuition. In 1810 he bought the estate of Tellow near Rostock, and lived there till his death in 1850, farming it in exemplary fashion. His chief published work, *Der isolierte Staat in Beziehung auf Landwirtschaft und Nationalökonomie*, was published in 1826. (Second edition, Rostock, 1842–1863, reprinted, Jena, 1921.) Cf. S. Schumacher, *J. H. Thünen, ein Forscherleben*, second edition, Rostock, 1883.

α. *Varieties of Agriculture in the Isolated State.* The assumptions made by Thünen for his study of the localisation of the various systems of agricultural production are the following: "Let us suppose that there is a large town in the middle of a fertile plain. . . . The soil of this plain is everywhere of the same quality. . . . At a great distance from the town the plain ends in an uncultivated wild, by which the town is wholly cut off fron the rest of the world."

The question now arises, how, under these conditions, agriculture would be carried on in various regions at different distances from the town, that is to say from the market. Thünen's reply may be summarised thus: Since a greater distance from the market involves heavier cost of freightage, the effect is equivalent to that of lower prices for produce (where the distance from the market remains the same). Consequently, as the distance from the market increases, there must be a transition to those methods of agriculture which, while less productive, demand less expenditure of capital and labour, inasmuch as they leave an increasing proportion of the process of production to nature's unaided activities. In short, as distance from the market increases, intensive agriculture gives place more and more to extensive. The upshot is, writes

Thünen, "that, near the town, produce must be grown which is heavy in proportion to its value, . . . and which involves such high costs for transport that to grow it at a considerable distance from the market would no longer be a paying proposition; and also produce which is so perishable that transport from any great distance is out of the question, must be grown near the town." Thus the various types of culture will be arranged in concentric zones around the city, a particular type of produce being the chief one in each zone, as shown in the diagram:

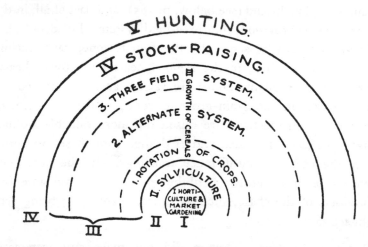

In the innermost circle there must be grown such things as will not bear transport at all, or for which freight charges would be disproportionate to their value: green vegetables, dairy-farming (stall-fed cows), sale of hay and straw (corn being only a by-product), clover, root-crops. Here, then, we have horticulture and market gardening, i.e. intensive culture carried on with the aid of manure from the town.—In the second zone there must be sylviculture, for the supply of the town with fuel and building timber; and in the region nearer the town the preference will be given to growing wood for fuel whilst farther off there will be raised the timber needed for building, since big tree-trunks, being more valuable, can bear higher transport charges.—In the next zone there are three subdivisions; for, though grain is the main product in them all, it is the outcome of a less and less intensive culture as we proceed outwards from the town. First of all, in the innermost subdivision we have the most intensive culture of the three, the one demanding the greatest expenditure of labour and capital, namely a fully developed system of rotation of the crops; next comes the alternate system of pasture-land and plough-land (see below, p. 185); and, last of all, in the outermost subdivision, the three-field system. (For details, see below, pp. 185 et seq.)—In the fourth zone, cattle-raising predominates. Here, in the regions nearest the town, beasts bred for the slaughterhouse are raised, and are fattened for the market in the grain-growing zone; whilst at a greater distance from the town are raised the more valuable animals used as beasts of burden and of draught, for these can better pay the cost of long-distance transport.—In the outermost zone, the only industry will be hunting; the valuable by-products of the chase, such as hides, horns, etc., being sent thence to the market.

β. *Other Teachings*. Thünen did not make any systematic advance upon Ricardo's theory of value, although he showed it to be inadequate. Nevertheless he explained interest and wages in ways which departed altogether from the Ricardian platform, and foreshadowed the subsequent theory of marginal utility, minus its errors. (See below, p. 175.) As regards both capital and labour, he distinguished clearly between the utilities that accrue from the first and the last item of expenditure respectively. In lifting potatoes, for instance, the labour and the pains must not be carried beyond the point at which the last increment of labour expended will be repaid by the addition it brings to the yield. [1]—The rate of interest "is determined

---

[1] *Der isolierte Staat*, second edition, ii/1, pp. 11 and 175.

by the utility of the last-utilised portion of capital". (Böhm-Bawerk has put forward the same theory of interest in our own day. See below, p. 272.)—The relation between interest and wages, as two kinds of income, is as follows: "The decline in interest attendant on the accumulation of capital [as an outcome of the working of the law of interest] is advantageous to the worker and increases wages"—a healthy contrast to Ricardo's law of distribution.

Thünen's theory of wages is likewise typical of his economic thought-trend. He regards the iron law of wages as "revolting" He tries to discover a formula for a wage which shall be simultaneously natural and just. A wage can only be natural when the wage labour which furnishes use-goods (out of its products) is as highly paid as the labour which produces capital-goods. In this way we get the celebrated formula

$$\sqrt{ap}$$

in which a represents the "necessary demand", that is to say the cost of reproducing the labour expressed in quantities or in money, and p the product expressed in quantities or money. This wage is at the same time a maximal value, in which the excess (y) over the necessary demand is greatest.—Another law of wages that is entirely conformable to modern teaching was developed by Thünen in connexion with his discussion of the size of enterprises. "Since it is to the entrepreneur's interest (no matter whether he be an agriculturist or a manufacturer) to go on increasing the number of the workers he employs so long as this increase continues to be advantageous to him, the limit of increase is not reached until the supplementary production realised through the engagement of a supplementary worker ceases to exceed the amount this worker's wages add to the general wage-bill. Conversely, the wages of labour are equal to the product of the last worker engaged;[1] i.e. the wages of the last worker are normative in this sense,[2] that the extension of the enterprise finds its limit at a point whereof he is one of the determinants.

Thus Thünen introduced into the discussion of the application of capital and labour that idea of the margin which, in the subsequent theory of marginal utility, was erroneously

[1] *Der isolierte Staat*, second edition, ii/1, pp. 177 et seq.
[2] *Ibid.*, ii/1, p. 182.

formulated by Menger as "marginal utility" and by Wieser as "marginal productivity". Whereas Thünen determined the margin of an economic enterprise with reference to its aggregate structure and its total functioning, on the other hand the champions of the doctrine of marginal utility want to define the enterprise with reference to its parts and their supposed "marginal value"—i.e. to delimit it from below upwards.

Surányi-Unger describes Thünen as forerunner of the mathematical school. In a restricted sense only can this be said, for in Thünen's writings the mathematical method is used only for illustration and for general guidance; and a non-mathematical investigation always holds precedence.

γ. *Applied Economics.* Originally, Thünen was a free-trader. Later he attacked the Smith-Ricardo theory of free trade on grounds akin to those of List, though Thünen did not elaborate them so fully. The main point was that he drew attention to the reciprocity of "industrial profit" and landrent. He was in favour of a protective tariff.[1] Thünen also paid close attention to the social problem, as his theory of wages shows. He may be considered the first among German social politicians to have an equal interest in theories and in their practical application.

b. VALUATION

a. *Inferences from Thünen's Theory of Localisation (Law of Returns, Comparative Soundness of the Varieties of Agriculture, Theory of Landrent).* From Thünen's zonal theory of the localisation of the various types of agriculture there is deducible a confirmation of the laws of increasing and diminishing returns. The working of the law of diminishing returns is illustrated by the cereal zone, for only if a comparatively extensive culture (on the alternate system, for example) demands less expenditure per unit of product, is it able to meet the greater charge for transport, and only then can it be more rational when prices are lower; and, on the other hand, the law of increasing returns is illustrated by the passage from one zone to another (as transition to a new optimum). Further-

[1] *Der isolierte Staat*, second edition, vol. ii, part ii, p. 92 et seq.

more, when we pass from the poorly capitalised zone of sylviculture, either inward to the richly capitalised zone of market gardening or outward to the richly capitalised zone of rotation of the crops, in both cases we are passing to a zone of more abundant output.

In addition, Thünen's zonal diagram shows us that the advantages possessed by one method of agriculture over another are relative merely, not absolute. As against Albrecht Thaer (1752–1828), who was at that date extolling the rotation of the crops and the stall-feeding of cattle as the only sound methods, Thünen declared it untrue to say that, economically considered, the technically best and the most intensive system of agriculture and the one that produced the maximum output was always the most desirable. Which method of production was economically the most advantageous, depended on economic considerations—on the articulation of economic life in general and on prices.

This applies to industrial technique as well as to agricultural, but in industry different conditions are decisive, and, above all, the size of the market. (See below, p. 228.)

From the doctrine that the soundness of the various methods of agriculture is relative only, not absolute, there automatically follows a theory of landrent. Thünen discusses mainly the rent of situation, but in addition the interrelated rent of the intensity of agriculture, whereas Ricardo was chiefly interested in the rent of the natural fertility of the soil. Situation nearer to the market gives land an advantage (rent), because (transport charges being lower) the producer pockets a larger proportion of the price, whilst for the producer whose land is farther from the market, there is a larger deduction from prices under that head. Besides this, land nearer the market draws an additional rent because more intensive culture is carried on there. At the margin of the isolated State, landrent falls to zero.—Rent

M

of situation is to-day the fundamental item in the explanation of urban groundrents and houserents.

β. *Empirical Validity of the Theory of Localisation.* Thünen's zonal theory is still the most outstanding theoretical foundation of agricultural practice. It is, of course, only true upon certain assumptions which can never be wholly realised—upon the assumption of a homogeneous soil and of homogeneous transport conditions. Still, actual experience often furnishes close approximations to Thünen's imaginative picture. Any one who leaves a great city by train can see for himself the innermost zone of horticulture and market-gardening. Going back into history, we find that in the Middle Ages the great towns were encircles by zones showing Thünen's succession of agricultural methods. We can trace this, for instance, in the environs of Berlin. The reason why such a schematisation no longer holds good, is that the growth of railways and the development of other means of cheap transport have brought remote places into close touch with the market. (South America supplies Germany with grain.) Consequently Thünen's idea of zonal localisation no longer applies to the environs of particular towns; but it does apply in broad lines to the aggregate system of countries having intimate trade relations one with another. Thickly populated and predominantly industrial lands like England and Germany have become markets for distant, thinly populated, and mainly agricultural lands. The result is that, round the great towns of the present day, only the first, the proximate zone, is clearly recognisable. Take Vienna, for which this zone is comprised by the whole of Lower Austria, southern Moravia, and northern Styria, whence the Austrian capital is supplied with green vegetables, milk, etc. We may go so far as to say that nowadays the greater part of western and central Europe and the British Isles lie within the first zone, at any rate as regards areas with good railway

communication, and where soil and climate are satisfactory.—
As far as particular places are concerned, in view of the
extremely complicated conditions of transport (a place forty
miles from a railway station and only a hundred miles from
the market, may, economically speaking, be farther from the
market than one close to a railway station and a thousand
miles from the market), the "localities" are interspersed in the
most confusing way by differences in soil, climate, etc.

Knies has supplemented Thünen's theory by formulating a
law to the effect that in regions which have been far from the
market and are then brought near to the market by improved
communications, land rises in price, thanks to the possibility of
inaugurating a system of more intensive culture; whereas in
the regions already near to the market the price of land now
falls, owing to the fact that the aggregate output increases.

In matters of detail, there is much to be said in the way of
justifying and developing Thünen's theory of localisation.
First of all, it is necessary to point out that agriculture generates
petty industrial centres of its own (market towns), a fact to
which Dühring drew attention (*Kursus der Nationalökonomie*,
third edition, 1892, pp. 251 et seq.). Zones necessarily form
around these markets.—There is another matter to which I
should like to refer in this connexion. When distilleries,
sugar mills, and other industrial centres arise in association
with agriculture, they furnish by-products which serve as
food for stock; then stock-raising is introduced into the middle
of the most intensive grain-growing zone, so that (quite apart
from the circumstance that these industrial centres are markets)
the zonal system undergoes transformation from within.—
In other respects, too, a special explanation is needed as
concerns the position of the stock-raising zone. In Germany
for a long time we have had more stock-raising than can be
accounted for in terms of Thünen's theory of localisation.

This is explained by the wrong-headed tariff policy which protects stock more than grain, so that the cereal zone is driven outward while the stock-raising zone is drawn inward. It is important to remember that stock-raising has less power of absorbing population than grain-growing has.—We find Thünen's deductions justified when we come to consider the size of enterprises. Recent experience of attempts at homeland colonisation have shown that, under like conditions, different types of agricultural production vary in their effectiveness from product to product. Speaking generally, on any particular area of land, peasant enterprise will be more successful in stock-raising, whereas large-scale agriculture will produce a larger quantity of grain per acre. The magnitude of an enterprise, moreover, gives it only a relative superiority, not an absolute one. Large-scale enterprises and small-scale, respectively, will tend, according to circumstances, to promote the expansion of one zone or another to a greater extent than Thünen foresaw. Large-scale enterprises will promote the growth of the cereal zone; small-scale enterprises, that of the stock-raising zone.—Finally, owing to the discovery of novel modes of transport, many of Thünen's deductions need reconsideration. Since milk, butter, meat, live stock, green vegetables, etc., thanks to accelerated transport and the use of modern methods of preservation, can now be successfully conveyed to market from even enormous distances (Siberian butter, Argentine meat, Australian and Californian fruit, vegetables carried on special freight-trains from Hungary to Berlin!), these goods need no longer be produced, as when Thünen wrote, in close proximity to the great city where they are consumed. Dairy-farming, therefore, which of old, when carried on for the urban market, had to be associated with suburban market-gardening, can now be conducted at a distance from the town, in conjunction with pasturage-farming.

Notwithstanding all this, Thünen's deductions are, fundamentally, incontrovertible. The only one with regard to which
I feel a doubt is that which relates to sylviculture. Yet Thünen
was right in giving forestry the striking place he did, in the
second zone, though Goltz criticised him for this (in Schönberg's *Handbuch der politischen Oekonomie*, vol. ii, part 1).
Wood is less easily transportable than grain. If it is not our
practice to have a zone of sylviculture immediately surrounding
the zone of most intensive culture, this is because we have,
here, there, and everywhere, areas of cheap and poor land
fitted only for afforestation. That is why timber is grown in
regions remote from the theoretically appropriate area for
sylviculture. The Alps, the Carpathians, the Bohemian Forest,
etc., are our natural sources of supply. But since wood as fuel
is being replaced more and more by coal and gas, the zone of
building timber is to-day of more importance than the zone
of wood for burning.—It is noteworthy that in latter-day
Hungary, deprived of its Carpathian forests in 1918, timber is
being grown in the midst of the corn lands.

γ. Thünen and the Present-day Theory of Localisation. Subsequent economists have paid little heed to Thünen's theory
of localisation, and they have failed to elaborate a kindred
theory as regards manufacturing industry. The present author,
in his criticism of Marx, has done his best to show that in the
methóds of industrial production (whether large-scale or small-
scale) large enterprises are no more than comparatively sound,
and do not possess a rigidly mechanical superiority; and he
has pointed out that, among the conditions which decide
whether a large enterprise or a small one will be more successful,
the most influential one is the size of the market. (See below,
p. 228; also *Der wahre Staat*, second edition, pp. 149 et seq.)

Moreover, people are apt to forget that in economics the
idea of localisation can never be a spatial or geographical one,
When Thünen speaks of "distance from the market", he is not
thinking of such and such a number of miles, but of cost of
transport. What does this mean, in the last analysis? Not,
once more, the mere magnitude of expenditure expressed in

numerical terms. When we look at the matter from the outlook of organic economics, it means a particular kind of articulation of the particular economic enterprise into the aggregate structure of institutions, into the entirety of the branches of agricultural production. The aggregate is, overtly or latently, always presupposed; and the individual enterprise has its method of articulation into the whole, determined with reference to all the other economic elements of that whole—be those elements cost of transport or what you will.

If, then, the cost of transport merely supplies a pointer as to the way in which a particular agricultural enterprise in the "isolated State" has to be articulated into the aggregate structure of agriculture (rotation of crops, it may be, or the alternate system)—this does not imply the determination of a particular situation, a geographical localisation, but that of a qualitative relationship of articulation, which can decide the specific locale only in a secondary and derivative way.—That is why Alfred Weber's [1] clever attempt to ascertain by mathematical calculation where particular industries will be located, to decide this in terms of the "orientation of raw materials, of articles of consumption, and of labour" (under the guidance of his "ultimate factors of localisation", namely "cost of transport and cost of labour") was foredoomed to failure. Although mathematics is certainly applicable to such investigations, it can never have in them the unimpeachable validity that, for example, Newton's formula $\dfrac{m^{\mathrm{I}} m^{\mathrm{I}}}{r^2}$ has in mechanics. If we conceive these "orientations" to be particular articulations of enterprises, we shall easily recognise that there are supplementary factors which cannot be expressed in mathematical terms: for instance, personal relations with those who can supply capital, and with business colleagues (whose place of residence may often determine the localisation of an enterprise); also and especially the abundant but not numerically estimable "capital of higher grade", which distinguishes national areas one from another, and local areas as well. More than all, however, Alfred Weber and his followers and critics, who use this mathematical method, fail to understand that "cost" of transport, etc., is not a mere mechanical item, but is dependent upon the nature of the enterprise and upon the articulated structure

[1] Alfred Weber, *Über den Standort der Industrien*, 1909.

of agriculture in general. (It was very different with Thünen, for whom the aggregate articulations of agriculture were primary data.) Values, like goods, are always reciprocal. The orientation of labour and the orientation of consumption have, therefore, no "weights" of their own, for they only acquire them in their articulate relationship to the economy as a whole —while the articulate structure which makes such a relationship possible evolves only through the establishment and localisation of enterprises. That is likewise the significance of the much-talked-of "historical development" and "historical determination" of localisation. These conceptions must be free from all elements which conflict with a sound theory; for they must—to be acceptable—explain the purely conditional and not mathematically calculable validity of the factors of localisation. The "historical development" of the localisations does not signify that there has been any sort of "forcing out by material orientation" or some such process; it signifies that localisation is not a preexistent datum, but has to develop —through incorporation into the extant articulate structure of industry, or through the further development of some existent articulate part of economic life.

All these considerations point to the same conclusion. There is no tenable theory of the "local determination" of enterprises, or of geographical localisation; the only possible theory is one of factors of interarticulation, which work themselves out (indirectly) as localising factors. Consequently, a purely mathematical or mechanical treatment of the theory of localisation is out of the question.

8. *Theory of the Just Wage.*[1] Thünen was so strongly convinced of the importance of his formula for the ideal wage, $\sqrt{a\,p}$, that he actually wanted to have it engraved on his tombstone. Modern economists reject it foolishly, without understanding it. Knies has shown it to be mathematically unsound,[2] but has failed to recognise the kernel of truth it contains—the

---

[1] Among modern British writers who lay stress on the idea of the "just price" and the "just wage" (the latter being only a particular case of the former), especial mention may be made of Arthur J. Penty.—Various writings, and above all the chapter on "The Just and Fixed Price" in *Towards a Christian Sociology*, George Allen & Unwin, Ltd., London, 1923.— TRANSLATORS' NOTE.   [2] *Kredit*, second half, viii, 6.

important truth overlooked by Ricardo, and only to-day gaining acceptance, that wages increase with the increasing productivity of labour (p). (See above, the criticism of the iron law of wages, and below, pp. 264 et seq.)

On this depends the possibility of profit-sharing; and so does the whole development of the modern wage system, which —in various kinds of piece-work rates, premium-systems, etc.— has worked out ways of paying labour (individual workers) according to productivity. In all these methods, and also in the sliding scale of wages (wages rising or falling as the price of the product rises or falls), the value p is a constituent.

ε. *Thünen's Method.* Whereas the method of Quesnay, Smith, and Ricardo is entirely atomistic and mechanical, using the solitary Robinson Crusoe abstracted from society, on his island as chief illustration, and regarding value as the main economic enigma to be elucidated—Thünen's method, while no less abstract (thanks be! for what would become of science without abstraction), is a world away. Thünen's zones portray the whole cosmos of types of agriculture, the multiformity and copiousness of the ways of turning the land to man's account, the organic interconnexions among the various economic procedures. Boldly as he uses the tool of abstraction, he keeps his feet firmly planked on realities, and shows a truly Shakespearean group of the actual world. In him, the universalist spirit is at work. The theory of economic calculation (the mere theory of value) is disregarded; and the organised, articulated structure and functioning of economic life become the essential objects of study.

In Thünen's method we already find full allowance for the distinction on which so much stress has been laid in recent years between conservative (static) and progressive (dynamic) economy. (Cf. *Der isolierte Staat*, second edition, ii/1, pp. 153 et seq.)

Although in certain respects Thünen is obviously dependent upon Smith, and especially so in the matter of the theory of value, it may be said that Thünen could never have written as he did, had not Adam Müller preceded him. His principal achievement, the theory of agriculture, is really nothing more than a further development of the basic ideas of Adam Müller. (See above, pp. 165 et seq.)—Regarding Thünen and the theory of marginal utility, see above, pp. 174 et seq.

c. BRIEF EXPLANATION OF THE LEADING SYSTEMS OF AGRICULTURE[1]

For the full understanding of Thünen, the following explanations will be helpful:

I. *The Three-Field System.* This was in use from the ninth century to the nineteenth. The plough-lands are divided into three parts, and in rotation one of the parts is left fallow for a year, the second part is sown with corn in the autumn, the third in the spring. Beside the ploughs, there are permanent pastures and meadows.—*The Improved Three-Field System.* To facilitate the keeping of more live stock, and the provision of a larger quantity of manure, the plough-lands are subdivided into six, nine, or more fields. One third of these are sown with corn in autumn, another third in spring, and the remainder, instead of being left fallow, is wholly or partly put under forage crops. (This system is still in use on many peasant farms.)

II. *The Alternate System.*[2] The land of a farm is kept

---

[1] Cf. von der Goltz, "Ackerbausysteme", *Handwörterbuch der Staatswissenschaften*, third edition, Jena, 1909; Areboe, *Allgemeine landwirtschaftliche Betriebslehre*, sixth edition, Berlin, 1923.

[2] The German term is *Feldgraswirtschaft*, or *Koppelwirtschaft*. The latter is by the dictionaries incorrectly translated "rotation of crops". This last, described under iii below, is called by the Germans *Fruchtwechselwirtschaft*. The system we are now considering is a sort of half-way house between the three-field system and a fully developed rotation of the crops. The three-field system is obsolete in Britain. What in the text we have called the *alternate system* is practised on a good many British farms, but there does

alternately under pasture and under corn, for several years in each case, and with a succession of different grain crops for the part under corn. We must distinguish between two varieties. There is the "unregulated alternate system" (*die wilde Feldgraswirtschaft*), when part of the land is planted with cereals year after year so long as the yield is sufficient, and then it is put under grass, while a corresponding area of what has for some years been pasture is ploughed up again for the sowing of corn. (In former days this method was practised side by side with the three-field system.) There is also the "regulated alternate system" (*die geregelte Feldgraswirtschaft*), in which on the part of the farm used for the time being as arable there is an orderly succession of crops—cereals, legumens, root-crops. This is a combination of rotation of crops with the alternate system.—A variety of the alternate system is "fallow culture" (*Egartenwirtschaft*), practised to-day in the Alps and in the mountain regions of South Germany. After being planted for several years in succession with cereals, etc., the land is left to the growth of natural grass (*Egartenwiese* = fallow pasture).

III. *Rotation of Crops.* In this there is an orderly succession of grain crops, legumens, roots, fodder—as contrasted with the alternation of cereals and grass. For example, in the Hohenheimer rotation we have: (1) fallow; (2) rape-seed; (3) autumn-sown cereal; (4) roots; (5) spring-sown cereal; (6) clover; (7) autumn-sown cereal. In this system, the various crops are to dovetail into one another, as far as possible, in their demand for nutrients. (The use of leguminous plants in increasing the nitrogenous content of the soil comes under consideration here.) Rotation of the crops was first practised in England early in the nineteenth century. It is a method of intensive culture, for it necessitates a high expenditure of capital and labour (frequent ploughing, the liberal use of manure, etc.).

IV. *Pasturage Farming.* For this, most of the land is under grass, the agriculturist's main concern being to raise stock (for dairy-farming or for the meat market). This must always

not seem to be any name for it in general use among British farmers. Fream writes (*Elements of Agriculture*, tenth edition, 1918, p. 279): "Grass land is either temporary or permanent. In the former case, often spoken of as a 'temporary ley', seeds of grasses and clovers are sown, and after a period of variable length the land is ploughed up again."—TRANSLATORS' NOTE.

rank as a form of extensive culture. It predominates in the Alps and other mountainous regions, because the conditions of soil and climate favour it there; but also in fenlands, where the opportunities for marketing the stock are often determinative in the choice of this method, over and above peculiarities of the soil. In the Alps, dairy-farming is the usual form; in the German fenlands, on the other hand, stock is fattened for the market.

V. *Free Culture (freie Wirtschaft).*[1] The distinction between this form of culture and rotation of crops is that in free culture there is no fixed succession, but the crop chosen for a particular piece of land is selected year by year in accordance with the dictates of local market conditions. It is the most intensive form of culture, and can be best carried out on farms of medium size made up of areas on which the soil varies considerably from one area to another.

C. FRIEDRICH LIST

a. ECONOMICO-HISTORICAL RETROSPECT

In Germany there had now for a considerable time been a cleavage, a conflict, between the practical need for the protection of developing large-scale industry, on the one hand, and the dominant free-trade theory, on the other.

Since the days of the Federal Act, adopted at the Congress of Vienna on June 8, 1815, the individual States of the Germanic Federation had inagurated a high-tariff policy. Inasmuch, however, as these States were too small to provide adequate markets for large-scale industries, the protection furnished by their tariffs was inadequate to foster the growth of such industries. As early as 1816, indeed, Prussia had abolished many of her internal tolls, thus creating at least a comparatively free home market; and in 1818 she had introduced a very moderate tariff upon imports, the rate being from 10 to 15 per cent ad valorem. But the other States formed detached markets of their own, and

[1] The term "free culture", a literal translation of the German *freie Wirtschaft*, is not acclimatised in England. *Freie Wirtschaft* was practised in Thünen's innermost zone (see above, p. 173), for the adjacent urban market. This is what we know as "market gardening".—TRANSLATORS' NOTE.

even in Austria the various crown lands were cut off one from another by customs barriers. As early as 1819, the manufacturers of central and southern Germany had signed a famous petition, drafted by Friedrich List, asking for "the abolition of the internal customs dues of Germany", and for "the establishment of a universal German customs system, based on the principle of retaliatory duties"—so that the signatories of this petition were still actuated by a free-trade spirit. Thus List was the spiritual father of the German Customs Union, which, despite Metternich's opposition, came into being in the year 1833 under the auspices of the Prussian statesmen Motz and Eichhorn, and upon the basis of the Prussian customs system. Austria remained outside the new Customs Union. This was in essentials a preparation for the subsequent exclusion of Austria from the German realm [when the new German empire came into being in 1871], though Austria in the eighteen-thirties was still politically preponderant over Prussia; and it marked the birth of the Little-German idea which is still the scourge of the German people.

At the time when the German Customs Union was founded, Adam Smith's doctrines held almost undisputed sway in the economic world, and therewith the free-trade theory was dominant among German men of science and civil servants. But the moderate tariff, averaging 10 per cent ad valorem, though introduced by the Customs Union in the belief that it would be a prelude to free trade, tended more and more to develop automatically into a typical protective tariff, the original values being insisted on for the purpose of estimating duties during a period when commodities were being considerably cheapened. Thus arithmetically the duties were still reckoned at 10 per cent ad valorem when they had really become much higher. The free-traders, however, strongly objected to this, and the gulf between theory and actuality continued to widen. Then Friedrich List stepped forward, and endeavoured to solve the contradiction by formulating a new theory of commercial policy.

b. EXPOSITION

Friedrich List, the son of a master tanner, was born at Reutlingen in 1789. He won a higher position for himself by self-tuition, and in 1817 was appointed professor of economics and political science at the University of Tübingen. He had already become convinced that the Continental System, as practised during the Napoleonic wars, had been favourable to the growth of German industry, for it had protected Germany from the competition of the more highly developed large-scale industry of Great Britain. "The remarkable results", says List, "were then too recent and too obvious for me to be able to overlook them." In 1819, his advocacy of the abolition of internal customs dues made him suspect to the Würtemberg government, and he had to resign his professorship. Three years later, owing to his advocacy of a customs union and other needful reforms, he was sentenced to ten months' imprisonment in a fortress. Released before the term was up on giving a promise to emigrate, in 1825 he removed with his family to the United States.

In that country, as List was quick to realise, there was an even sharper contrast between commercio-political practice and the theory of free trade. In 1827, he wrote two pamphlets in which he attempted to formulate the theory of a protective tariff. In 1832, an ardent patriot, he returned to Germany, where he worked indefatigably on behalf of the idea of a customs union, and also to promote railway development.[1] Most of the pioneer German railway lines (the Dresden-Leipzig Railway among them) were built at his instigation.

Ere long recognition came to List, more especially thanks to Nebenius, the Badenese privy councillor—though his economic colleagues were slow to admit his merits (Hildebrand [1848] and subsequently Eugen Dühring being notable exceptions). His chief work, *Das nationale System der politischen Oekonomie* (Stuttgart and Tübingen, 1841), speedily ran through several editions. Nevertheless his financial position was embarrassed,

[1] In this matter List comes into line with Joseph von Baader (brother of Franz von Baader), whom recent investigations have shown to have been one of the doughtiest champions of railway construction in Germany. See Sauter, *Baaders Schriften zur Gesellschaftsphilosophie*, Jena, 1925, pp. 851–870 and 925 et seq.; also "Jahrbucher für Nationalökonomie und Statistik", vol. cxxiv, 1926, pp. 61 et seq., *Ein vergessenes Kapitel aus der Geschichte der Eisenbahnen.*

and prematurely his health became undermined. In 1846, he shot himself at Kufstein in Tyrol, whither he had gone for change of air. The List Society founded in 1925 is now engaged in publishing a collected edition of his works in eight volumes— a belated expression of gratitude on the part of the author's fatherland. A collection of the lesser writings, *Kleinere Schriften*, edited by Lenz, appeared at Jena in 1926 in the "Herdflamme" collection.—There have been two English translations of *Das nationale System*: one (American) in 1856, by G. A. Matile, with a preface by S. Colwell, and the other by Sampson S. Lloyd, *The National System of Political Economy*, with a memoir of the author, Longmans, London, 1885.

List animadverts against Smith's and Ricardo's conception of economics, and does so for reasons that are akin to those voiced by Adam Müller. Smith, said List, had been content to study exchange-value, and nothing but the exchange-value of concrete goods; and had regarded bodily labour as the exclusive force of production. This "theory of values" must be supplemented by a theory of the productive forces that lie behind values. "The prosperity of a nation is great, not in proportion to the accumulation of wealth, but in proportion to the development of the productive forces." If we speak of a "theory of values", we mean nothing more than a theory of the value and the price of products that are already finished; but if we speak of a "theory of productive forces" we mean, in addition, a knowledge of the conditions of the origination and reproduction of national wealth. For assuredly the causes of wealth must be something very different from wealth itself!

According to List, productive forces are: the laws of a State, its public institutions, science and the arts, religion, morality, intelligence and culture, the maintenance of public order, the political power of the State, and (above all) the harmonious cooperation of agriculture, manufacturing industry, and commerce. Again: "The Christian religion, monogamy, . . . hereditability of the throne, the discovery of the alphabetic

method of writing, the invention of printing, the postal system,
. . . and the introduction of improved means of transport,
are bountiful sources of productive force. . . . In order to
estimate the influence of freedom of conscience upon the
productive forces, . . . we need merely turn from the history
of England to the history of Spain. The publicity of legal
proceedings, parliamentary legislation, . . . ensure for the
citizens, and for the State authority as well, an aggregate of
energy and force which they could hardly expect to obtain
in any other way. It is difficult to conceive . . . of a law which
can fail either to increase or to diminish the forces of
production." [1]

We learn from these considerations, declares List, that the
free-trade doctrine is untenable. It is not true, he says, that
a nation, like the private trader, ought to buy in the cheapest
market; it is not true that protective duties serve only to
establish a monopoly for the benefit of industrialists at the
cost of the nation. First of all, and above all, it is not true,
because the infant industries that are fostered by such protection become interarticulated parts of the mutuality of economic
life, and promote the fructification of energy throughout the
whole of the body economic. How does this come to pass?
Thus: the protective duty does not protect one or another
large-scale enterprise in particular, but the entire aggregate
of the national industry.

This great idea of List's regarding the fruitfulness of mutuality
may be clarified as follows. The coalmines will thrive best when
the coal from them can be marketed to smelting works situated
close at hand; the smelting works, when there are affiliated
or adjacent rolling mills to use the pig iron; the rolling mills,
again, when they are sure of finding a market near by in
machine-making works, railways in course of construction,
building industries, etc.; the machine-making works, when
they can place the machines in easily accessible factories which
have a use for them; the factories, when they have no difficulty
in finding consumers for their products. The upshot is that

[1] *Das nationale System*, etc., 1841, p. 209; Lloyd's translation, p. 139.

no one of these enterprises can get on without all the rest. Those who supply raw materials, need those who elaborate raw materials a stage; these latter need those who elaborate still farther; and so on. Similar relations exist among all the enterprises that elaborate raw materials. If, for example, the manufacture of artificial dyes is rendered possible by a protective duty on foreign dyes, then (though the dyes will be dearer), the textile industries of the homeland will find a new market among the workers in the new chemical works. In this way, since the market has expanded, the burden of the increased cost of the dyes can readily be borne by the textile industry, though perhaps at the cost of a slight increase in the price of textiles.—There is a like interdependence between agriculture and large-scale industry. Large-scale industry is a customer for agriculture, and is the better customer the nearer the seat of industry is. In this matter List comes to the same conclusion as Thünen, that the productiveness of agriculture increases as the market draws nearer. A large-scale enterprise close at hand is the most natural patron of agriculture, and that is why industrialists are apt to regard a protective tariff for agriculture as superfluous. Agriculture and industry are by nature predestined to live "in perpetual peace" each with the other. (This is in sharp contrast with the Ricardian doctrine, according to which the prosperity of industry and that of agriculture are mutually antagonistic.)—In like manner, according to List, there is an internal connexion between industry and transport. Through a well-developed transport system with an abundance of ramifications, the market is expanded, and this fosters the growth of large-scale industry.

Secondly, the free-trade principle that we should buy in the cheapest market, is not applicable to the body economic as a whole. As soon as the forces of production have been developed by protection, the protected industries produce more cheaply instead of more expensively. "In course of time, the products of a nation capable of developing integral manufacturing energies can be made at home more cheaply than they can be imported from abroad." The loss of exchange-values, which the country suffers at the outset owing to the protective tariff, is to be regarded as capital invested upon the education of industry. By transient sacrifices, the country is endowed with permanent productive forces. The customs dues are payments made for educational purposes.

"Should England at this juncture undertake to supply Germany with a sufficiency of manufactured goods free, gratis, and for nothing, it would be inadvisable to accept the boon. If, thanks to new inventions, the English should become able to manufacture linen 40 per cent cheaper than the Germans (keeping to the old methods) could make it, and if the new methods were able to give them only a few years' start of the Germans, unless a protective tariff were promptly imposed the most important and oldest branch of German manufacturing industry would perish—the result being much the same as if a limb had been lopped from the German nation. Would a man be consoled for the loss of an arm by the assurance that thereby he had been enabled to buy his shirts 40 per cent cheaper?" [1]

Even for List, free trade, in so far as it can be accounted a means for educating the forces of the nation, remains an ulti-mate ideal. But before a free-trade system can work in a natural way, the backward nations must advance in industrial development until they stand on an equal footing with the most forward ones. (At that time, England was far ahead in the race.) Thus the nation, the national economy, steps in between the individual and mankind at large. The full develop-ment of the division of labour has to begin in the nation. "That nation will have the maximum productive power, and will consequently be the richest, which has developed to the utmost within its own area all the forces of manufacture in all their ramifications, and whose territory and agricultural production are big enough to provide its manufacturing population with the bulk of the necessary raw materials and means of subsistence."

[1] *Das nationale System*, etc., 1841, pp. 218–219; Lloyd's translation, pp. 146–147.

N

Thus, as an advocate of protection, List only accepts the theoretical kernel of the free-trade doctrine, for he considers free trade attainable solely as a sequel of a protectionist era, and only realisable between nations on the same economic level and therefore able to compete on equal terms. An [unprotected] agricultural State surrounded by highly developed industrial States cannot possibly establish thriving industrial enterprises. The industries of long standing have very great advantages as compared with the aspiring new ones: experienced entrepreneurs, customary markets, trained workers, an abundance of capital seeking investment, and an excellent transport system. On the other hand, it is unquestionably an error to suppose that only exceptional nations, such as the English and the French, are predestined to undergo far-reaching industrial expansion. Every nation becomes capable of this as soon as it has a sufficiency of surplus capital and surplus population.

If only for the reason that the nations pass through various phases of economic evolution, and pass through them at different times, it seemed to List absurd to suppose that one and the same commercio-political principle could be applicable at all times and to all peoples. In this way he happened upon the doctrine of "economic phases".

List distinguishes five phases or stages of economic development: (1) that of hunting tribes; (2) that of pastoral communities; (3) that of the agricultural commonwealth; (4) that of the agricultural and manufacturing State; (5) that of the agricultural and manufacturing and commercial State. The last is the ideal, for it is the perfected economic State, wherein "native manufactured products are exchanged for native agricultural products". In each successive phase a new commercial policy will be needed. Free trade is suitable for all the first three. In the two most primitive stages, and also in the purely agricultural State (where the population is too thin and where surplus capital is too scanty for any hopeful prospect of large-scale industrial developments), free trade signifies the advantageous exchange of home products for foreign manufactured articles. But as soon as agriculture has produced the necessary surplus of capital and population, the former can be invested and the latter set to work upon the establishment of an industry or industries. When, at long last, after a lengthy period of protection, the stage of a perfected economic State has been reached, protective measures will have become superfluous and perhaps even injurious, seeing that foreign competition will now be desirable as a spur to further advance. Free trade is the final aim, being the most expedient economic policy in the last phase, just as in the early phases, of economic development.—List said that in his day Italy, Spain, Portugal, Turkey, and Russia were in the agricultural phase. Germany and North America were in the agricultural and manufacturing phase; evidence of this as far as Germany was concerned being given by the great subdivision of farming land and by extensive emigration. Great Britain was in the last phase; and so, to a considerable extent, was France. Germany could not pass into the last phase without an enlargement of territory, and for this reason List advocated (in addition to protection) the expansion of the Customs Union to the sea-coast in the south and the north; also the passing of Navigation Acts, and the growth of German naval power. But his political aims were wider even than this. He dreamed of a united German realm stretching from Dunkirk to Riga and from the North Sea to the Adriatic.

List's theory of population is interconnected with the foregoing theory of social evolution. He considers that each economic order has its own peculiar faculty for absorbing population, the so-called "capacity for population", this latter increasing as economic development progresses. Consequently, and because it seems to him that there are no visible limits to the technical advances possible in agriculture and industry, List rejects the Malthusian theory of overpopulation. He writes in his opus magnum: "If in any nation population outstrips the production of the necessaries of life, and if capital accumulates to such an extent that it can no longer find investment at home, . . . this merely shows that nature no longer wishes industry, civilisation, wealth, and power to redound to the exclusive advantage of any one nation, or that a great part of the cultivable land in the world shall be inhabited by animals alone."[1] Elsewhere he writes: "In our days, a nation which does not grow must perish, seeing that all other nations are growing from day to day."[2]

c. Valuation of List, Especially as Concerns the Theories of Free Trade and Protection

We are helped to an appraisement of List's teachings by drawing a contrast between free trade and protection.

The free-trade ideal is a most alluring one; the ideal of an international division of labour, thanks to which commodities will always be produced where the conditions for their production are most favourable, so that they can be made as cheaply as possible. (This is the basis of Smith's advocacy of free trade. As to Ricardo's reasons for supporting it, see above, p. 140.) Here we have the principle of industrial freedom translated into the domain of the worldwide economy. National and international freedom of industry and division of labour are to mean exactly the same! List adduced, in answer to this notion, the reciprocal determinism of the various branches of production; and he insisted that the different forces of production must be educated before the regime of free competition could begin.—Contemporary economic science continues to swing like a pendulum between the two theories, and is wont to content itself with the hazy formula that the question of free trade versus protection cannot be decided in general terms, but must be independently argued in each particular case. From the "organic" standpoint there can be no doubt that the theory of protection contains a much larger measure of truth. The theory of free trade is an arid and artificial construction, which sets out from the standpoint that goods are to be looked upon as arithmetically calculable data (List

[1] *Das nationale System*, etc., 1841, p. 197; Lloyd's translation, p. 129.
[2] *Kleinere Schriften*, edited by F. Lenz, vol. i, 1926, p. 521.

calls this the "theory of values") instead of as entities which come into being through reciprocity alone.—Furthermore, the free-trade doctrine is only applicable if we envisage the world-market as "intercourse", as the place where numerous individual economic agents are gathered together. But if we recognise, as the champions of every organic doctrine recognise, that the national economics are specialised subordinate aggregates of the world economic aggregate, then we shall agree, as a matter of principle, in the suitability for each of a protective tariff tending to develop the whole. (In the present writer's view, for each of them this also functions as a comprehensive "capital of higher grade" peculiar to each.—See below, p. 279.)

I demur, in especial, to the free-traders' contention that when two nations exchange goods, both derive equal benefit from the exchange. The varying amount of capitalised energy with which the respective nations work will always produce a difference in the national benefit, for the one endowed with more capitalised energy will have a natural advantage. Moreover, just as the commercial profit differs in the two cases, so there must be a difference as regards the dependence of the two nations each on the other. (Hildebrand.)

Incorrect, on the other hand, is List's assumption that, after customs dues have exercised their educative influence for a sufficient period, the return to free trade will be a simple and easy matter. With a protective tariff or without, there is always a gradation of enterprises (graded in accordance with the varying effects of conditions peculiar to each), and when there is a protective tariff the less favourably placed of these enterprises are only enabled to keep going under the ægis of that tariff. Its suppression will inevitably be followed by their ruin. That is why the transition from protection to free trade is always a very difficult matter!—But apart from this, there will often be a danger that unqualified freedom of trade will expose even vigorous and thoroughly healthy large-scale enterprises to grave dangers. In the struggles of international competition, the industries that have the greatest command of capital and the most considerable natural advantages have a privileged position, and for this reason under free trade productive forces which in a particular country have been notably expanded at the cost of great sacrifices may be threatened with destruction by rivalry in a more advantageously situated land.

The seamy side of protection is that, inasmuch as it is impossible for all branches of production in a country to have equal advantages in respect of plant, situation, climate, and available capital, under a protective tariff, it is easy for large quantities of capital and labour power to be sterilised more or less by being devoted to "forcing-house industries", at the expense of more genuinely profitable kinds of enterprise. Before the war, Lujo Brentano drew special attention to this danger. The criticism, however, relates to the degree of protection, and to the success of this or that item in a tariff; it does not bear upon the general question of the soundness of protectionist doctrine, or refute the teaching of List. The two most notable constituents of that teaching are List's insistence upon the evolution of productive prices and their education under a protective system, and his stressing of mutuality as the fundamental determinant in such cases. These two leading thoughts become a permanent part of economic science in proportion as that science frees itself from atomistic conceptions, looks behind the superficial data of the hour, reaches out in universalist fashion to the reciprocities and living interconnexions that underlie these data; in proportion as it effects a genuine advance from an atomistic theory of values to a universalist theory of functions or achievements. Post-war conditions, which have made protection against imports as a supplement to the ordinary tariffs an elementary necessity for the weakened national economies, give the best possible proof of the soundness of List's doctrine.

Before all, List is of outstanding importance thanks to his method. He was little concerned with systematised investigation rigidly confined to the theoretic plane; but by none of his predecessors except Adam Müller had he been excelled or equalled in respect of a vivid way of contemplating economics historically. By making his views on the exchange of goods between the various national economics dependent on the state of economic development in each—the abundance of capital, the experience of entrepreneurs, the skill of workers, etc.— he advanced beyond the abstract, atomistic outlook of Smith and Ricardo. Methodologically, this procedure is rounded off by the introduction of the concept of the concrete cultural community, the idea of the nation—as contrasted with the idea of unrestricted, cosmopolitan, intercourse between individuals.

Hildebrand goes so far as to write: "List pricked the economists of Germany on to historical study." The affiliations of the historical school to Müller and List are likewise illustrated by the following remark of Knies: "The writings of Adam Müller and Friedrich List had an unmistakable influence even on those who repudiated their teachings. . . . We may be well aware that some of Müller's conclusions were erroneous, and none the less be willing to follow him in the endeavour, . . . when we are making calculations about concrete material goods, . . . to avoid ignoring moral and political needs." [1] In actual fact, List produced a very powerful impression by the abundant supply of historical proofs (although in this respect he is hardly to be compared with Adam Müller). By instances drawn from the history of Italy, England, France, and other countries, he tried to show how the growth of industry had been promoted by mercantile protection; and by the examples of Amalfi, Genoa, Venice, Pisa, and the German Hansa towns, that they had decayed owing to the lack of

[1] Knies, *Die politische Oekonomie*, etc., second edition, p. 311.

national unity and of the full development of their productive forces.—It would, however, be going too far to ascribe to List a historical methodology in the study of economics. He did not practise this in the strict sense of the term.

The kinship between the views of List and those of Adam Müller is, however, impaired by the fact that List never completely departed from a liberal standpoint, never fully abandoned the doctrine of natural right, and had to the last an inclination towards centralist views. Nor did he adopt the philosophy of German idealism. His idea that what matters is, not exchange-values alone, but also (and more) the spiritual and moral forces that determine the processes of value, and furthermore the organic composition of the aggregate and the relations of the parts to the whole—all this is the, greatly elaborated, thought of Adam Müller. In the latter's writings, too, we find passages closely resembling List's formulations. For instance, in the *Versuche einer neuen Theorie des Geldes* (Lieser's edition, p. 2) we read: "State property does not by any means consist exclusively of the returns from the land owned by the State, etc., or of the capitalised value of such incomes. All the defensive powers of human beings and of the land; armies, fortresses, weapons, the administrative art of the civilian State in its entirety; even the constitution, the laws, and the national memories—are constituents of State property." List would have said that these same things are parts of the forces of production. List and Müller were not merely at one in the use of such ideas to confute Smith, for they used them also constructively in the formulation of their own doctrines. All that List did (apart from his deductions concerning the theory of foreign trade) was to carry out Müller's leading notion in fuller detail, especially by showing how the various branches of industry were interconnected in a way which determined and intensified production, and further by demonstrating the links between agriculture and industry; these being matters in which the general theoretical connexion had already been pointed out by Adam Müller. No doubt in Müller's writings the whole train of thought is directed towards a strictly organic (universalist) conception of the State, whereas in List we often note an inclination towards a liberating application of universalism. Certainly, too, we find that Müller is always aiming at the establishment of corporative relations, based on personal elements, and giving a privileged position to the

landed gentry; whilst List is always working for the development of a modern monetary economy and of large-scale
industry, of a system in which no preference would be given
to the landowners, whose interests in existing circumstances
would, he considered, be safeguarded by the establishment of
large-scale industry as an adjacent market for agricultural
produce. But the two economists are at one again in the stress
they lay upon the principle of duration.

Although nowadays the close connexion between List and
Müller is usually overlooked, shortly after their own time,
when their influence was still strong, it was generally recognised. Thus Hildebrand wrote (*Nationalökonomie der Gegenwart
und Zukunft*, 1848, p. 69): "List has been compared to
Burke, and has even been termed the Luther of the economic
world; on the other hand, some have described him as an
ignoramus and a charlatan, asserting that what few good things
there are in his writings were pilfered from Müller, and have
been garbled in the reproduction." The detailed account (not
wholly accurate) which Hildebrand (*op. cit.*, pp. 59–62) gives
of the relation between List and Müller, confirms me in my
opinion.—Finally, List knew Müller personally in Vienna,
and must therefore have been acquainted with Müller's writings.
—As regards the affiliation of List to Franz von Baader, cf.
Sauter, *Baaders Schriften zur Gesellschaftsphilosophie*, Jena,
1925, pp. 816–833.

Not wholly correct is the general opinion that List's teaching
amounts to nothing more than a neomercantilism. Agreed that
there is an inner kinship between List and the mercantilists;
but the doctrine of the productive forces and of the reciprocal
interaction between all the branches of economic life is something very different from a mere refurbishing of the mercantile
theory of customs duties. Whereas the latter aims at promoting
the import of money, at establishing a favourable balance of
trade, and at getting rid of a natural economy, List's theories
are based on the principle of industrial mutuality and the
promotion of industry by education. Again, whilst for List, free
trade was the ultimate goal, and protective tariffs were only
means to that end, the mercantilists knew nothing of such a
distinction.

Regarding List's influence on Bernhardi, see immediately
below; regarding his influence upon Carey, see below p. 205;
and regarding his criticism of Malthus, see above, p. 128.

D. Germano-Russian Economists

It is desirable here to make a brief reference to the so-called "Germano-Russian School." This name is applied by Roscher to a group of early nineteenth-century economists, who do not really form a unified school. The chief representatives of this trend are Storch, Kankrin, and Bernhardi[1] (1802–1885). The last-named was the most notable of the three, and his chief published work, *Versuch einer Kritik der Gründe, welche für grosses und kleines Grundeigentum angeführt werden* (St. Petersburg, 1849), is the most notable product of the group.[2]

The name of the book notwithstanding, the main content of the *Versuch* is a general critique of economic dogma. Bernhardi attacks the theories of Smith and Ricardo, and runs atilt against their individualism. He contraposes to this (§ 5 et passim) a universalism of a somewhat confused character, for a genuine universalism does not consist in a sacrifice of the individual to the aggregate, but in a proper, that is to say an articulated, construction of the aggregate. He objects to the preference for large-scale landed proprietorship shown by the classical economists. Since large-scale, medium-scale, and small-scale landed proprietorship have their respective advantages, not one of these forms should receive an absolute preference, but all should as far as possible be supported and maintained to a suitable extent.—Bernhardi, whose mother was a sister of Ludwig Tieck, held views akin to those of the German idealists, and had unquestionable affiliations to Adam Müller (anti-individualist standpoint, conception of duration), List (duties on grain, but Bernhardi did not favour a tariff on manufactured articles), and the earlier historical school (a juster distribution of income through economic ties).

[1] Felix Theodor Bernhardi, the diplomatist and economist, must not be confused with his son, General Friedrich von Bernhardi (b. 1849), whose work *Germany and the Next War*, published in 1912, attracted so much attention in England.—Translators' Note.

[2] Concerning Bernhardi, see K. Diehl, in the preface to the reissue of the *Versuch*, Leipzig,

CHAPTER NINE

CAREY'S OPTIMISM AND ITS COUNTERPARTS ON THE CONTINENT OF EUROPE

1. Carey's Teachings

NORTH AMERICA'S main contribution to economics is to be found in the system of Henry Charles Carey.

Carey (1793–1879) was the son of an Irish immigrant, Matthew Carey, who in his transatlantic home attained note as a publisher. H. C. Carey's chief works were the *Principles of Political Economy*, three vols., 1837–1840 (when he penned this, he was still a free-trader), and *Principles of Social Science*, three vols., 1858–1859).

His doctrine was permeated with the notion of harmony and the feeling of optimism. The authorised German translation of the *Social Science* bears as motto Kepler's dictum: "The world-edifice is a harmonious whole".

Carey, like List, regards national wealth as consisting of the sum of all utilities—contrasted with the sum of all exchange-values. Utility is man's power over nature; value is nature's power over man, that is to say "the measure of the resistance to be overcome in obtaining things required for use". Value is, therefore, tantamount to the cost of reproduction. Man's power over nature is continually increasing; nature's resistance is decreasing. Hence, while wealth increases, values fall. Land has no special position among the means of production, for land, economically considered, is only a tool fashioned by human hands. Just as a steam-engine is made out of iron by labour, so the soil is transmuted into a means of production, is made cultivable. Since from this standpoint land is seen to be no more than one "artificially made" instrument among many, landownership is merely the ownership of capital; is only the possession of a particular kind of labour stored up in the soil. Landrent, therefore, is not as Ricardo declared, a plum falling from heaven into the landowner's mouth, but interest on capital. Agricultural production, consequently, is subject to the law that is valid throughout the domain of economics—the law that the usefulness of labour continually increases, while the exchange-values of products continually fall.

Carey attacks Malthus and Ricardo. It is not true, he declares, that owing to the increase of population man is forced to bring under cultivation land of steadily worsening quality, so that new and ever new landrents are originated. Observation of the actual process of cultivation proves the opposite. The first land to be tilled is not the best, but the worst; just as, in the case of the other means of production, men began with the use of the most inadequate. The stone axe was made long before the iron one. To begin with, people cultivate land at a considerable altitude, land that is dry and that has a light soil; the lower slopes of the mountains from which the water runs off of itself. Not until later do they see what they can make of the low-lying and marshy, though more fertile, regions, prone to inundation, and afflicted with an unhealthy climate. The history of the settling of new land, from Egypt to America, shows this clearly.

Thus Carey finds it possible to escape from the pessimism inherent in the earlier view of the evolution of the individualist economic order and to substantiate an optimistic outlook. The trend of development, he thinks, is towards an increasingly favourable distribution of the aggregate product. Since, as previously explained, the power of man over nature is growing, the importance of the labour factor must increase.

He arrives at the following law of distribution. In course of time, the interest of capital and the rent of land must fall lower and lower, while the part of the net product that accrues to labour will continually increase. In other words, landrent and the rent payable to other kinds of capital will decline owing to a steady diminution in the cost of the produce of the soil. Nevertheless, the capitalist class will continue to play its part in promoting the course of economic development. The share of interest will be smaller, but the absolute amount will increase, because of the great increase in productivity. Thus there will be a beautifully harmonious interadaptation of the various social interests.

This harmony is consolidated by "the law of the relative increase in the numbers of mankind, and in the supply of food and other commodities required for their support". Malthus was wrong in assuming the reproductive function to be a constant quantity. In actual fact, "fecundity is in the inverse ratio of organisation", and the "cerebral and generative powers of man mature together".[1] Thanks to the increasing fruitfulness of capital, the means of subsistence increase faster than population. (For a fuller discussion of this question, see above, p. 129.)

Oncken has not inaptly termed Carey "a List of the agrarian world", for, whilst the two men have kindred notions as to the nature of wealth, Carey gives the first place among the branches of production to agriculture, and holds that it is agriculture which needs protection by an import tariff. A steady and equable advance of all classes can, in his opinion, only be secured by ultimately returning to the soil all the mineral constituents that are taken from it in the crops, for in default of this it will in the end become hopelessly impoverished. He writes (echoing Liebig): "It is singular that modern political economy should have so entirely overlooked the fact that man is a mere borrower from the earth, and that when he does not pay his debts, she acts as do all other creditors, and expels him from his holding." This return of mineral constituents to the soil can only be effected when producer and consumer live close together, when

[1] *Principles of Social Science*, vol. iii, p. ix.

agriculture and manufacturing industry are carried on side by side. That implies, moreover, the "decentralisation of production", which at the same time reduces the intervention of middlemen in trade.

From this follows, according to Carey, the need for "a protective system as understood by Colbert"; and also the existence of a community of interests between landowners and manual workers, seeing that both land and labour command higher prices under a protective system; but it likewise follows that the interest of the trading class is divergent from that of the agriculturists and the workers. In other respects, Carey is strongly in favour of a system of natural freedom, is a supporter of laissez-faire.—He elaborated his own theories of money and credit.

2. VALUATION OF CAREY

Carey's teaching displays numerous flashes of insight, but lacks systematic elaboration. His optimism was accordant with the conditions prevailing at that date in a progressive country richly endowed with natural resources, but it cannot be regarded as proof at all points against criticism. One of his basic ideas, that land is on all fours with every other kind of capital and is therefore increasingly fruitful, cannot be fully sustained. The other, that the power of man over nature is continually increasing, is sound as far as it goes; but it underestimates the antagonistic influences inherent in the diminishing returns from land, in the increase of population, and in the unhappy consequences of the imperfect organisation of economic life (crises, proletarianisation). Hence there is inadequate justification for his generalising trend towards optimism and a faith in social harmony. In my opinion, the most effective refutation of Carey is to be drawn from Thünen's zonal theory. Any one who intelligently applies what was said in previous pages anent that theory, will be able to distinguish easily between the grain and the chaff in Carey. That Carey should think of the "relative utility of economic systems", rather than of equable intensification, speaks volumes.

As to details, the following remarks may be made. Since all economic goods are but transformed natural materials, it is doubtless time that this applies as regards the land, no less than elsewhere. Carey insists on the point, following Liebig. But for practical purposes the multipliability of the soil is much less considerable than that of the majority of movable means of production, and is of a very different kind. (See above, pp. 122 et seq., concerning the law of diminishing returns from land.) Inasmuch as, concurrently with the increase of population, it oftens becomes necessary to have recourse to more costly methods of agricultural production (whether because less fertile land has to be brought under cultivation, or because additional capital has to be less fruitfully utilised on land already cultivated), land occupies a peculiar position as compared with mobile capital. The law of diminishing returns applies more comprehensively to land than to mobile means of production. Carey makes much play with the notion that technical advances in agriculture suffice to compensate, and more, the working of the law of diminishing returns. (See above, p. 129.) But this is only true in certain labile historical periods, when great leaps to new systems are being made. (Consider Thünen's zones!) Besides, the over-compensation referred to by Carey is soon outweighed, in its turn, by the increase of population. We may agree that there are sound elements in Carey's account of the historical development of agriculture. But this has little bearing on the theory of rent. Even when we look at the matter historically, we find that the land under cultivation at any particular time is always the best land available; and for that reason, in the extant technical conditions, recourse to technically less favourable land is continually becoming necessary. If we want to criticise the Ricardian theory of landrent to good effect, we must seek other grounds than Carey's. (See above, p. 143.)

For the rest, however, Carey tried to look at economics, not in abstract isolation, but as a living social reality. For this reason his doctrine, in contrast with Ricardo's atomistic constructions, has a bountifulness, a vigour, and an organic coherence, which make it akin to that of Adam Müller and List. Carey, indeed, often refers to List, and also to Thünen and Liebig. But he fails, just as Dühring fails, to solve the contradiction between economico-political individualism and the universalist idea of protection.

As concerns Carey's arguments against Malthus, which are chiefly based upon the effect of advances in the technique of agriculture, see above, pp. 129 et seq.

3. Counterparts on the Continent of Europe

Carey's doctrine was adopted in Germany—with important modifications, especially in the matter of practical application to social reform—by Eugen Dühring (1833–1921), an unattached scientist who, one-sided though he was, attained considerable note as mathematician, physicist, philosopher, and political economist.

Dühring's economic works are: *Careys Umwälzung der Sozialwissenschaft und Volkswirtschaftslehre*, Munich, 1865; *Kritische Grundlegung der Volkswirtschaftslehre*, 1866; *Kursus der National- und Sozialökonomie*, Berlin, 1873, fourth edition, edited by Ulrich Dühring, Leipzig, 1925. Dühring must be thanked for certain important services. He was the first to appreciate List duly, and was also first in the field as critic of Marxism. He had considerable originality; displayed keen insight; and was a man of pure and incorruptible aspirations who had to suffer much injustice at the hands of academic critics. Nevertheless, we cannot accept him at his own valuation as a pioneer. He was but a caricature of Schopenhauer. That philosopher's pungent censure often degenerated in Dühring into embittered railing; and Schopenhauer's genius found a counterpart in Dühring only as talent, many-sided, indeed, but inharmonious, and fatally infected by the positivism of his day.

In France, Frédéric Bastiat (1801–1850) represented the same thought-trend as Carey, and influenced a wider public than Dühring was able to do. His chief work, *Les harmonies économiques*, 1850, was left unfinished at his death.

Dühring and others have accused Bastiat of plagiarising from Carey. The opinion is now widely diffused, and there is a core of truth in it. (For the other side of the case, see Gide and Rist, *Histoire des doctrines économiques*, Paris, 1908.)

Bastiat's teaching, eloquently phrased, exerted much political influence in Germany as well as France. In Germany, where in the meanwhile protectionism had become dominant, it gave impetus to the free-trade reaction. Under the leadership of Prince-Smith, the German translator of Bastiat, O. Michaelis, J. Faucher, Léon Faucher, Michel Chevalier, and others, there originated from 1846 onwards in France and Germany a powerful free-trade party, which had some striking successes in the campaign against protection (the Franco-British commercial treaty of 1860). There were some other economists who followed in the footsteps of Bastiat and Carey, but held aloof from the free-trade party. Max Wirth (1822–1900) was one of these.

To the same trend as that which found expression in the German romanticist movement belong two famous Englishmen, Thomas Carlyle and John Ruskin. Carlyle (1795–1881; *Sartor Resartus*, 1835; etc.) was, as a social reformer, a vigorous opponent of the individualism of the British school. Ruskin (1819–1900; *Unto this Last*, 1862; etc.) championed a moralist conception of economics, advocated an ennoblement of the conduct of life, and promoted a return to the artistic handicrafts as against machine production.

CHAPTER TEN

A SHORT ACCOUNT OF THE EVOLUTION
OF SOCIALISM

THIS section has perforce been extremely condensed. For its better understanding, the student should, before beginning it, reread the account of Ricardo (pp. 134 et·seq.), and the fourth chapter, "Individualism versus Universalism", pp. 59 et seq. References to the literature of socialism will be found below, under Marx, and elsewhere throughout the chapter.[1]

A. THE CONCEPT OF SOCIALISM

> The power to distinguish good
> from ill,
> And joy on earth where sadness
> lingers still,
> Give thou to those who seek thee
> with good will!
>
> EICHENDORFF

The history of socialism lies beyond the scope of this book. A cursory glance at its origins and connexions must suffice. Socialism is not, properly speaking, a theory of the economic process. It is, rather, a moral concept, a demand that economic life should have a particular trend. Only for that reason have socialists any use for economic doctrines—usually those of other theoreticians, their own contributions to economic theory consisting almost exclusively of criticism of the existing order. In *Sozialismus und soziale Bewegung im neunzehnten Jahrhun-*

---

[1] On the general topic of the evolution of socialism, the most valuable work now available in English is Harry W. Laidler's *A History of Socialist Thought*, Crowell, New York, 1927, Constable, London, 1927.—TRANSLATORS' NOTE.

dert, eighth edition, 1919, p. 25,[1] Sombart quotes a motto of Weitling's which might well be that of socialist literature in general: "We wish to be free as birds on the wing; to make our way through life as they through the air, untrammelled, cheerful, and harmonious." The basic idea of socialism is that of making all men happy. But the essential thing, according to the socialists, is that this universal happiness can only be established through the economic process. The primary needs are community of property and equality of incomes. Private ownership (of the means of production) must be done away with; the right of inheritance and the right to receive an income without working for it must be abolished (no more landrent and no more interest on capital); and in this way the "right to the full product of labour" will be established. An associated demand is that of the right to existence—to existence on the same terms for all.

Can socialism be regarded as a purely universalist system? No, it cannot. The abolition of private property and the modification of economic life on collectivist lines are, in a sense, universalistic; but the insistence upon the "right to the whole product of labour", taking the name of universalism in vain, is in truth wholly individualistic. The idea that every one is to have and to enjoy the fruit of his labour for himself alone, is individualistically conceived and presupposes an economic process so ordered as to render this possible. It involves the individualistic notion of economic activities that are detached, isolated, self-governing. The "right to equality", on the other hand, is a hybrid notion (pure individualists would demand arbitrary inequality; pure universalists, graduated inequality).

[1] There have been two English translations of this book, both entitled *Socialism and the Social Movement in the Nineteenth Century*: one from the first edition, by A. P. Atterbury, Putnam, New York, 1898; the other from the sixth edition, by M. Epstein, Dent, London, 1909. (See also below, pp. 219, 235, and 242.)—TRANSLATORS' NOTE.

Demands for democracy and liberty are, once more, wholly individualistic. In general, socialism discloses itself as an unorganic hybrid form in which individualistic and universalistic ways of thinking are commingled. (See below, p. 231.) —Socialism can, however, also be regarded as existing in various grades. Land reform (see below, p. 237) and social reform might be termed lower grades of socialism, inasmuch as they both aim in one way or another at the organisation of economic life.

B. Socialism in the Classical World

Ancient socialism is not, as people are apt to declare to-day, fundamentally different from modern. In antiquity there already existed genuine capitalism, a social problem of the same character as the one we now have to solve, and a socialist theory closely resembling our own.[1] Even bolshevism had its counterpart in those days. Ancient socialism came to its climax in the utopias of Euhemerus (flourished about 300 B.C.) and Iambulus (Hellenistic period). The latter is extraordinarily "modern". I need not go into details.[2] It will be well, however, to allude to the converse error of supposing that Plato, in his *Republic*,[3] was advocating socialism in the latter-day sense of the term. This "republic" was not properly speaking socialistic, for it was not democratic but authoritative, its rulers or "guardians" being the best and the wisest. The "best" decide, not the "will of the masses"; and there is no question of equality.

C. The Chief Exponents of Socialism before Rodbertus[4]

In modern times, socialist movements have become more and more active in proportion as the individualist economic order

---

[1] Cf. Pöhlmann, *Geschichte der sozialen Frage und des Sozialismus in der antiken Welt*, two vols., third edition, Beck, Munich, 1925. See especially vol. ii, p. 410; vol. i, pp. 425 et seq. For these, see Pöhlmann.

[3] English translations by Jowett, by Davies and Vaughan, and by H. Spens (in Everyman's Library).

[4] Cf. Lorenz von Stein, *Geschichte der sozialen Bewegung in Frankreich bis auf unsere Tage*, three vols., Leipzig, 1848, new edition, Munich, 1921. See below, p. 247.

has become established. Modern economico-scientific socialism first appeared in the days of the great French revolution, when the fourth estate began to voice its demands persistently. But even before the revolution, modern socialism had had its exponents. The socialist theoreticians Morelly (flourished in the middle of the eighteenth century) and Mably (1709–1785) had advocated the communistic equality of all; and Rousseau (1712–1778), as we have already learned, taught that all had been equal in the state of nature to which he recommended a return. During the revolution, communist aspirations found practical expression under the leadership of François Noël ("Gracchus") Babeuf (1764–1797), who aimed at the abolition of private property and the establishment of a community of goods. The "conspiracy of the equals" was, however, betrayed to the Directory, and the contemplated insurrection missed fire. When Babeuf and his friend Darthé were sentenced to the guillotine, they stabbed one another.[1]

As a critic of the extant social order, Bernard de Mandeville (1670–1733) may, in a sense, be considered a forerunner of the socialism of the Enlightenment. In his *Fable of the Bees, or Private Vices Public Benefits*,[2] starting from Hobbes' view that morality was based on self-interest, Mandeville inferred that vice was necessary to the prosperity of the commonwealth, and that the pinch of hunger for some redounded to the advantage of the whole. He maintained, further, that the interests of the individual and those of the community were incompatible, and therefore urged that wages should be kept down. There is no folly too extreme to find a place in the history of the social sciences!

The first socialist systematist of note was Count Henri de Saint-Simon (1760–1825; *Nouveau christianisme*, 1825; translation by the Rev. J. E. Smith, London, 1834; *Oeuvres choisies*, three vols., Brussels, 1859). He was the first to insist that there

---

[1] See Philippe Buonarroti, *Conspiration pour l'égalité dite de Babeuf*, two vols., Brussels, 1928; J. Bronterre O'Brien, *Buonarroti's History of Babeuf's Conspiracy*, London, 1836; E. Belfort Bax, *The Last Episode of the French Revolution*, London, 1911.—TRANSLATORS' NOTE.

[2] The first draft appeared in 1705 as *The Grumbling Hive, or Knaves Turned Honest*. As the *Fable*, it appeared anonymously in 1714, and with the author's name in 1723. It was primarily written as a political satire on the state of England in 1705, when the Tories were accusing Marlborough and the ministry of advocating the French war for personal reasons.—TRANSLATORS' NOTE.

is an intrinsic opposition between capital and labour. He had a number of enthusiastic disciples, who developed the socialist aspects of his teaching. The most important among these disciples were Enfantin (1796–1864) and Bazard (1791–1832). The latter formulated Saint-Simon's leading thought in the following terms: "To every one according to his capacity, and to every capacity according to its achievement." (The right to the whole product of labour.)

Charles Fourier (1772–1837), when working as a clerk at Marseilles in 1799, was told by his chief to arrange for the sinking of a ship-load of rice in the harbour, in order to keep up prices. This incident made a powerful impression on his mind. Like so many of the champions of the Enlightenment, he assumed that perfect harmony exists in nature and society. This latter is to be organised—without compulsion—in cooperative groups of moderate size, numbering from 500 to 2,000 persons each, called "phalanxes". His principle was, "Les attractions sont proportionelles aux destinées". What this means is that, for each kind of labour, persons must be found who are designed for it, are competent to perform it, and are willing to undertake it. Work must be a pleasure. As to the distribution of the product, according to Fourier, a just allotment would be: to labour, five-twelfths; to talent, four-twelfths; and to capital, three-twelfths.—Fourier's most notable disciple was Victor Considérant (1808–1893).

Robert Owen (1771–1858) likewise expected to realise his socialist schemes through the establishment of small cooperative commonwealths. (*A New View of Society*, 1813.) For him, as for Rousseau, human character was the outcome of education and economic position. It followed that the governments, by judicious modifications of social circumstances, could make human beings perfectly happy, and could supply a superfluity of goods. Production should be organised on the basis of productive cooperatives.—Owen did yeoman's service by the transformation he effected in the working and living conditions of the operatives and their families at the cotton mill of New Lanark, where he was superintendent, and also by his promulgation of the idea of voluntary cooperatives, both for production and consumption.[1]—One of the best-known of his followers was William Thompson (1785–1833), *An Inquiry*

[1] Lives of Robert Owen, by Joseph McCabe, 1920, Frank Podmore, 1923, G. D. H. Cole, 1925.—TRANSLATORS' NOTE.

into the Principles of the Distribution of Wealth most conducive to Human Happiness (1824). The producer was to receive the whole product of his labour. Thompson clearly foreshadowed the notion of surplus value. (See below, under Marx, p. 220.)

The Genevese Simonde de Sismondi (1773–1842; *Nouveau principes d'économie politique*, Paris, 1819; English translation, *Political Economy, and the Philosophy of Government*, London, 1847) must be numbered among the critics of individualist economics, rather than among the socialists proper. He adopted the system of Adam Smith, but was greatly influenced by German romanticism as well as by British utilitarianism, and this has an important bearing on the German origin of modern social reform. Sismondi demands systematic State action for the protection of the poor, but without collectivisation of production. ("System of regulative State intervention.")

Louis Blanc (1813–1882; *Organisation du travail*, 1839; English translation, *The Organisation of Labour*, London, 1848) did not advocate a social revolution, but a gradual development of the extant social order into the new one, by the establishment of workers' associations for cooperative production. Like Marx subsequently, he considered history to be a succession of class struggles. He founded a labour party, and in 1848 was a member of the provisional government, but was unable to carry his plans into effect, and had to take refuge in Belgium during the autumn of 1848. He was one of the few socialists who have accepted the Malthusian theory of population.

Pierre Joseph Proudhon was born in 1809 and died in 1865. His principal writings were: *Système des contradictions économiques ou philosophie de la misère*, 1846 (this was the book against which Karl Marx polemised in his *La misère de la philosophie*, 1847); and *Qu'est-ce que la propriété?* 1840 (English translation by B. R. Tucker, *What is Property?*, two vols., 1898–1902). In this earlier work, to his own question, "What is property?" Proudhon had answered, "Property is theft!" Proudhon considers that the root of all economic evil is to be found in the interest upon capital, and, more generally, in rent and money of every kind. Proudhon recommended as a remedy the establishment of a bank of exchange, which was to buy from every producer the goods he had made, giving him as payment a note proportional to the amount of labour that had been expended; and the bank was to give credit without charging for the accommodation. If there were such a bank, no one would borrow from the capitalists money for which interest would have to be paid, and the only thing left for the capitalists to do would be to set to work themselves. Free competition was to continue. In that matter, Proudhon aimed at a unification of liberalism and collectivism, and differed from all other socialists.

In Germany it was at one time usual to class among the socialists the philosopher Johann Gottlieb Fichte (1762–1814; *Der geschlossene Handelsstaat*, 1800; *System der Rechtslehre*, 1812), whom we have to thank for the refutation of the doctrine of natural right (*Grundlage des Naturrechts*, 1796) and for the formulation of a consistently universalist idea of the State. But Fichte was not a socialist. He defined property, not as a right to things, but as an exclusive right to a particular activity. In *Der geschlossene Handelsstaat*, he was pioneer in recognising that any economic community is necessarily to some degree secluded from the rest of the world, thus fortifying the idea that such a community should as far as possible supply its own needs instead of having recourse to foreign trade. From his conception of the State he tried to deduce the outlines of a just economic order. The State measures the economic activities of production and trade, and assigns them to the various organised estates in such a way that all the citizens are enabled to live according to much the same standard. Foreign commerce, which might tend to upset the balance of this organisation, is to be reduced to a minimum. (Cf. Baxa, *Einführung in die romantische Staatswissenschaft*, Jena, 1923.)—Karl Georg Winkelblech (1810–1865), who wrote under the pen-name of Karl Marlo, had economic ideas that stand midway between feudalism and socialism. His most notable book was *Untersuchungen über die Organisation der Arbeit oder das System der Weltökonomie*, four vols., 1850–1859. In this he recommended a federative system linking up craft-guilds.—Wilhelm Weitling was a journeyman tailor, born in Magdeburg, 1808, died in New York, 1871. He wrote *Garantien der Harmonie und Freiheit*, 1842, putting forward a communistic doctrine which, though naïve and confused, had a fairly solid philosophical foundation. He had a good deal to do with the organisation of the German labour movement.

D. RODBERTUS

Building upon Ricardo, Proudhon, and Saint-Simon, the distinguished theoretician Karl Johann Rodbertus-Jagetzow (1805–1875) was the real founder of scientic socialism in Germany.

His chief writings were: *Zur Erkenntnis unserer staatswissenschaftlichen Zustände*, 1842; *Soziale Briefe an von Kirchmann*, 1850; *Zur Erklärung und Abhülfe der heutigen Kreditnot des Grundbesitzes*, 1869; *Kleine Schriften*, edited by Wirth, Berlin, 1890.

Setting out from Ricardo's theories of value and of wages, Rodbertus discovers the fundamental defect of the capitalist system in what he calls the "law of the falling share of wages", according to which the absolute share of the working class in the national income remains constant at a time when the aggregate yield of the joint economic activities of the community is increasing, whereas the share of the landowners and the capitalists continues to increase. Thus the share of the workers grows continually smaller, that of the owners of land and capital grows ever larger. (For a criticism of this view, see above, pp. 147 et seq.)

Rodbertus believes this to be the cause both of poverty and of crises. (Theory of under-consumption.) The only way of putting an end to such a regime of injustice is to make land and capital the property of the State, and to bring production under unified management. In this way rent and interest will be abolished, and the right to the whole product of labour will be assured.—But it will take a hundred years to realise this State-socialist ideal, and the realisation will be effected through a socialist monarchy of the Hohenzollerns. Meanwhile we should strive to bring about reforms, the most important of which will be the State regulation of wages. Instead of the present time-working-day, there must be a work-working-day, with a minimum wage, supplemented in proportion to productivity. Both wages and the prices of all commodities are to be fixed in terms of normal working hours (labour money)—much as, to quote a modern instance, maximum prices were fixed for prime necessaries during the late war. For the organisation of agriculture he formulates a "principle of rent", which culminates in a proposal to replace, mortgaging by irredeemable "Rentenbriefe" (rent letters or charters). The modern "Rentengut" (rent-estate)[1] has grown out of this. Unlike Marx, Rodbertus was opposed to free trade, and in politics was on the whole a conservative. Although he had much less influence than Marx, he was a more original thinker and a more outstanding investigator. Like Marx, however, Rodbertus considered labour to be the sole factor of production. See below, pp. 220 and 226.

E. KARL MARX

The acme of scientific socialism was reached in the teaching of Karl Marx.

Marx was born at Treves in 1818. His father was a Prussian K.C., a convert from Judaism to Christianity. When in Brussels at the close of the year 1847, and during the early months of 1848, in conjunction with Friedrich Engels (1820–1895), Karl Marx wrote the famous *Communist Manifesto*. In Cologne, he edited the "Neue Rheinische Zeitung". When this was suppressed, he went in 1849 to Paris, and shortly afterwards to London, which became his permanent home, and where he died in 1883. His chief works were as follows: *Das Kapital, Kritik der politischen Oekonomie*, vol. i, 1867, vols. ii and iii being posthumously published by Friedrich Engels. (English translations: from the third German edition of vol. i, by S. Moore and E. Aveling, London, 1887; from the second German edition of vol. ii, by E. Untermann, Chicago, 1907; from the first German edition of vol. iii, by E. Untermann, Chicago, 1909. Also a new translation of vol. i, from the fourth German edition, by Eden and Cedar Paul, London, 1928.) *Zur Kritik der politischen Oekonomie*, 1859; English translation by N. I. Stone, *A Contribution to the Critique of Political Economy*,

[1] A "Rentengut", in West Prussia and Posen, is a holding leased out by the government to German colonists, or more usually sold to them against the payment of a fixed annual rent redeemable only with the consent of both the contracting parties.—TRANSLATORS' NOTE.

New York and London, 1904; *Theorien über den Mehrwert*, published posthumously by Karl Kautsky, Stuttgart, 1920. A collected edition of the works of Marx and Engels, edited by D. Ryazanoff of the Marx-Engels Institute in Moscow, is now in course of publication, the first volume having been issued at Frankfort-on-the-Main in 1925.—Marx's friend Friedrich Engels contributed a little to the elaboration of the former's doctrines, but his main work was as populariser. Among his independent writings may be mentioned, *Herr Eugen Dührings Umwälzung der Wissenschaft*, 1877. [English translation of part of the foregoing, by E. Aveling, *Socialism, Utopian and Scientific*, 1892.]

From among the immense literature of Marxism, I can refer only to the following:

1. Marxian in trend. Karl Kautsky, *Karl Marx' ökonomische Lehren* (Dietz, Stuttgart), an "orthodox" work, and may well serve as a useful introduction to Marx, for it embodies the genuine Marxism of the old school which it is important to understand as contrasted with the arbitrary interpretations of the neo-Marxists. Hilferding, *Das Finanzkapital*, Vienna, 1911, second edition, 1920. [Translation of Otto Bauer's detailed review of this book published as appendix to Hilferding's *Boehm-Bawerk's Criticism of Marx*, Socialist Labour Press, Glasgow, 1920.]

2. Critical, but still socialistic in trend. Anton Menger, *Das Recht auf den vollen Arbeitsertrag*, third edition, Stuttgart, 1906; English translation by M. E. Tanner, with an introduction by H. S. Foxwell, *The Right to the Whole Produce of Labour*, London, 1899.

3. Critical. A detailed criticism of Marxian teaching as a whole will be found in my *Der wahre Staat*, first edition, 1921, second edition, 1923; also in Werner Sombart, *Der proletarische Sozialismus* ("*Marxismus*"), two vols., Jena, 1924[1]; A. Voigt, *Die sozialistische Utopien*, Leipzig, 1906; Muhs, *Anti-Marx*, 1927.

1. EXPOSITION

In Marx's teaching we must distinguish between his theory of economics and his economico-sociological interpretation

---

[1] See above, p. 211; also below, p. 235 and p. 242.

of history—the latter being what is known as "historical materialism"

a. Theory of Economics.—Marx's theory of economics is built almost entirely upon the foundation laid by Ricardo. His conception of wealth is as rigidly mechanical as Smith's and Ricardo's. *Capital* opens with the words: "The wealth of societies in which the capitalist method of production prevails, takes the form of an immense accumulation of commodities, wherein individual commodities are the elementary units." Only concrete objects are commodities (goods). In his theory of value there is no place for considerations of scarcity and utility (to which Ricardo still assigned a modest role), so that Marx puts the finishing touches to the mechanical outlook of the classical economists. Value is for him an objective substance. [See note, p. 239.] It is congealed labour. Here Marx has dug deeper than Ricardo. The value of commodities is determined, not simply by labour, but by the "average socially necessary labour" expended on their production. Human labour is the only factor in the production of goods. The value of labour power itself—wages—depends, for Marx as for Ricardo, upon the amount of labour needed for the production of the means of supporting and educating the worker. Now, if goods are exchanged in accordance with the quantities of labour they respectively embody (this being for Marx the only measure of value), and if the workers receive out of the product of their (let us suppose) eight hours' labour only so much, or its equivalent in wages, as is necessary for their maintenance, etc. (the "cost of reproducing the labour power"—say, the equivalent of four hours' labour), there is a difference amounting to the value produced in four hours' work, the "surplus value" which the capitalist puts in his pocket. It follows that the capitalist method of production is based on the appropriation of unpaid labour on the

"exploitation" of the worker. The workers and the entrepreneurs confront one another as producing class and exploiting
class.

This is strictly in line with the classical economists' view of
productivity. Nothing but living labour is productive—not
capital, not land, not the entrepreneur's organisational thought.
If, for example, a commodity embodies 24 hours of labour, and
if 12 of these represent substituted capital (i.e. in Marxian
terminology, labour-value transferred from the machinery, for
instance, which is partly used up in the process of production),
and 12 represent new labour, these latter alone are productive,
since they need for their replacement only, say, 4 hours of
labour. The surplus of 8 hours' labour (the surplus value) consequently derives from the exclusive fertility of the living
labour, which—since the only commodities, the only goods,
are the concrete outcome of labour—cannot be anything but
manual labour. Thus manual labour is the only productive
labour.—For Marx, the value of commodities is wholly comprised of the substituted capital (previous labour embodied in
the means of production) and the living labour added when
these means of production are being used; it follows, therefore,
that interest on capital, entrepreneur's profit, landrent, traders'
work, etc., must all be paid out of surplus value. Every such
income is, in Marx's view, no more than a "phenomenal form
of surplus value".

The most important law of the capitalist method of production, one which is at the same time a law of evolution, is the
law of the concentration of capital. In the stress of competition,
the victory goes more and more to the wealthiest capitalists, to
the enterprises which work with the best machinery, the most
abundant resources, the most far-reaching division of labour.
The course of this concentration is such that an increasingly
large proportion of capital ("constant capital") is embodied in
the machinery or the buildings used in production, or devoted
to the purchase of raw materials, whilst an ever smaller proportion ("variable capital") is devoted to the payment of wages.

Owing to this decline in the proportion of variable capital, workers are continually being dismissed, and swell the ranks of the unemployed. The unemployed contingent is a relatively redundant population, and comprises what Marx calls the "industrial reserve army", but it is not, in his opinion, a true surplus population in the Malthusian sense. (See above, pp. 116 et seq.) Owing to the steady increase of the industrial reserve army, exercising a perpetual pressure upon the wages of the employed workers, there occurs, as economic evolution continues, a progressive impoverishment of the masses. Hand in hand with the "accumulation of capital" there marches an "accumulation of poverty". This is the famous "theory of increasing misery". Furthermore, the concentration of capital involves repeatedly renewed disturbances of the market, with consequent crises.

At long last, however, the development of capitalist society will inevitably lead to the destruction of capitalism. The ultimate result of the concentration of capital will be that a mere handful of capitalists will confront the huge mass of impoverished proletarians. The latter will not hesitate to make an end of the contradiction between the method of production, which is social and cooperative, and the method of appropriation and exchange, which is individualistic. The workers will take over the means of production, and will place them in the hands of the community. "The knell of capitalist private property sounds. The expropriators are expropriated." Then will follow the "dictatorship of the proletariat", as transition to a "free association of individuals", to a "classless society". Every producer will receive the full product of his labour, undiminished by any rent or revenue paid to idle non-producers. The final aim, however, is that from the superfluity of products every one shall receive according to his needs.—Marx deliberately refrained from attempting to give a detailed description of the way in which production was to be transformed and a collectivist system brought into being. Nor did he tell us how distribution was to be effected, and the society of the future to be organised.

β. *Historical Materialism.*—In his philosophy of history Marx built, not on Ricardo, but on Hegel.

Hegel's fundamental notion was that the world-reason dominated history ("whatever is, is rational"); and that every historical phenomenon is to be comprehended as the necessary consequence of an inner automatic movement of the thought-content of an epoch (proceeding through the opposites of thesis and antithesis to a synthesis—this being the "dialectic method"). Marx, adopting the notion, and giving it a twist of his own, substituted a material mechanism for Hegel's metaphysical foundation of the universe, for the "idea" or world-reason. Such was the origin of his "materialist conception of history".

According to this materialist conception (or interpretation) of history, the whole of historical evolution is determined, all the processes of history are determined, by the development of economic life. According to Marx, the action of men and their thoughts are wholly dependent upon economics; and are, speaking generally, to be regarded as a product of their environment. "It is not the consciousness of human beings that determines their existence, but, conversely, it is their social existence that determines their consciousness."[1] Here we have a wholly "environmental" doctrine. This conception of history culminates in the proposition that the "production of the means of subsistences and, next to production, the exchange of the things which have been produced, are the bases of the whole social structure; that in every society which has appeared in history, the manner in which wealth is distributed and society

[1] Marx, *Zur Kritik der politischen Oekonomie*, 1859, preface.

divided into classes or estates, is dependent on what is produced, how it is produced, and how the products are exchanged. Consequently, the final causes of all social changes and political revolutions are to be sought, not in men's brains, not in men's better insight into eternal truth and justice, but in changes in the methods of production and exchange. They are to be sought, not in the philosophy, but in the economics of each particular epoch".[1] The spiritual content of a society is "ideology", self-deception. The extant economic order (the feudal system, or the capitalist system) determines the whole structure of society—political, legal, scientific, artistic, and religious! Furthermore, inasmuch as ever since the super-session of primitive communism the economic structure of society has been determined by the class oppositions prevailing in any particular epoch (barons and serfs, capitalists and workers), the history of mankind has throughout this long period been at bottom the history of economic class struggles.

It follows that present-day society will inevitably, under stress of the evolutionary trends inherent in its economic structure, transform itself into a socialist society. As previously explained, the concentration of capital must perforce (according to Marxian theory) automatically lead to a collectivist society. In this way Marx establishes socialism upon the unqualified necessitarianism of all social happenings, upon a mechanical succession of causes and effects; whereas in Hegel's scheme the metaphysical necessity of the idea was dominant. "For Hegel", wrote Marx in the preface to the second edition of the first volume of *Capital*, "the thought process [the world-reason] . . . is the demiurge [creator] of the real; and for him the real is

---

[1] Friedrich Engels, *Socialism, Utopian and Scientific* (German original 1877, E. Aveling's translation, 1892), George Allen & Unwin's Social Science Series, p. 45.

only the outward manifestation of the idea. In my view, on the other hand, the ideal is nothing other than the material when it has been transposed and translated inside the human head."

2. CRITIQUE

Every one knows how immense has been the influence exercised by Marx on the workers throughout the world, the workers whom he assembled to fight against capitalism under the battle-cry "Proletarians of all lands, unite!" But what about the soundness of his teaching?

Well, the remarkable thing is that every one of his theories is faulty. Marx's idea of wealth is open to the same criticism as Smith's. He, too, looked upon wealth as a mere aggregate of material commodities; looked upon wealth mechanically, atomistically, and therefore individualistically (see above, pp. 109 and 162): whereas Adam Müller, whom Marx despised, laid stress upon the organic composition and the spiritual elements of wealth. (See above, pp. 162 et seq.) Since Marx's theory of value is based on the notion that value has a substantial nature (see note p. 239), it is open to the same annihilating objection as Ricardo's theory (see above, pp. 133 et seq., and below, p. 281); for there is no such "substance" of value, but value inheres in utility. The same criticism applies to the doctrine of surplus value, which is nothing other than the residual magnitude to which Ricardo gave the name of "profit". But the doctrine of surplus value is not only deprived of its theoretical foundation by the fact that Marx's theory of value is erroneous; it is also convicted of fallacy because wages are not determined by the "cost of reproducing the commodity labour power". In actuality, the aggregate amount paid in wages is an average share of the total output of the national labour, and the productivity of labour is therefore one of its co-determinants.—Yet there remains in the doctrine this kernel of truth, that the capitalist enjoys an income as leader of an enterprise, receiving that income in the form of interest on capital and entrepreneur's profit. In fine, though the economic notion of a "surplus value" is theoretically unsound, Marx nevertheless did good service by drawing attention to the inequality of the treatment meted out to worker and to entrepreneur respectively in the individualist order of society.

Marx's calculation of the constituents of price—value of product = substituted capital + expenditure of labour (the latter item consisting of wages + surplus value)—is childish. In addition, Marx, like Rodbertus before him, and Ricardo before Rodbertus, maintains that labour is the exclusive factor of production, and that only living labour (not capital, which is the stored product of previous labour, and is merely "substituted" or "replaced" in the new labour process) is productive. —The constituents of price are far more numerous, being as follows: wages of labour; replacement of capital; interest; entrepreneur's wages; salaried employees' wages, and expenses of management (the unseen cooperation of the managerial and bookkeeping staff in the work done by the manual operative at the bench); the State's wages (taxes = replacement of the national productive capital, of the higher-grade capital represented by the various superposed aggregates); insurance against risk. In addition, out of the total yield of the enterprise there must still be paid: the educational capital for the increase of population ("wages" in the Marxian sense contain at most the costs of educating the population that will replace the present numbers, without provision for increase); productive capital (machinery, tools, etc.), for the increase of workers; absolute increase of capital for economic advance (attainable only by lengthening the detours of production [see below, p. 270], that is to say, by multiplying capital). Only what is left over after the payment of all the foregoing, can constitute the real entrepreneur's profit, which is, fundamentally, secured not by exploitation but by preeminent achievement. The national economy as a part of the world-wide economy, the particular enterprise as a part of the national economy, the individual

worker as a part of the particular enterprise—one and all of
them get shares in the output of the higher aggregates, receive
so-called rents. But these "rents" are not deducted from the
yield of others' labour. (See above, pp. 143 et seq.)—When we
bear in mind that the achievement of those who are led is only
rendered possible by the leaders, and that the work of the
latter often remains unpaid, we shall be inclined, rather, to
speak of an inversion of what the doctrine of surplus value
proclaims, and especially of a misappropriation of the fruit of
unpaid mental work. Consider, for example, lapsed patents;
recall how many inventors and artists have died in penury
when others were enjoying the product of their labour.—In
later years Marx had an inkling that his doctrine was untenable
and spoke of "socially necessary surplus value".

The Marxian theory of wages is only Ricardo's iron law of
wages (the theory that wages represents the cost of reproducing the labour). In so far, however, as the pressure of the
"industrial reserve army" comes into consideration, it would
seem to be possible for wages to be forced permanently down
below the level necessary for subsistence! Thus Marx actually
outdoes the iron law of wages, which, in our study of Ricardo, we
have already seen to be fallacious. (See above, pp. 147 et seq.)

The difficulties which this way of explaining value and profit
(surplus value) has to face are, then, the very same that we discussed in our study of Ricardo. (See above, pp. 142 et seq.)
The only difference is that now they are intensified. For, since,
by hypothesis, entrepreneurs live solely by exploiting the
workers, the entrepreneur who engages only a few workers
and uses a great deal of machinery (the owner of a rolling-mill,
for instance) must get little surplus value, and the entrepreneur
who employs many workers and uses little machinery (say, the
owner of a dressmaking establishment) must get much. So
paradoxical a result would certainly interfere with the concentration of capital.

Marx in due course became aware of all these difficulties, and
in the third volume of *Capital* he really let his theory of value

go by the board, for he admitted that only in exceptional cases does the price of commodities coincide with their "labour value". According to this later development of the Marxian theory of value, surplus value is contained in the mass of profit received by the capitalist class as a whole, and this mass of profit is equalised or averaged through competition among the various undertakings—an untenable figment.[1]

The most important part of Marxian doctrine is the "law of the concentration of capital", which had already been formulated by Pecqueur and Louis Blanc. This "law" being based on an unsound generalisation, is true only to a limited extent. Thus we find that the development of large-scale industry creates a middle class anew; and not only a class of salaried employees, but also a middle class of industrialists, as when the growth of great factories in which sewing-machines and bicycles are made leads to the appearance of thousands of small independent workshops where sewing-machines and bicycles are repaired by hand. In fact, large-scale industry is not in all respects superior to small-scale. The latter has the advantage wherever small markets are dominant, as in places with poor facilities for transport, in repairing industries, and in artistic crafts. A small enterprise can serve a small market best; a large enterprise, a large market. Furthermore, mechanical production on an extended scale is inapplicable to "fine industries", those whose products have to be exceptionally tasteful, or characterised by unusual durability. Finally, the small market is apt to dominate in agriculture, so that here, likewise, small-scale production is often more successful than large-scale.—Even when extreme concentration of an industry has occurred, the owners are still multitudinous, thanks to the way in which capitalists are accustomed to

[1] A detailed criticism of the Marxian theory of value will be found in Böhm-Bawerk's *Geschichte und Kritik der Kapitalzinstheorien*, third edition, 1914, pp. 486 et seq. and 501 et seq.

"generalise their interests". We see this in the great combines and trusts.

There is a noteworthy contradiction between the theory of surplus value and the theory of the concentration of capital. Inasmuch as concentration lessens the ratio of variable capital to constant, the entrepreneurs who amalgamate several small factories into one great factory must (if the Marxian theory be sound) dry up some of the sources from which they have been drawing surplus value.—The theory of the concentration of capital likewise conflicts with the theory that only living labour is productive. If the latter contention were true, it would be impossible for a large-scale enterprise, using a comparatively large amount of machinery and employing a comparatively small number of workers, to have (as Marx himself says it has) the advantage over a small-scale enterprise.

The effective importance of the theory of the concentration of capital has arisen from its association with the materialist conception of history, thanks to which the view has prevailed that the concentration of enterprises will bring about a transformation of our capitalist society into a socialist one. In this way the "law" has been transmogrified from one merely descriptive of industrial forms into one enabling us to foretell the course of social evolution, and has become the main pillar of the Marxian edifice. But the flaw already pointed out is fatal. Seeing that the concentration of capital cannot be thoroughgoing (not even in the course of a whole century, inasmuch as ever and again the process of concentration is creating a new middle class), the collectivisation of production thus brought about cannot be thoroughgoing either. Another plain demonstration of this is afforded by the difficulties of the latter-day "problem of socialisation".

Utterly fallacious, therefore, is the theory of increasing misery, which came to outbid the Ricardian law of wages, and was based on the false premise of the unqualified concentration of capital. Yet another defect of this theory is that it ignores the marked stratification within the working class, the cleavage between skilled workers and unskilled, and so on.

Finally, it was a basic error on Marx's part to maintain that in the matter of production, above all, the collective enterprise of the coming socialist society would excel that of the "planless" individualist economy of to-day. Only in the matter of a juster distribution could we expect a socialist society to show its superiority to our own; for as regards production, capitalist enterprise, despite its lack of centralised plan, must always be more effective than socialist. Capitalism has developed the forces of production to an extent unexampled in history. To-day, socialists grudgingly admit this, for they tell us that economic life, which was shattered during the Great War, must be reconstructed under capitalism before it can be socialised.

Superadded to these errors in the domain of theory is the defiance of nature involved in the principle that there are to be no class segregations in the society of the future, and that all are to be equal (these demands being voiced in the same breath with the conflicting assertion of the right to the whole product of labour!). True universalism looks for an organic multiplicity, for inequality. A society characterised by the "total absence of authoritative governance", and by the "free association of individuals", is a utopia. Here "scientific socialism" has rounded the circle, and has got back to anarchist utopism!

Implicit in the materialist conception of history is, indeed, the sublime Hegelian notion that all the processes of history and all the subdivisions of human society are organically interconnected. Upon this depends its greatness as well as its methodological significance. But its general content, and the spirit which animates it, make of it the most tragical doctrine of the century. Even sociologically considered, it is full of contradictions. Its ideal of the coming "society", as one in which the State will have "died out", and as one in which "no man will hold sway over another", is purely individualistic: and yet at the same time its champions preach a collective method of advance, a method typically universalistic; while its view of the general course of history is an expression of the orthodox collectivist opinion that the thoughts of men are determined by the externals of their existence, and are a mere reflex of that existence. (The environmental theory.) For the rest, this last is but a parroting of Rousseau, the banality of the rationalist "Enlightenment", crude materialism.

Still more important, however, seem to me the following considerations. The reader must clearly realise that the formulation of the materialist conception of history only became possible because Marx lapsed from the idealism of Kant, Fichte, and Hegel, into positivism, nay, into materialism. When we are reckoning up the debit side of Marx's balance-sheet, we are concerned, not so much with the economic mistakes he made, as with the stamp he gave these errors, the barbaric spirit which made him degrade the ideal to "ideology", the spiritual content of society to a mere "superstructure" resting upon an economic groundwork—while exalting the economic process into an independent mechanism, which ticked out its predestined movement like a huge clock, and contained within itself the mainspring that moved the whole. Marx failed to see that economics exists only as spiritual usage, only as a means towards the achievement of man's ends. What desolation has been wrought by this way of regarding socialism. (How different a way from that of Plato, Fichte, even Lassalle!) Instead of comprehending civilisation and culture as outward expressions of an essential core of truth, the apostles of historical materialism teach that science is in the last resort only the science of a class, that religion is but priestcraft, that morality and law are nothing but a hotchpotch of class interests, and that even art must be subdivided into "bourgeois" and "proletarian"! When we have grasped all this, we shall have

become aware of the utter barbarism of such a hideous caricature of the eternal verities that underlie the great ideas of all
ages; and we shall be able to appraise the cleavage which the
doctrine of the "class struggle" must make in the life of a
nation. Into how dread a vacuum, too, are proletarians thrust
by this dreary doctrine; into a world where all that we regard
as right, and truth, and beauty has become non-existent, and
where life, torn from its roots, can no longer find any ideal
purpose. Marx himself had gone hopelessly astray, turning to
the crass naturalism of Feuerbach,[1] and abandoning the
idealism of Hegel. In truth, Marx learned nothing from Hegel,
remaining a mechanist, a champion of the Enlightenment, an
individualist. His intellectual (purely intellectual) gifts must not
blind his readers, who should never forget what Aristotle said
long ago, that not thought simply as thought is the sublimest
thing in the world, but only thought as thought of the best.[2]

As Wilbrandt has rightly insisted, Marx's personality was to a
very large extent the expression of his sympathies. But if these
led him, from being an idealist, to become a revolutionist, that
did not suffice to make him a genius. Sympathy determines,
but genius creates. Marx was not the original producer of a
single one of the main elements of his teaching. He merely
huddled together whatever his predecessors had excogitated in
the way of criticism of the existing order. In his dissection of
the economic process he was but a follower of Ricardo; and as
regards the doctrine of surplus value, Anton Menger points
out that the true discoverers of this were "Godwin, Hall, and
especially Thompson".[3] In my view, however, Ricardo, with

[1] Ludwig Feuerbach's *Das Wesen des Christentums* was published in 1841.
English translation by Marian Evans (George Eliot), *The Essence of Christianity*, 1853.　　　　　　　　　　　　　　　[2] Aristotle, *Metaphysics*, xii.

[3] William Godwin, 1756–1836, Shelley's father-in-law, author of *En-
quiry concerning Political Justice*, 1793; Charles Hall, M.D., ?1745–?1825,
author of *The Effects of Civilisation in European States*, 1805; William
Thompson, see above, p. 214. The quotation from Menger is from *Das
Recht auf den vollen Arbeitsertrag*, third edition, 1906, p. 100.—TRANSLATORS'
NOTE.

his concept of "profit", is the true spiritual father of the notion of surplus value. (See above, p. 113 and 143.) The theory of the concentration of capital was formulated before Marx by Pecqueur. Even Rodbertus complains of having his thoughts plagiarised by Marx.[1] We have seen that historical materialism ultimately derives from Hegel; the Enlightenment, with its environmental theory, and Feuerbach, with his philosophical materialism, having been the two corruptors of Hegel's magnificent basic idea. As for the notion of the class struggle, this had already been enunciated by Adam Smith, and still more emphatically by Lorenz von Stein; also by Pecqueur.

Marx's leading doctrines, therefore, were not original. Let us turn to examine their inner nature. As to this, there can be but one opinion. They are platitudes born out of hatred!— True genius sees into the inner heart of reality, discerns the spiritual factors of history and society. But Marx declared all spirituality to be a function of economics, to be class illusion, to be "ideology". In answer, hear Meister Eckehart: "The first thing one should know is that the sage and wisdom, . . . the good man and goodness, . . . are closely akin", this meaning that wisdom and goodness have their own essence independent of all economic considerations.[2] Thus speaks the true genius, who discerns the perdurability of spiritual and moral values.

If we ask how it has come to pass that so faulty a doctrine has had so tremendous an effect, and has indeed achieved a momentous historical task in promoting unanimity throughout the working class of all nations, we shall find the ultimate reason in the grave defects of the prevailing individualist order of society and in the oppositional or negative attitude of Marx —for destructive criticism is always much easier than constructive activity. Where the malady of liberal [individualist] economics prevails there also shall we find the suppurative inflammation of Marxism; and both of them are diseases of the soul. The flaws we can discover in Marx's economic doctrines invalidate his arguments doubtless, and yet they do not touch the root of the trouble. The poverty of the workers and their lack of a firm standing-ground in society the [conditions which

[1] Menger, op. cit., p. 82.
[2] Buch der göttlichen Tröstung, 1 (Bernhardt's modernised version, in the Kösel collection, Lehmann, Göttingen, 1924)

aroused Marx's sympathies, and determined his revolutionary trend] still remain. The longing to bring redemption was more potent than logical criticism. The individualist economic order automatically and all too easily conjured up against itself the no less individualist spectre of revolution. Furthermore—and this mainly accounts for the success of Marxism—individualist society was too aimless, too disintegrated, and too hopelessly materialistic, to present an unbroken front against so compact a doctrine. Had not such men as Feuerbach, Büchner, Mole-schott, and their successors the positivists (the narrow-minded charlatans who still flourish among us), expelled our idealist philosophy from the domain of German culture, Marxian teaching would never have become dominant, and capitalism would not have undergone so far-reaching a degeneration. It was only owing to the reasons here analysed that Marxism was able, despite its alliance with sensualism and materialism, to cut as bold a figure in the field of social science as Darwinism in the field of biological.

After he has taken the foregoing criticism to heart, the reader's main concern will doubtless be with the question, what is to replace the untenable doctrines of Marxism? That question, unfortunately, cannot be discussed here. Suffice it to say that the organisation of economic life, an organisation now in the making, will not be, as Marx assumed, the outcome of the concentration of capital. It will arise because untrammelled, individualist economic activities conflict with the very nature of economic life. That is why individualistic economy must be replaced by organised economy. Enough indications have already been given in the present work to show that this organisation cannot take the form of a straightforward, unified, and thoroughgoing collectivisation. Owing to the spiritual multiformity of society, it will necessarily be a mobile and restricted collectivisation—one endowed with a corporative character.[1]

[1] Cf. Spann, *Der wahre Staat, Vorlesungen über Abbruch und Neubau der Gesellschaft*, Leipzig, 1923. See also below, p. 247.

3. POLITICAL DEVELOPMENT OF MARXISM

The labour parties in most countries adopted Marx's teaching, and thenceforward called themselves social democratic parties. Nothing but bitter need, however, in conjunction with their situation as parties continually in sharp opposition to their respective governments, made it possible for them to ignore the numerous contradictions inherent in the doctrine they professed. Nor were these contradictions everywhere ignored. In Germany, even before the war, there emerged a school of socialists who stressed the evolutionary [as contrasted with the revolutionary] aspects of Marxism, that part of the system which is a deduction from the theory of the concentration of capital. The followers of this trend came to form a group having the characteristics of a radical-socialist party, and were styled "revisionists". In the general view, revisionism was given its first impetus in 1899 by the publication of Eduard Bernstein's book, *Die Voraussetzungen des Sozialismus* (English translation by Edith C. Harvey, *Evolutionary Socialism*, I.L.P. Socialist Library, 1909). But an indispensable preliminary had been Werner Sombart's critique of Marxism.[1] (See also under Dühring, above, p. 209.)—In France at about the same time there originated a trend of the opposite kind, a revolutionary movement appealing to the ideas of a reign of terror and a general strike. This was known as "syndicalism". The war, unfortunately, interfered with the revisionist movement in the German Social Democratic Party.—When, after the war, the social democrats obtained political power, it was inevitable that the internal contradictions of Marxism should become conspicuous once more. There now came to the front a group of moderates (the "majority socialists"), convinced democrats who did not propose to bring about any sudden overthrow of the extant order but were prepared to work along evolutionary lines. These were faced by the "spartacists", socialists who were seriously determined to effect the speedy establishment

---

[1] *Zur Kritik des ökonomischen Systems von Karl Marx*, "Archiv für Sozial-wissenschaft", 1894; *Sozialismus und soziale Bewegung*, first edition 1896,, ninth edition, 1922. (See pp. 211, 219, and 242.) This latter work has been translated into twenty-four languages. It made a powerful impression upon Marxists everywhere, especially on the Russian but also on the German Marxists.

of a communist society through the instrumentality of the dictatorship of the proletariat, and who therefore adopted bolshevism as their creed, and repudiated democracy. A middle position was occupied by the "independents", who, however, soon ceased to exist as a political party.[1]

F. LASSALLE

In Germany, meanwhile, an independent labour party had come into existence, thanks mainly to the activities, not of Marx and Engels, but of another socialist, Ferdinand Lassalle.

Lassalle (1825–1864), of Jewish extraction, was son of a Breslau merchant. He studied philosophy and literature at various universities. In 1863, in his famous *Offenes Antwortschreiben*, he sketched a political programme for the workers, and flung himself into the career of an agitator. He founded Der Allgemeine Deutsche Arbeiter Verein (General Union of German Workers), the forerunner of the German Social Democratic Party. In August 1864, while in the full swing of his multifarious activities, he was killed in a duel. His chief writings were: *System der erworbenen Rechte* (System of Acquired Rights), 1861; *Herr Bastiat-Schulze von Delitzsch, der ökonomische Julian*, 1864. A complete edition of his works in twelve volumes, edited by Eduard Bernstein, was published in Berlin, 1919, and subsequent years.

Lassalle's views on economics are centred in the Ricardian law of wages—called by Lassalle the "iron law of wages"—according to which the average wage of labour can never rise above what is necessary for the worker's bare subsistence. (See above, p. 147.) There is only one way in which the workers can escape that law; they must combine to form productive associations, and this should be made possible for them by

[1] Recent books on Marx and Marxism, available in English translation by E. and C. Paul are: Achille Loria, *Karl Marx*, George Allen & Unwin, Ltd., London, 1920 (semi-Marxian, but critical); *Karl Marx, Man, Thinker, and Revolutionist*, a symposium, edited by D. Ryazanoff; Henry de Man, *The Psychology of Socialism*, George Allen & Unwin, Ltd., London, 1928 (*Au delà du Marxisme*, " Beyond Marxism", is the title of the French version); and Otto Rühle, *Karl Marx, his Life and Work*, George Allen & Unwin, Ltd., London, 1929 (contains extensive quotations from Marx's writings). The two last-named works are greatly influenced by the New Psychology.— TRANSLATORS' NOTE.

the provision of State credit. In order to force the State to make them the necessary advances, the workers must form an independent political party of the working-class, and must make it their first aim to secure the establishment of universal [manhood] suffrage.

As the reader will have seen for himself, Lassalle had adopted Louis Blanc's leading tenet. He was tempéramentally averse from Marxism, for not only was his notion of the community universalistic on the whole, but it was sustained by a high appreciation of the functions of the State; and, besides, his sentiments were nationalist, and he did not accept the economic interpretation of history. In philosophical matters, Lassalle was better trained than Marx, and he had adopted the standpoint of the Fichtean and post-Kantian philosophy. He was a man bubbling over with energy, and a brilliant orator. His importance in the history of socialism depends rather on his political activities, and his connexion with the founding of the German labour party, than upon his contributions to socialist theory.[1]

G. LAND REFORM

The American writer Henry George (*Progress and Poverty*, 1879), accepting as gospel Ricardo's theory of landrent, sees in landrent the source of all social miseries, and especially of low wages and commercial crises. Consequently, the absorption of landrent by taxation (the "single tax") would put an end to poverty. Similar opinions were voiced by Flürscheim (*Der einzige Rettungsweg*, 1890), Stamm, Samter, Hertzka (*Freiland*, 1890; English translation by A. Ransom, *Freeland*, 1891), and others.

In Germany, since the turn of the century, Adolf Damaschke has been presenting George's views in such a way as to bring them within the domain of practical politics. (*Die Bodenreform*, nineteenth edition, Jena, 1922; *Aufgaben der Gemeindepolitik*, tenth edition, Jena, 1922.) He rejects the "single tax", distinguishing between "landrent of yesterday" and "landrent of to-day". The former is to be regarded as an accepted datum; the latter, being a "Zuwachsrente" ["augmentation rent",

---

[1] Concerning Lassalle's life and writings, see Arno Schirokauer, *Lassalle die Macht der Illusion, die Illusion der Macht*, Paul List, Leipzig, 1928; English translation by Eden and Cedar Paul, *Lassalle, the Power of Illusion and the Illusion of Power*, George Allen & Unwin, Ltd.; London, 1930.— TRANSLATORS' NOTE.

equivalent to what British reformers speak of as "unearned increment"] should accrue to the community. This is to be achieved (especially as regards urban groundrents) by the taxation of unearned increments, by the taxation of land values, by the extension of the municipal ownership of land, by national and municipal housing schemes, and so on.

Damaschke has done good service by familiarising the idea of such practical reforms wherever the German tongue is spoken. But on the theoretical side, his teaching is no less untenable than that of Henry George. "Landrent is social property." Thus saith Damaschke; and he goes on to tell us: "If only the community were to take possession of it" in all its forms, "there would be an end to unmerited poverty (!), for all the children of man could develop their capacities to the uttermost" (*Bodenreform*, 1922, p. 60).—We see that Damaschke clings to the fundamental notion that landrent is the essential cause of poverty. I should like, therefore, to adduce the following considerations. (1) In point of theory, there is no ground whatever for the belief that the appropriation of landrent by the community would abolish poverty. (2) There is no sound reason for drawing a sharp distinction between rent of land and rent of capital; the attempt to do so is based on a mistake of Ricardo's; "rents" originate everywhere, rents of capital and labour just as much as rent of land. (See above, critique of the notion of rent, pp. 143 and 226.) (3) The taxation proposed by these land reformers is, therefore, one-sided. It ignores the rent of capital (which a graduated taxation of capital would annex); and it makes the great mistake of being directed towards things instead of persons, so that it would often tend to be graduated in the wrong direction, i.e. to burden small incomes more heavily than large. Every one knows that percentage taxes on houserent and on the necessaries of life bear more heavily on small incomes than on large ones. (Cf. p. 252.—Concerning the nature of urban groundrents and houserents, see Pohle, *Die Wohnungsfrage*, second edition, 1920, in Göschen's collection.)

H. National Socialism

The economic idea underlying national socialism (I say nothing here of the political content of the doctrine) is outlined by

Gottfried Feder in *Der deutsche Staat auf nationaler und sozialer Grundlage*, third edition, Munich, 1924. Feder considers the dominance of financial capital to be the chief cause of the economic and social distresses of central Europe. As remedies he advocates: (1) the nationalisation of the currency system and the note-issuing banks; and (2) the avoidance of the issue of government loans. The State is to finance its undertakings (railways, etc.) by the issue of non-interest-bearing certificates. Feder does not regard this as coming within the category of inflation, seeing that the certificates will be redeemed out of the profits of the enterprises.—Bold as the idea may seem, every economist except those who have taken their stand upon metallism (see above, p. 40, and below, p. 288) or upon the quantity theory (see below, p. 288), will be prepared to recognise that it has a sound kernel so far as theory goes.—If we assume that, to ensure correct book-keeping, a proper discount is charged up to the productive undertakings with which we are concerned (in actual practice, additional restrictions would be needed), we can compare the core of Feder's theory with the "bank theory" or "banking principle" (see below, p. 291), which rightly states that a bank-note covered by the exchange of goods has no such inflational effect as a note that is not covered by any substantial economic values. Certainly the purpose for which a new note is put into circulation is not an indifferent matter. The vital question is, whether the creation of new money is or is not based upon an economic expansion. (See above, under John Law, p. 74, and below, under theory of the channels of outflow or paths of inflation, p. 289.)

[TRANSLATORS' NOTE to pp. 220 and 225. The translators demurred to the author's contention that Marxian "value" is an "objective substance" (p. 220), or has "a substantial nature" (p. 225), quoting from *Capital* (Part One, section 3) Marx's own words: "Not an atom of matter enters into the reality of value". Dr. Spann replied: "I cannot agree with your criticism. I consider Marxian value 'substantial'. Nowhere do I say that it has a physical or material substantiality. But it is plain enough that we are concerned with a 'labour-time substance'. Not a substance that is palpable, like crude matter; but nevertheless a substance which, because it is composed of labour-time, is mathematically calculable. Compare Marx's own phrase that value is 'congealed labour'. Please append this explanation in a footnote."]

CHAPTER ELEVEN

THE HISTORICAL SCHOOL, SOCIAL REFORM, THE THEORY OF MARGINAL UTILITY

A. The Rise of the Historical Schools, and the Disputes about Method

a. The Historical Schools.—As we have learned, in the classical political economy the deductive method prevailed. The economists of the classical school, regarding economic individuals atomistically, and conceiving them to be actuated exclusively by self-interest, were able on this presupposition to formulate for themselves a unified general picture of economic life. It would be more correct, however, to style this method of the classical economists "abstractly isolative" rather than "deductive", for the crucial element in their procedure was the endeavour to contemplate economic processes undiluted, that is to say, abstracted from their setting, and completely isolated. That is the important point here, and not any question as to the preponderance of inductive or deductive constituents.

The body of doctrines excogitated by Quesnay, Smith, and Ricardo, was subsequently enriched and improved in various ways; but it still contained a number of arid, devitalised, and artificial ingredients, which made it contrast pitifully with the stormtossed evolution of reality, and (above all) rendered it inadequate to cope with the social and political needs of the time.

Furthermore, the causes which had led to the appearance of the romantic school—causes rooted in the philosophical and conservative trends of the day—continued to operate, though in modified forms, giving a powerful impetus towards a departure from individualist classicism and its appropriate method.

These considerations account for the origin of the historical school in Germany.

After the brilliant speculations of German idealist philosophy, and in particular after the triumph of Hegel and his school, there came a reaction that was hostile to every kind of metaphysics. Interest in natural science, a materialist outlook, became dominant. The nation turned away from inner culture to the performance of objective tasks. In ethics and philosophy, the crude empiricism of the British schools made headway. But it was a decisive matter for German science that the universalist spirit of romanticism and of the philosophy of Schelling and Hegel had struck deep roots in the method known as historism. Thence, in the fields of jurisprudence and of social and political science, there originated, early in the nineteenth century, under the leadership of Savigny, Eichhorn, and Puchta (see above, p. 156), the "historical school of jurisprudence", which rejected the idea of rationalistic and abstract natural right, and took actual, positive law, as historically recorded, for its topic of study. In economics, too, there came a kindred endeavour to substitute a historical induction for the purely abstract and arbitrary constructions of the classical theory.—Wilhelm Roscher (1817–1894)[1], Karl Knies (1821–1898),[2] and Bruno Hildebrand[3] were the three economists who, in the middle of the nineteenth century, under the stimulus of the historical school of jurisprudence, and influenced likewise by the teaching of Adam Müller, Baader, and List, first took

---

[1] *Grundriss zu Vorlesungen über die Staatswirtschaft nach geschichtlicher Methode*, 1843, and *System der Volkswirtschaft*, vol. i, first edition, 1854, twenty-sixth edition, 1922; English translation by J. J. Lalor, *Principles of Political Economy*, two vols., New York, 1878.

[2] *Die politische Oekonomie vom Standpunkt der geschichtlichen Methode*, Brunswick, 1853; second edition, entitled *Die politische Oekonomie vom Standpunkt der Geschichte*, 1883.

[3] *Die Nationaloekonomie der Gegenwart und Zukunft*, Frankfort-on-the-Main, 1848.

this line, and attempted to return to the evolutionary laws of economics, to the historical actualities of economic life. They were the founders of what is known as the "older historical school" of political economy.

In the eighteen-seventies came a further development, with the appearance of the "younger historical school" of political economy, which aimed at an even more objectively historical and statistically realistic method of research, and had, further, a predominantly sociological trend. The chief members of this school are Gustav Schmoller (1838–1917)[1], Lujo Brentano[2], Knapp[3], Schönberg, Bücher, Held, Gothein, and Max Weber.[4] —Among recent economists of note, Werner Sombart occupies a position peculiar to himself. He is the author of *Der moderne Kapitalismus*, third edition, four vols., 1919–1927. Originally a Marxian socialist, in *Der proletarische Sozialismus (Marxismus)*, two vols., Jena, 1924, he takes up a position definitely opposed to Marxism.[5] His achievement is synthetic, and passes beyond the scope of the Schmollerian, or younger historical, school. He differentiates between a number of historically extant economic systems, each having its own economic disposition or complexion ("Wirtschaftsgesinnung"). For him, "political economy is the study of economic systems". (See below, p. 278.)

The older historical school was mainly concerned with theoretical questions, as contrasted with the trend of the

[1] *Grundriss der Volkswirtschaftslehre*, vol. i, 1900, vol. ii, 1904.

[2] *Die Arbeitergilden der Gegenwart*, two vols., 1871–1872.

[3] *Die Bauernbefreiung und der Ursprung der Landarbeiter in den älteren Teilen Preussens*, two vols., 1887.

[4] *Protestantische Ethik und Geist des Kapitalismus*, "Archiv für Sozialwissenschaft", 1905.

[5] The gradual development of Sombart's views in a direction adverse to Marxism may be interestingly traced in the successive editions of *Sozialismus und soziale Bewegung im neunzehnten Jahrhundert*, of which *Der proletarische Sozialismus* is but a final redrafting. See footnote, p. 211, and footnote, p. 235.—TRANSLATORS' NOTE.

younger school. It aimed at effecting some sort of synthesis between the regulative tendencies of mercantilism and the principle of laissez-faire. The investigations of the younger school, on the other hand, related more and more to the history of economics and took the form of descriptive monographs. This went so far that among the last generation of German economists interest in the traditional theories of political economy seemed to have evaporated. At the same time, the study of philosophical fundamentals was neglected. This lack of an adequate attention to economic theory was largely responsible for the defencelessness of academic political economy in face of so amateurish a doctrine as Marxism. In like manner, the younger historical school had only a feeble resistance to put up against the new theories emanating from Austria, and it is now in a state of utter decay. But it did good and lasting service in one respect; it initiated a vigorous and wisely planned social-reform movement. (See below, p. 247.) Unfortunately, however, the universalist and sociological factors of that movement remained in great measure unconscious, and were therefore not cultivated as they should have been. If the historical school is to-day ceasing to exist, this is due, not so much to the want of strong personalities among its members, to their lack of philosophical training and of an all-round knowledge of economic theory, to their narrow-minded devotion to "hard fact"—as to the essential weakness of their position.

b. The Abstract School.—The younger historical school was soon confronted by a new trend, generally spoken of as "deductive", but which it would be better to term "abstract", for its champions regarded economics as fundamentally an abstractly isolative science. The initiator of this movement was Karl Menger, who, in 1883, strenuously attacked the historical school. Thus was founded what is known as the "Austrian school", to which (with reserves in varying degrees) belong the writers mentioned on p. 262 in the first sentence under the heading "Literature of the Doctrine of Marginal Utility". To begin with, Alfred Amonn and the author of the present work were more or less in sympathy with this school as far as the theory of value was concerned. (See below, p. 279.)—Theoreticians who do not belong to the Austrian school, but whose writings give expression to the same abstract trend, are H. Dietzel, Adolf Wagner, Wilhelm Pohle, Andreas Voigt, Gustav Cassel.

c. The Problem of Method.—Considerations of space make it impossible here to undertake a full discussion of the problem of method. Still, something must be said in supplement to the remarks made upon this topic in the account of Quesnay (above, p. 75), Smith (p. 113), Ricardo (p. 146, and pp. 150 et seq.), and Adam Müller (pp. 154 et seq.).

Economics is only a province, a department, of society, existing side by side with State, law, religion, etc. This brings us up against the basic problem of method. The question, in what way economics should be studied, is not an idle one, for it involves the even more vital question as to the very nature of economics. What we have to ask ourselves is this. Can the laws of the internal structure and the evolution of political economy be studied as if they existed "by themselves", as if they formed a closed and self-determining system, originating out of purely economic causation (individual self-interest); or should we, rather, regard economics as inseparably interconnected with the other provinces of society, and therefore not subject to laws peculiar to itself, but participating in the historically conditioned structure and development of society as a whole—which, for the very reason that they are historically conditioned, are individual, and therefore not in strict conformity with law? If we adopt the former alternative, if (as did Ricardo and Karl Menger) we assume economics to exist apart, pure, and disconnected from the historical process, we shall choose a method which ignores social and historical configurations. It will be isolative or abstract; it will be one which, setting out from the self-regarding activities of individuals, expects to demonstrate that economic processes occur in strict accordance with law. (The method will be predominantly deductive, but it will not reject induction.) If we adopt the latter alternative, after the manner of the historical school, which is concerned only with concrete historical realities, we shall choose a method directed towards the study of these. It will not only be historical, statistical, and realist, but it will endeavour to understand the present as an outcome of the past. Necessarily it will renounce any attempt to comprehend economics in terms of theory. Those who adopt it will consider that, strictly speaking, there can be no laws of value, price, and wages. Whatever regulative principles of this kind it is possible to observe, will merge into evolutionary trends or other uniform successions.

According to the younger historical school, the question of method was a question of the relative extent to which induction and deduction were used. This way of looking at the matter is erroneous, for any method must use a fair amount of both. Karl Menger had a much sounder way of formulating the basic problem of method. The important question, according to him, was, whether the object of economic study was to be the whole body economic, empirically extant, as the outcome of historical and social modification—or a purely abstract and partial element of society.

Still, even this formulation does not yet touch the root of the matter. In my view another relationship, that of economics to society, that of the part to the whole, is ultimately decisive as to method. In the last analysis, the question is one of a universalist as against an individualist conception of society. If we probe to the bottom of this relationship, we see: (1) that according to the individualist conception of economics and society, the individual economic agent is to be regarded as a self-governing, atom-like force, which appears in the market, is independent, exists for itself alone, and is therefore to be studied by the abstract, isolative method. (For a purely abstract, self-existent economic force will continue to work in a purely economic environment, in an economic domain set apart from society at large.) (2) However, such an isolative contemplation of the individual economic agent becomes impossible when we have come to consider that he does not really exist as an individual apart, when we cannot conceive him as individualistically self-governing, but as indissolubly interconnected with other social manifestations—when we can only conceive him universalistically. Then the individual, the commodity, demand, value, and so on, will no longer appear to us as things simply extant in the market, as self-governing, self-existent entities; we shall see them only in their places in the interconnected aggregate of economic means, aims, and productive forces! It is a mere assumption, made for the purposes of the investigation, that commodities, values, etc., exist per se. Consequently, Menger's abstract method subsists only in virtue of an individualist postulate, upon the supposition that all economic forces are self-governing, like atoms self-moving in the void. The historical method, conversely, rests upon the supposition that there is a universalistic interconnexion between all apparently discrete economic forces, and that all are historically conditioned. The weakness of the historical method is chiefly upon the theoretical side. The weakness of the abstract method lies in this, that it can explain the exchange of extant supplies and demands, but cannot explain the origin of demand; that it cannot explain production; and that it cannot explain a circumscribed economic system in which exchange does not occur. (See above, under Smith.)—Logically, both ways of regarding economic phenomena are indispensable; but the essential thing is to bring them into mutual organic interconnexion. (See below, p. 279.)

If, therefore, the problem of method is ultimately one of an individualist versus a universalist explanation, the key to its solution is to be found in sociology. A sociological attitude, a sociological method, must be substituted for a purely abstract or a purely historical method.—In respect of their historical outlook, the two historical schools of economics embodied a powerful and healthy reaction against the atomistic aridity of the individualism of the Manchester school. But the economists of the younger historical school neglected conceptual thought so grievously that economics in contemporary Germany has sunk to a deplorably low ebb.

As regards the literature of economic method, I may refer to: Karl Menger, *Untersuchungen über die Methode der Sozialwissenschaften und der politischen Oekonomie insbesondere*, 1883; Schmoller, "Volkswirtschaftslehre" in *Handwörterbuch der Staatswissenschaften*; Spann, *Wirtschaft und Gesellschaft*, Dresden, 1907. There is a detailed account of the matter in my *Fundament der Volkswirtschaftslehre*, fourth edition, Jena, 1929; and in Baxa, *Einführung in die romantische Staatswissenschaft*, Jena, 1923. As to the writings of Gottl, Amonn, and others, see below, p. 278.

B. THE SOCIAL-REFORM MOVEMENT [1]

a. Origin and Nature.—The movement for social reform is the grandchild of the romantic school and the child of the younger historical school.

The "social harmony" which the individualists had looked for as the outcome of free competition had failed to make its appearance. "Instead of the expected equality of the classes", writes Lorenz von Stein, "competition had evoked an ever-increasing inequality". The introduction of machinery, the development of large-scale industry, the growth of the towns, the unlooked-for expansion of the labour of women and children, had atomised the workers and ground them down. Formerly they had been united, incorporated in the guilds: now they were a vast and often terribly impoverished proletariat. Some remedy must be found.

We know (see above, pp. 154 et seq.) that the repudiation of the individualist conception of society was consummated in the German idealist philosophy; that Fichte, Schelling, Baader, Schleiermacher, the romanticists generally, and Hegel, had elaborated a universalistic notion of the State; that romanticist political economy involved a criticism of the economics of the individualist schools; and that, under these auspices, with the

[1] Philippovich, *Das Eindringen der sozialpolitischen Ideen in die Literatur* (in *Entwicklung der deutschen Volkswirtschaftslehre im neunzehnten Jahrhundert*, 1908). As to the history of the social-reform movement, see Gehrig, *Die Begründung des Prinzips der Sozialreform*, Jena, 1914.

development towards historism there was necessarily associated a trend towards universalism in political and social science. The historical school of jurisprudence, which had broken away from the doctrine of natural right, exercised a persistent influence. Juristic philosophy (Stahl, Ahrens, Röder) had since the days of Hegel and Schleiermacher been devising a system for the promotion of State activity to regulate the workings of society. Even before this, Adam Müller, Baader, and Friedrich List had taken up the cudgels against individualist economics.

The French socialists' criticisms of extant social conditions were also making a profound impression. Saint-Simon, Sismondi, Fourier, and Proudhon had been the most notable spokesmen, in the French tongue, of a movement which in Germany was shortly thereafter to find its advocates in Rodbertus and (paradoxically enough upon the basis of the Hegelian philosophy) in Marx and Engels.

Superadded, in the practical field, was the influence of the cooperative movement. Initiated by Robert Owen, and fostered in Germany by Victor Aimé Huber, Schulze-Delitzsch, and Raiffeisen, it assumed a more or less anti-individualist character.

As a primary offshoot of German philosophical development has to be considered the "Gesellschaftslehre" (social theory) of Stein and Mohl (not to be confounded with modern "sociology", also known in German as "Gesellschaftslehre"). This "social theory" was founded in the eighteen-forties by Lorenz von Stein[1], and was further developed by Robert von Mohl and others. This "social theory" posits, between the body economic and the State, "society", which is the sum of relationships of dependence and other personal relationships between individuals, as conditioned by property, mode of work, and family. Further, according to Mohl, this science must include a "theory of social purposiveness" or "policy of social reform". Philippovich has rightly pointed out that this introduction of the concept of.society was of great moment for the furtherance of practical political demands, and thus for the inauguration of the social-reform movement. Stein's "social theory" is really

[1] *Der Sozialismus und Kommunismus des heutigen Frankreichs*, 1842; *Die Geschichte der sozialen Bewegung in Frankreich bis auf unsere Tage*, three vols., 1848; *System der Staatswissenschaft*, vol. ii, *Gesellschaftslehre*, 1856. Concerning Stein, see E. Grünfeld, *Lorenz von Stein und die Gesellschaftslehre*, Jena, 1910.

much the same as Hegel's philosophy of the State, with its doctrine of the "objective spirit," which in the third stage (that of morality) discloses itself as "family", "civil society", and the "State". This "civil society" of Hegel's, this and nothing else, is the subject matter of the "social theory" of Stein and Mohl—a doctrine foredoomed to sterility despite its inner unity.—Herbart, Krause, and Schleiermacher have likewise, in their several fashions, expounded the theory of society.

Philippovich and others have expressed the view that the above described beginnings of the movement towards social reform were the effect of pre-Marxian socialism. This contention must be rejected. Though it may be true that the study of French socialism was a contributory factor in inducing Stein to formulate his "social theory", that theory did not (as Philippovich declares) introduce a new element into German social and political science. Stein drew his spiritual sustenance from Hegel. The real source of the German movement on behalf of social reform is to be found in the ideas of the State and the community that are inherent in German idealist philosophy.

Nevertheless, the doctrines of Smith and Ricardo were still dominant in economics. At length, however, thanks to the growth of the historical school, a change ensued, not only in respect of method, but also in the political applications of economics. Now that a description of living economic reality and of its evolution had come to be considered of supreme importance, it was inevitable that an individualist and abstract outlook upon the application of economics to politics should seem inadequate. To abstract economics there had been superadded concrete economics and the living processes of society and history as objects of study. "In this way, political economists were led to contemplate the individual, not merely as an individual, but also as part of an organised community; and they were induced to do justice to his role in economic life" (Philippovich, *op. cit.*). Thus an organic and universalist way of looking at these matters, as contrasted with an individualist and abstract one, came into vogue, with the result that people soon became inclined to make society as a whole responsible for evils prevailing in its parts, and to substitute ideas of solidarity and justice for the idea of unrestricted individual liberty. "At the same time, the individual must not be regarded as a being who pursues his private interest alone, but as a personality subject to the moral law". (Philippovich, *op. cit.*). The younger historical school laid especial stress on this ethical side. As a result there originated the trend towards social reform (sometimes mockingly styled "Kathedersozialismus"—socialism of the professorial chair), a movement to which economists not directly associated with the historical school such as Schäffle, and those who were in other respects individualist, like Adolf Wagner, adhered. In 1873, under the leadership of a number of German professors, headed by Schmoller, this movement culminated in the foundation of the Verein für Sozialpolitik (Social Reform League). Ever since then, nearly the whole body of professorial economists has been associated with the League.[1]

The foregoing historical survey throws light on the nature of social reform. It is a reaction on the part of the community against the pressure of unfortunate social conditions upon some of its individual members or upon certain groups; and whereas, according to the liberal conception of the State, for the relief of these troubles we must look only to "self-help", the social reformers insist that help must also come from the State and from various organisations (municipalities, corporations, etc.). It is essential to realise that such a demand was only rendered possible by a considerable change in peoples' ideas regarding the nature of the State. They had become animated by the conception of a higher solidarity among the members of the State, by the notion of a moral community among us all, one not existing for business purposes exclusively, and one which makes the aggregate responsible for the welfare of the individual. Thus, as previously explained, the movement for social reform originated primarily out of a victory of the universalist idea of the State over the individualist idea, the former having itself sprung from the German classical philosophy.

But the mere fact that a measure is born out of the notion

[1] Cf. Boese, *Der Verein für Sozialpolitik*, 1872–1922, Munich, 1922.

that the State is a solidarised unity of all classes—such a measure, let us say, as an import tariff for the protection of agriculture—does not suffice to bring it within the category of social reform. In the proper sense of the term, when we speak of social reform we imply that the community is deliberately intervening on behalf of those of its constituent groups or members that are being fundamentally and permanently injured in the economic struggle. Propertyless urban operatives, the ruck of landworkers, lower-grade employees in shops and offices, home workers, semi-independent persons engaged in petty industries, these and their congeners appear to be permanently handicapped in life's race as compared with the capitalists and the well-to-do. A further decisive criterion of what we term social reform is that measures which come under this head are not, like poor relief and charity, directed towards helping individuals as such, but are designed to ensure that people shall receive the aid of society while they are themselves exercising their social functions. They are aided and protected when entering into labour contracts, or as consumers (housing reform, etc.), or when engaged in the task of bringing up their children (government schools, family help), or what not. But here we reach as it were the "dead point", the margin where social-reform measures and poor relief shade into one another. Well-planned poor relief aims always at overstepping this margin, at surpassing this "dead point", in the direction of social reform, by the avoidance of giving mere monetary help to indigent persons, who should rather be wisely assisted towards the performance of some useful activity (e.g. by providing a poor sempstress with a sewing-machine, etc.).

b. Classification.—These considerations give us pointers for a classification of social reform under various heads. (1) Social reform concerned with labour contracts and working conditions. This includes legal regulation of the length of the working day, of mealtimes, regulation week-end rests, child labour, night work, period of notice before discharge, also compulsory insurance of the workers against sickness, accident, permanent disablement, old age, death of bread-winners, unemployment, motherhood, etc. (Bismarck introduced compulsory insurance in the eighteen-eighties. This comprehensive and far-reaching reform measure would have been impossible unless public opinion had first been influenced by the "professorial socialists"). (2) Social reform which aims at increasing the value of labour power (technical education, scholarships, etc.). (3) Social reform concerned with the family and with the upbringing of children (vocational training, health visiting, children's courts).[1] (4) Social reform concerned with consumption, i.e. with the use of the output of labour (housing reform, building schemes, the establishment of consumers' cooperatives, public gardens and playgrounds, instruction in domestic economy and personal hygiene, e.g. the temperance and teetotal movements). Neither this branch of social reform nor yet the previous one (that which concerns the family) has hitherto been adequately developed. (5) Social reform which operates through the adjustment of taxation so that it will bear less hardly on those citizens who are less well-to-do (specification of a subsistence income which shall be exempt from taxation, graduated taxation of income and property, taxation of groundrents and other forms of unearned increment, in the case of indirect taxation heed to its relative incidence on the respective budgets of rich and poor with due regard also to the "law of Engel and Schwabe" according to which the wealthy expend a lesser proportion of their incomes upon food and housing than do the poor. (6) Social reform that helps handicapped groups to have their interests properly represented and to practise self-help, through the instrumentality of workers' councils and factory committees, through the legalisation of trade unions and strikes, and through the establishment of conciliation and arbitration boards. (7) Social reform in the shape of welfare work, and poor relief and rescue work for acute and hopeless cases (hospitals, cripples' homes, etc.)—these activities being, as already said, in the borderland where rationally devised social reform merges into personal aid and simple humanitarianism.

[1] Cf. Spann, *Die Erweiterung der Sozialpolitik durch die Berufsvormundschaft*, Tübingen, 1912.

c. Developmental Trends of the Modern Social-Reform Movement.—The modern tendency is to pass beyond the remedying of individual instances of hardship in order to establish general ties, which gradually acquire a corporative form, so that (unconsciously) an endeavour is being made to move towards a quasi-feudalist ordering of society deemed to consist of a number of associated estates. Thus at the outset of the social-reform movement there was legislation in the form of detailed special enactments relating to hours of labour, week-end rests, etc.; whereas in later years great self-governing organisations came into being to carry out the provisions of the compulsory insurance acts. In earlier days, the truck system was prohibited by legislation; but now we leave it to the trade unions to enter into collective bargains with the employers' associations. (Cf. Spann, *Der wahre Staat*, second edition, 1923, pp. 95 et seq., pp. 257 et seq., p. 272, et passim.

d. Theoretical Possibility of Social Reform and of Applied Economics.—From the outlook of individualist economics the question arises, in what sense social reform and applied economics are possible. According to the doctrine of the old classical school, and also according to that of the neo-classical school (Karl Menger, Gustav Cassel, etc.), prices are determined by mechanical laws. Distribution, and, above all, the rates of wages (with which social reform is especially concerned), are supposed to be conditioned by these "natural laws" of the formation of prices. This problem of theory has been summarised by Böhm-Bawerk under the catchword, "force, or economic law?"[1]

According to this line of reasoning, the old liberal school and the neo-liberal school are agreed in believing that no measure of social reform or applied economics can have a lasting effect on prices or on distribution. That was why the individualists enunciated the doctrine that social reform established a "vicious

[1] *Macht oder Oekonomisches Gesetz* is the title of an article by Böhm-Bawerk in the Viennese "Zeitschrift für Volkswirtschaft", 1914. For the first principles of the matter, consult Karl Menger, *Untersuchungen über die Methode der Sozialwissenschaften*, 1883.

circle". It made commodities dearer, and in this way used up any supplementary purchasing power it might have given to the workers. They taught, too, that if unearned increment were to be taxed, the cost would ultimately be borne by the consumer; and so on. An English writer recently declared that to fight against the law of supply and demand was to "bay the moon".[1] Böhm-Bawerk says that force can only make its influence felt within the limits imposed by the economic laws of prices (*op. cit.*).

The economists of the historical school, on the other hand, those who were the main protagonists of social reform, failed to give serious attention to this theoretical problem. As practical workers, they were content with the assumption that public institutions (such as labour-protection laws, building regulations, etc.) would of themselves have the power to bring about the desired changes in price and distribution. Although in the field of practice they excelled their rivals of the liberal school, in the domain of theory they were weaponless, and devoid of a firm scientific platform.[2]

According to the universalist doctrine advocated by the author of the present work, social reform and applied economics are, on principle, thoroughly practicable. The body economic is an articulated structure of interlinked means to economic ends, and has its internal connected purpose, its rationale, just as the links in a chain of argument have an unambiguous interconnexion. But for that very reason the body economic can be modified by a process of rearticulation. A badly articulated economy can be transformed into a well articulated one; and, by a change of aims, invalid means can be made valid. If, for example, as a sequel of the temperance movement, the State should, by taxation, compel the transformation of breweries into jam factories, by changing production it will have also brought about a change in the distribution of the total product. A similar thing happens when, through the introduction of a system of compulsory insurance, a part of the aggregate income which has hitherto been devoted to the formation of capital is devoted to consumption. The economic community in which this occurs will build fewer new factories, but will spend more upon hospitals, upon feeding the unemployed, etc.—The

---

[1] Hubert D. Henderson, *Supply and Demand*, Nisbet, London, 1922, p. 19.
[2] Cf. Andreas Voigt's polemic, *Kleinhaus oder Mietkaserne*, 1905; also Pohle, *Die Wohnungsprage*, in the Göschen collection.

fundamental error of the liberal school is that it regards economics from the standpoint of the formation of prices, and holds that the regulation of prices is effected by the working of the natural laws of mechanical causation. Price, however, is only an expression of the articulation of economic means; is only an indicator, not a primary phenomenon. Besides, we are not concerned with the absolute net product (with its money price), but with the purposiveness of the net product, that is with its relationship to the aims of the State and of civilisation. The apostles of the doctrine of self-interest forget this!

Alike in theory and in practice, therefore, the body economic can be influenced by social reform and by applied economics in all sorts of ways that are in harmony with its articulated structure and with its developmental possibilities (the possibilities of rearticulation). An unsatisfactory type of articulation can be transformed into a satisfactory one, and an unsound price expression into a sound one. The sound price expression and the satisfactory articulation are—the just price![1]

C. The Earlier German School of Use-Value, and the Theory of Marginal Utility

1. EXPOSITION

In Germany the earlier school of economists who in general accepted the teaching of Adam Smith, did not adopt the mechanical labour-cost theory of value, but formulated a use-value theory of its own. This applies to Jakob, Soden, Lotz, Hufeland, Storch, Adam Müller, Rau, and Hermann. Similarly with the historical school; with Hildebrand, Roscher, and Knies.[2] This use-value theory set out from the importance of the various kinds of wants (want of food, want of luxuries, and so

---

[1] Cf., in this connexion, my article *Gleichwichtigkeit gegen Grenznutzen*, "Jahrbücher für Nationalökonomie und Statistik", vol. cxxiii, Fischer, Jena, 1925, p. 289; also *Tote und lebendige Wissenschaft*, third edition, Jena, 1929, p. 68. See below, p. 281. See also above, p. 183, footnote on writings of A. J. Penty.

[2] Concerning the works of these various authors, see above, pp. 109, 158, and 241.

on), and from the specific utilities of goods (for instance, essential foodstuffs are more important than luxuries), but was unable thence to find an explanation of the ratios between the values of certain goods obtainable in definite quantities, and those of other goods likewise obtainable in definite quantities (food and water had always the same specific utilities). It was inevitable that a theory of use-value should break down so long as the disharmony between utility and price remained unexplained; and so long as the difficult problem of finding a measure for utility had not been solved, so that there was no explanation of Smith's paradox that bread was useful but cheap whereas diamonds were useless but dear.—Nevertheless, Hildebrand, Knies[1], and Hermann[2] came to the conclusion that, whilst the total value of any kind of commodity (such as water) was constant, the value was variously allotted to the fractions of the whole. But this doctrine, according to which the use-value of a commodity was inversely proportional to its quantity, was too general. The theory of marginal utility was needed.

The fundamental idea of the theory of marginal utility was conceived almost simultaneously by three different economists. One of them was the German, Karl Menger, professor of economics in Vienna, who died on February 26, 1921.[3] The second was the Englishman, W. Stanley Jevons.[4] The third was the Swiss, Walras.[5] But earlier than any of these, the German, Gossen, had developed similar ideas, in a work which remained practically unnoticed, until Jevons rescued it from oblivion.[6] So, even earlier, had, to a degree, the mathematician

---

[1] *Die nationalökonomische Lehre vom Werthe*, "Tübinger Zeitschrift für die gesamten Staatswissenschaften", 1855.

[2] *Staatswirtschaftliche Untersuchungen*, first edition, 1832

[3] Author of *Grundsätze der Volkswirtschaftslehre*, vol. i (the only one), Vienna, 1871, second edition (posthumous), 1923.

[4] *Theory of Political Economy*, London, 1871, third edition, 1888.

[5] *Eléments d'économie politique pure*, Lausanne, 1874–1877; *Théorie mathématique de la richesse sociale*, Lausanne, 1883.

[6] *Entwicklung der Gesetze des menschlichen Verkehrs*, Brunswick, 1854; republished, Berlin, 1889.—See below, p. 274.

Daniel Bernoulli (*Commentarii*, 1738). Notable foreshadowings of the doctrine are found also in Bruno Hildebrand (*Die Nationalökonomie der Gegenwart und Zukunft*, Frankfort-on-the-Main, 1848, pp. 318 et seq.); and, indeed, Ricardo's theory of landrent and Thünen's theory of wages and the interest on capital depend on kindred notions. (See also below, under "The Mathematical School", pp. 274 et seq.)

a. KARL MENGER'S FUNDAMENTAL NOTION

According to Menger, economic goods are to be regarded as things that satisfy human wants, and the importance they thus acquire constitutes their economic value. What underlies the concept of value is, therefore, this concrete dependence on the satisfaction of a want, and not a merely potential utility (Smith's "use-value"), nor yet an objective substance (such as the quantity of labour a commodity has incorporated). Menger classifies goods in two grades, those of a lower grade (goods of consumption or enjoyment) and those of a higher grade (goods of production); and these latter, if they are to possess full utility, must be present in complementary quantities—bricks for the building of a house cannot develop their full utility unless there be also available sufficient quantities of sand, lime, etc. (this Menger terms the "complementary quality of goods").—Underlying Menger's theory of value is the "law of the satisfaction of wants" which Wieser subsequently (reviving the memory of a forgotten doctrine) christened "Gossen's law". According to this law, within a period of want (such as the period during which a meal is being eaten) successive portions of a quantity of goods develop varying utilities—for the progressive satisfaction of the want is continually reducing its intensity. "Within any period of want, each successive act of satisfaction will be esteemed less highly than the previous one" (Wieser). The utility developed by that portion of the quantity of goods that is last consumed in the series, is therefore termed a marginal utility. (The expression "marginal utility" is Wieser's; Menger did not coin a special name for it.) To illustrate, let us suppose that the utility of the first part of the satisfaction of a want (the first glass of water drunk by a thirsty man) is estimated at 10, the second at 9, the third at 8, and following ones at 7, 6, 5, and so on. The greater the available

R

quantity of a good, the less is the last or "marginal" utility. This formulation of the doctrine of marginal utility must be completed by the statement of the "law of the equivalence of marginal utilities". What happens in actual practice is, not that particular wants are fully satisfied while other wants are left entirely unsatisfied, but that at a certain point the satisfaction of the primary or more important wants is interrupted in order that other wants may have a turn. Let us suppose certain essential wants ranged in order of importance thus, food I, clothing II, shelter III, and amusement IV, we shall get the following numerical table of utilities, in which each series ends with the marginal utility 7:[1]

I	II	III	IV
10	9	8	7
9	8	7	
8	7		
7			

In accordance with these basic phenomena, Menger declares marginal utility to be decisive in our estimate of the value of goods. When we renounce the consumption of the remainder of a quantity of goods, we are only renouncing the utility that is of least importance to us, the marginal utility. Hence we estimate the value of goods according to their marginal utilities.

There you have the marginal utility theory of value as contrasted with the cost of production theory of value put forward by Smith, Ricardo, and the socialists. We should note that the marginal utility theory is also a "subjective" theory of value, for the satisfaction of wants is a subjective canon: whereas the contrasted theory of value is an "objective" theory, for the costs on which it is based have as it were a substantial nature (quantity of labour, for instance); and it is furthermore a psychological canon, inasmuch as it is founded upon the course of the mental process of satisfaction.

The economists who promulgated the theory of marginal utility did not round it off into a complete body of doctrine, for Menger despaired of the continuance of his school, and his pupils were content to develop fragments of his teaching. (Wieser's attempt lacked clarity.) The main elements of this teaching will now be presented.

[1] Cf. Menger, *Grundsätze*, second edition, pp. 120 et seq.

b. THEORY OF PRICES

Under free competition and in an ideal market, price is determined upon the basis of the various subjective valuations which the different would-be purchasers form of the desired goods, and of the various subjective valuations which the different would-be sellers have formed of the goods they offer for sale. Suppose that ten equally good horses are brought to market by ten potential sellers, and that there are ten potential buyers, then, according to Böhm-Bawerk and Philippovich (who in this matter follow Menger closely) we may have:

Buyers' estimates of value	10	9	8	7	6	5	4	3	2	1
Sellers' estimates of value	1	2	3	4	5	6	7	8	9	10

In that case only five purchases will take place, the five most effective buyers (those who put the highest estimates on the value of the goods, because perhaps money is less essential to them than to the others) buying from the five most effective sellers (those who will sell cheapest); and the market price will be between 5 and 6. To explain this in fuller detail: if the price were to fall below 5, there would be six effective purchasers but only four effective sellers, and the purchasers would outbid one another until the price had risen above 5; and if it were to rise above 6, there would be only 4 effective purchasers, though there would be 6 effective sellers, who would therefore underbid one another until the price fell to somewhere between 6 and 5.—Böhm-Bawerk formulates as follows this law of the formation of prices: the market price lies between the subjective estimates of the marginal pairs of buyers and sellers. (Law of the marginal pairs.)

c. RELATIONSHIP TO COST

The first deduction from the idea of marginal utility is the proposition: cost goods or productive goods [Menger's "higher-grade goods or goods of production] derive their value from their fruits; and, inasmuch as a productive good can produce numerous commodities with various marginal utilities, the marginal utility of the marginal product (that is to say, of the least useful productive group) will decide the value and the price of the productive goods. (The formulation is Wieser's, but the idea comes from Menger. See *Grundsätze*, second edition, p. 157.) Costs, therefore, are not causes but effects of the price of the fruits. They must always be determined concomitantly with the marginal utilities of the fruits. To illustrate this: before a farmer buys a threshing machine, he considers whether its usefulness will repay its cost.

d. AGGREGATE VALUE

A separate question is that of the value of the total available supply of a commodity. Here Wieser's view and Böhm-Bawerk's are opposed. According to Wieser, all the units (or fractional quantities) of a total supply are to be endowed with the marginal-utility value, so that the aggregate value will be obtained when we multiply the marginal-utility value by the number of pieces or of fractional parts. (But here a difficulty arises, in that when the supply is very large, the marginal utility will sink so low that the aggregate value will work out at less than if the supply were much smaller!)—According to Böhm-Bawerk, we shall get the aggregate value by adding together the marginal-utility values of all the individual specimens of the supply, which, in virtue of Gossen's law, must vary one from another.—Jevons, Walras, Pareto, and Schumpeter, adopt a standpoint identical with Böhm-Bawerk's, and also in harmony with Menger's differential method; whereas Zuckerkandl, Clark, and F. A. Fetter, are at one with Wieser. The last-named bases his contention mainly on the fact that in actual business affairs the individual parts of a supply (such as each sack out of ten sacks of flour) are deemed to be of equal value.

e. ACCOUNTING

The extent to which the theory of marginal utility is applicable to the theory of distribution, depends in the last resort upon whether the value of the fruit (the output) can be assigned to, can be "charged up" to, the productive goods individually. The question of charging up the output was first considered in recent times (leaving Thünen, Say, etc., out of consideration) by Karl Menger; but we owe to Wieser the use of the term accounting ("Zurechnung") and the detailed consideration of the problem. Menger set out from the idea that the putting of one of the instruments of production out of action could never result in stopping the whole output of an enterprise, for the complementary instruments of production would continue to turn out their part of the yield. The part of the output assignable to a particular instrument was the difference between the total output when all the instruments were working, and the lessened output when the particular instrument was out of action.[1]—To this Wieser objects that the accounting must be based, not on the variations of a reduced productivity, but always and exclusively on what is, in actual fact, the most productive utilisation. In his *Theorie der gesellschaftlichen Wirtschaft*, he has recently drawn a distinction between "general" and "particular" accounting. "General accounting" applies to the cost elements of production, and generally therefore to capital and labour. If, for example, labour and wood can be utilised for making either a table or a cupboard from the varying results (assessed in money or in utility) the economic share of each in the output is calculable. If the applicabilities $x + y = 100$; $2x + 3z = 290$; $4y + 5z = 590$: then we calculate the value of x to be 40, that of y to be 60, and that of z to be 70. "Particular accounting" applies to particular elements of production, and as a rule to the land. The agriculturist calculates the landrent in this way, that from the aggregate yield of his land he deducts the cost value, and in doing so he charges up the cost factors at only the value which is assignable to them on the basis of their marginal utility in the national economy and the world economy, whilst the whole of the remainder of the product is accounted to the land. In like manner, every other preferential rent is calculated by deducting costs from yield.— In essentials, Böhm-Bawerk agrees with the foregoing, but Schumpeter and Clark do not. In connexion with this problem of accounting, Clark develops the following law: "To each agent a distinguishable share in production, and to each a corresponding reward—such is the natural law of distribution."[2]

f. THEORY OF DISTRIBUTION

This school of economists did not succeed in elaborating a systematised theory of distribution. Their leading notion, the one with whose aid they endeavoured to throw light on the nature of wages, landrent, and entrepreneur's profit, was the idea of the "marginal productivity" of labour, land, and the particular enterprise. As regards their views concerning

[1] Menger, *op. cit.*, p. 157.

[2] John Bates Clark, *The Distribution of Wealth, a Theory of Wages, Interest, and Profits*, Macmillan, New York and London, 1899, p. 3.

interest, see below, pp. 269 et seq. But, apart from the fact that Menger's disciples took divergent paths here, "marginal productivity" is not competent to explain the distribution of income.

Substantially, this theory of distribution is identical with Ricardo's. But whereas Ricardo discerned rent only in the case of areas of land (differing degrees of utility in accordance with relative scarcity), these later economists look upon Ricardian rent as no more than a special instance of the general formation of prices. Rents arise everywhere. Price is not determined solely by the last (i.e. the least effective) of the purchasers who must be invoked to absorb the product (thus endowing the more effective purchasers with a rent—"consumers' rent"). Co-determinants of price are also the qualitatively least effective, least productive, and therefore most expensive, worker; the least effective, and therefore most costly, machine; the most costly method of production, among all the methods used; the least effective enterprise among all those engaged in a branch of production; and so on. All of these endow the more effective workers, capitals, enterprises, etc., with a preferential rent.[1]

2. LITERATURE OF THE DOCTRINE OF MARGINAL UTILITY

Germany and Austria: Wieser (ob. 1926), *Ursprung und Hauptgesetze des wirtschaftlichen Wertes*, Vienna, 1884; *Der natürliche Wert*, Vienna, 1889; *Theorie der gesellschaftlichen Wirtschaft*, 1914, second edition, 1924; Zuckerkandl (ob. 1926), *Zur Theorie des Preises mit besonderer Berücksichtigung der geschichtlichen Entwicklung der Lehre*, Leipzig, 1889; Philippovich (ob. 1917), *Allgemeine Volkswirtschaftslehre*, fifteenth edition, Tübingen, 1920; the writings of Eugen von Böhm-Bawerk (see below, p. 269); the writings of Sax, Lehr, Schumpeter (see below, p. 274); L. Schönfeld, *Grenznutzen und Wirtschaftsrechnung*, Vienna, 1924 (this work has an "organic" trend on the basis of its author's general conceptions, but it is

---

[1] Among writers in the English language who have sedulously developed economic theory along these lines, and have done so with exceptional clarity, the most familiar name will be that of the American economist, General Francis Amasa Walker (1840–1897). Chief works: *Political Economy*, New York, 1883; *Money*, London, 1878; *The Wages Question*, New York, 1876; *First Lessons in Political Economy*, New York, 1889.—TRANSLATORS' NOTE.

one which, carried to its logical conclusion, liquidates marginal utility).—Holland: N. G. Pierson.—Italy: Pantaleoni, Ricca-Salerno, and Graziani.—France: Aftalion, *Les trois notions de la productivité et les revenus*, "Revue d'Economie Politique", 1911.—Sweden: Wicksell (volumes of lectures upon the foundations of the principle of marginal utility).—Great Britain and the United States of America: Marshall, *Principles of Economics*, fifth edition, 1907; Edgeworth; Hobson; Wicksteed; John Bates Clark, *The Distribution of Wealth, etc.*, New York, 1899, *Essentials of Economic Theory*, New York, 1907; Seligmann; Patten.[1]—Hungary: Wolfgang Heller, *Theoretische Volkswirtschaftslehre*, Leipzig, 1926, *Die Grundprobleme der volkswirtschaftlichen Theorie*, third edition, Leipzig, 1928. (Heller's attitude towards the marginal-utility theory is somewhat sceptical, and he is inclined to regard it as out of date.)—Regarding Gossen, Walras, and Jevons, see above, p. 256.—Additional literature is referred to under the Mathematical School (below, p. 274).

The British and American theoreticians of marginal utility are inclined, in some degree, to revert to the principle of cost as a factor of value, in that they try to amalgamate the unpleasantness of labour as cost-factor instead of, like Ricardo, the quantity of labour as cost-factor with the marginal-utility factor. This is the line taken already by Jevons. Marshall and Clark have tried to formulate a law to the effect that the value of goods fixes itself at the intersection between their utility and the disagreeables attendant upon the labour of producing them.—But this "disutility theory" is logically untenable. If, as a general principle, we regard utility as determinative of value, then labour (with the associated agreeable or disagreeable sensations) only comes into consideration as a means for creating utility, and cannot rank as a primary factor of value side by side with utility.

Among outspoken opponents of the theory of marginal utility, the first to appear on the scene was J. von Komorczynski, whose *Der Wert in der isolierten Wirtschaft* was published at Vienna in 1889. He did not, indeed, expressly repudiate the idea of marginal utility, but as concerned the application of that idea in the theory of value he made the sound objection that, fundamentally, all goods are to be looked

[1] As to the replacement of the marginal-utility school in the United States by the "institutional school", see below, p. 277.

upon as complementary, and that for this reason we cannot properly speak of the individual value of a good; further, that if there should be a lack of any particular commodity, some substitute-commodity or other would take its place, and that for this reason the original utility would not be nullified (as the theory of marginal utility assumes), and all that would happen would be that the utility of remoter substitute-commodities of comparatively little importance would be restricted.—Similar views have been expressed by Dietzel (see below, p. 279), Diehl, and Cassel (*Das Recht auf den vollen Arbeitsertrag*, Göttingen, 1900), Lexis (the article "Grenznutzen", in the *Wörterbuch der Volkswissenschaften*, third edition, Jena, 1911), Mohrmann (*Dogmengeschichte der Zurechnungslehre*, 1914), and Otto Neurath (*Nationalökonomie und Wertlehre*, "Zeitschrift für Volkswirtschaft", Vienna, vol. xx).

Wieser is forcibly criticised by Amonn, *Wiesers Theorie der gesellschaftlichen Wirtschaft*, in the "Archiv für Sozialwissenschaft", vol. liii, 1925. Amonn's criticism is all the more important in that, to begin with, he took his stand on the theory of marginal utility. See also Amonn, *Der Stand der reinen Theorie*, in *Festgabe für L. Brentano*, two vols., 1925.

Some of the Marxists have tried to effect a compromise between the marginal-utility theory and the labour-cost theory of value; for instance, Tugan-Baranowsky, Gelesnoff, and F. Oppenheimer (*Wert und Kapitalprofit*, 1916). Liefmann, whose criticism in *Grundsätze der Volkswirtschaftslehre*, Stuttgart, 1917, third edition, 1923, is vaguely expressed, makes the further mistake of thinking that his basic ideas are original. For a criticism of Liefmann himself, see Amonn, "Archiv für Sozialwissenschaft," vol. xlvi, pp. 367 et seq., and vol. xlvii, pp. 523 et seq.

3. CRITIQUE OF THE DOCTRINE OF MARGINAL UTILITY[1]

a. GOSSEN'S LAW

The fundamental notions upon which the doctrine of marginal utility has been built up are untenable. This becomes

[1] In amplification of this brief critique, see the present writer's article, *Gleichwichtigkeit gegen Grenznutzen*, "Jahrbücher für Nationalökonomie und Statistik", vol. cxxiii, Jena, 1925, p. 289, and the third and fourth essays in his *Tote und lebendige Wissenschaft*, second edition, 1925.

especially plain as soon as we make a careful study of "Gossen's law"—which at the first glance seems so plausible.

This law is approximately valid only when we are contemplating individual or isolated wants—and not always even then. But in actual fact there can be no such thing as the isolated satisfaction of a particular want. In the example given to illustrate the law (supra, p. 257), the first glass of water saves the traveller's life, whilst the tenth glass is practically valueless because by the ninth his thirst has already been fully quenched. Such is the assumption of the marginal-utility theory. But surely if our friend were unexpectedly to find yet another couple of glasses (making up the dozen), he would still have a use for them, since they could provide him with other enjoyments. For instance, he might like to have a wash; or to water his mule (gratifying a want of his own, in a sense, if he is fond of the beast); or to make some soup, thus using the water as a factor in the preparation of another enjoyable good. In like manner, a musically gifted young man who has to earn his livelihood as a clerk, and is deeply grieved because he has no chance of fostering his musical talent, may be lifted into the seventh heaven of delight by a modest legacy that will enable him, at a pinch, to study music for three or four years—though all that time he will have to live on short commons instead of living (we may suppose) pretty comfortably as a clerk. The windfall may seem to bring him the very crown of life, although thanks to it and the use he makes of it his elementary material needs are less adequately satisfied than they were before. The examples show that supplementary quantities of a commodity may be turned to account for the production of more utility than could be provided by the earlier quantities of the same commodity, in so far as they can be utilised in new ways, for the attainment of new ends.—Like considerations apply to the means of production. When the traveller uses the supplementary water to water his mule, this may save all his possessions. Or let us suppose that there is a forest difficult of access, but sufficiently supplied with water by a brook; now let the brook suddenly swell to become a navigable stream, and thereby the value of the timber will be increased many times over, since its transport will be greatly facilitated and consequently its utilisability intensified. Speaking generally we may say that, pending the attainment of the optimum, each additional increase in supply increases the utility of a commodity by furnishing fresh opportunities for its use. Besides, even optima as a rule are not absolute but merely relative. (See above, pp. 122 et seq.)

If Gossen's law is invalid, the "law of the equivalence of marginal utilities" must likewise be invalid, and therewith the whole notion of "marginality" falls to the ground. For now the magnitude of the last or marginal utility can no longer be decisive as to the value of the aggregate supply, and the values of commodities cannot be estimated in terms of marginal utilities. If the series of figures representing the successive degrees of utility be not a progressively declining one, but one liable to irregular increments; if it be not 10, 9, 8, 7, etc., but (assuming for the sake of argument that a numerical estimate of utilities is at all possible) 10, 9, 8, 12, etc.—then we must obviously be debarred from reckoning the aggregate utility on the basis of 12, the last figure in our hypothetical series.

b. Atomistic Nature of the Theory of Wants, Market, and Price

It is true that the notion of marginal utility contains an "organic" element within it, to this extent, that the doctrine implies the values of goods to be mutually interdependent; but the idea of this interdependence is not turned to account as it should be. Menger assumes, rather, as his starting-point, the atomistic nature of the wants of individual economic agents, and considers the economy as a whole to be a composite that results from the aggregation of their individual estimates and dealings. To all his arguments, therefore, the criticisms that have already been applied to the doctrine of the "ordre naturel" and to the doctrine of self-interest are equally applicable.[1]

[1] See above under Quesnay and Smith (pp. 109 et seq., p. 146, and pp. 150 et seq.); also my article "Eigennutz" in the *Handwörterbuch der Staats-wissenschaften*, fourth edition, vol. iii, p. 323.

Unsound, likewise, is the atomistic notion of the market as nothing but a place where individual economic agents are gathered together; and the "law of the marginal pairs" is also fallacious.

Price is not a composite product of the subjective estimates of individuals, and more especially it does not fix itself as a "price of equilibrium"—e.g. between 5 and 6 in the instance given above on p. 259. Were the considerations upon which that instance is based really valid, the price would equilibrate itself between 0 and 1. For the sellers and the buyers are not atomised masses, but form an interarticulated whole. The buyers are the predominant partners; and, in an economy based on the division of labour, sellers have as a rule an estimate of the value of their goods which tends towards zero. (What, for example, is the owner of a stud-farm to do with his horses if he cannot sell them?)[1]

c. THEORY OF DISTRIBUTION

Since the theory of marginal utility sets out from premises which are unsound both methodologically and in respect of their content, we are not surprised to find that it leads to erroneous conclusions in the matter of the theory of distribution.

The idea of "marginal productivity" cannot stand when the idea of marginal value (Gossen's law) falls, and the theory of wages must share the fate of both.—Moreover, we conceive the problem wrongly if we speak of "aggregate value". The total available supply of a commodity does not acquire its value through the summation of the individual utilities (the fractional quantities), nor yet through our multiplying the marginal-utility value by the number of pieces or of fractional parts: it acquires its value only as an effluent from the more exalted wholes of which it is a member. Values and prices cannot be explained from below upwards by summation, but only from above downwards by disarticulation or dissection, by an analysis of the extant higher economic aggregates—the national economy and finally the world economy.—An attempt at "accounting"

[1] A criticism of Böhm-Bawerk's formula of prices will be found in § 19 of my *Fundament der Volkswirtschaftslehre*.

has likewise been made atomistically from below upwards. Wieser was right in objecting to Menger's method of accounting by reckoning up the diminution in output when a particular instrument of production is put out of action; but his own solution of the difficulty amounts in the end to nothing more than an ordinary calculation of costs, like those made by every man of business. A calculation of costs is not an explanation of value! Apart from this, Wieser's method ignores the fact that when one element of unknown magnitude in a composite is changed, the change involves a simultaneous and proportional change in all the other elements. In economics, no magnitude is an atomistic datum, for all of them mutually condition one another. "Accounting" (if we retain the name) can only be worked out from above; the individual "magnitudes" must all be contemplated as parts of a whole. In that case (as I have shown elsewhere), we are concerned, not with the idea of a specifically different "productive contribution" furnished by each individual functioning factor (a purely technical factor), but with the idea of equilibrium or equivalence.[1] Further, a gulf yawns between "accounting" and the theory of the market price, seeing that the latter depends upon the gathering together of subjective estimates of value, whereas the former is always concerned with aggregates, such as supplies, industries, etc.

Whilst the classical economists' theory of distribution acquires a unity through the objective idea of cost (labour content), Menger's school, regarding the national income as a summation of individual incomes produced by the gathering together of subjective estimates of value, cannot achieve a like unity.

It is no doubt owing to the atomism and individualism of the theory of marginal utility that its champions have followed Smith and Ricardo in making the doctrine of value and of price the central pillar of economic theory. The worst of this way of looking at the subject is that it becomes impossible to formulate any theory of achievement, seeing that price is made primary while achievement remains secondary. From the organic standpoint, on the other hand, achievement is primary, price secondary. The concrete interarticulation of the means to an end comes first; magnitude of achievement (that is to say, value) and price are only deducible from achievement and its articulation (that is to say, distribution).

[1] Cf. my article *Gleichwichtigeit gegen Grenznutzen* in "Jahrbücher für Nationalökonomie", vol. cxxiii. See also below, p. 282.

For all these reasons, the theory of marginal utility has led only to the formulation of sterile pseudo-problems and to empty sophistications. Karl Menger, the founder of the school, despaired of the survival of his doctrine, and failed to follow up the first volume of his *Grundsätze* (1871) with a second— even refusing to have the first volume reprinted. Still more significant is it that Menger was antipathetic towards the further development of his doctrine by Wieser and Böhm-Bawerk. We know this, not merely from traditional talk in Vienna, but from what Menger had to say of Böhm-Bawerk after the latter's death,[1] and from the additions to the post-humous reissue of Menger's own book (Vienna, 1923). Apart from a handful of immediate disciples in Vienna, Menger had practically no supporters in German-speaking lands.—In England, it was from Jevons and not from Menger that the school of economists who espoused the doctrine of marginal utility took its rise.—In Teutonic countries to-day, the doctrine may almost be regarded as extinct.—In the United States of America, the school of its supporters has given place to the "institutional school". (See below, p. 277.)

None the less, the theory of marginal utility did one good service. In Germany, thanks to it and to it alone, during a period when attention to matters theoretical was at a low ebb, the tradition of theoretical thinking was maintained.

D. Böhm-Bawerk's Teaching

Böhm-Bawerk[2] (professor at the University of Vienna, ob. 1915), a man highly respected by foreign economists, was the most widely read representative of the Austrian school.

[1] Karl Menger, *Eugen von Böhm-Bawerk*, reprint from the "Almanach der Kaiserlichen Akademie der Wissenschaften", Vienna, 1915.

[2] Böhm-Bawerk's most important book is *Kapital und Kapitalzins*, Innsbruck, 1884–1889, translated by W. Smart in two parts as *Capital and Interest*, 1890, and *The Positive Theory of Capital*, 1891.

a. EXPOSITION

Böhm-Bawerk insists that in estimating the values of goods we must take into account prospective utility as well as present utility. The majority of goods, indeed, have it as their only purpose to produce other goods for future consumption; in a word, they are capital. Within this category of capital are subsumed all the intermediate products which come into being in the course of the aggregate process of production. Thus the extant capital of a national economy is an expression of the "devious paths of production", of the detours along which goods have to be made. For instance, men may draw water for themselves in the hollow of the hand; or, using a circuitous method, they may build an aqueduct to bring it whithersoever they please. By entering upon these devious paths of production, we gain the advantage of getting more extensive results for the same expenditure of energy, or the power of producing a good which could not be produced at all by a less circuitous method. (This is the "law of the superior productivity of the devious paths of production".)

The value of a capital is an anticipation of the value of the goods which will be brought into being by its aid. This leads us to the most important of Böhm-Bawerk's notions (formulated in connexion with an observation of Menger's, which has, however, been deleted from the second edition of the *Grundsätze*), the one on which he bases his explanation of interest. Present goods, he says, have subjectively a higher value than future goods, and consequently command a higher price. There are three reasons for this. First of all, there comes into play present scarcity, thanks to which present goods are always preferable to prospective ones, and thanks to which the demand for present goods always exceeds the supply. Secondly, there is an invariable tendency to underestimate future demand. Thirdly and lastly, there is a technical reason, inasmuch as the most fruitful methods of production are those which have to be carried out along time-expending devious paths, so that present goods have a productive superiority. Consequently the command of present goods gains enhanced importance, inasmuch as only one who enjoys that command over a sufficiency of them can enter the devious paths on which production can most advantageously be effected. Future goods, prospective goods, are of no use here.

Of these three reasons for valuing present goods more highly than prospective goods, sometimes one is more powerfully operative, sometimes another. But in any case the result is that the present goods attain higher prices than the prospective ones, and the tension that ensues upon the establishment of this difference, the premium payable upon the present goods, is the interest of capital. One who has present goods at his command, can secure in exchange for them the promise, not merely of an equivalent amount of prospective goods, but of a supplementary quantity, which is interest.

Where are the exchanges between present goods and prospective goods effected? What mainly happens is that entrepreneurs, through their money capital, have the disposal over articles of consumption, and supply to the workers as wages, to the landowners as landrent, and to the providers of raw materials and machinery as purchase prices, the means for buying the articles of consumption which these respectively need to keep themselves going. The economic process of production is unceasingly associated with acts of exchange as between articles of consumption and articles of production— or, in other words, as between present goods and prospective goods. The entrepreneur offers present goods in order to get prospective ones, and has therefore necessarily to take into account the premium or agio payable upon present goods— i.e. the market rate of interest. The capitalist is a merchant who has present commodities for sale; the worker is a merchant who has future commodities for sale.

As with production, so with loans. According to Böhm-Bawerk, loans for consumptive and loans for productive purposes consist of an exchange of present goods for prospective ones, and not (as is usually held) of the temporary relinquishment of assignable goods—a surrender taking the form of a pact or a deed of hire. Just as, in production, interest arises as profit on capital, so here we have interest on the loan.—The entrepreneur has present commodities for sale, and with them he buys the means of producing future commodities (labour power, machinery, etc.). But these means of producing commodities that will be consumed in days to come, are worth only what the commodities of the morrow are worth to-day. If, for example, the means of production of an area of land will be able to produce 100 bushels of wheat in a year, the value of the means of production is the value of next year's wheat, but that value is only the value of 95 bushels of extant wheat. In the course of the process of production, however, the prospective commodity gradually ripens into an extant commodity, and ultimately therefore attains its full value. The increase is the profit on capital (interest). A like growth in value from present commodities to future commodities occurs in the case of credit. A 100 pounds sterling to-day will have grown a year hence into 105 pounds sterling. The £5 interest is the increase, is the difference in values that will have ensued when goods that are now prospective shall have become actual. Every kind of interest is the premium, the agio, payable upon extant goods.

The rate of interest therefore (it is impossible here to summarise the whole train of reasoning) is subject to the following law: "Interest will be higher in proportion as the stored-up supplies of articles of consumption in a national economy are smaller, so that only the less devious and consequently less productive paths of production are practicable, and the greater therefore the supplementary yield that will attach to a lengthening of the detours. Conversely, interest will be lower when there is a bountiful store of articles of consumption, rendering more devious and consequently more productive paths of production practicable, so that a less extensive supplementary yield will be obtainable by any possible further lengthening of the detours. In brief, the rate of interest depends upon the supplementary yield of the last lengthening of the process of production," or in other words upon the marginal productivity of capital. (Thünen conveyed the same idea by saying that the rate of interest was "determined by the utility of the last-utilised portion of capital". (See above, p. 175.)

b. VALUATION OF BÖHM-BAWERK'S THEORY OF INTEREST

In this brilliantly elaborated theory, we have the first systematic study of the gradations in value as between prospective and extant goods. Herein lies its merit. But the fundamental notion of the theory, the idea that prospective goods are less valuable than present ones, is unsound. In a trustworthy economic calculation, the value of prospective commodities is precisely. estimated in accordance with the prospective possibilities of their utilisation. A sound economist likewise foresees that prospective goods will be just as scarce as present goods are. (Consider the foresight of a farmer who divides his crop into three parts, one for seed, a second for personal consumption, and a third for the market; and the manufacturer or the domestic economist looks ahead in just the same way.) It appertains to the very nature of economic planning, that there should be no underestimate of the value of future goods! Such an underestimate is made only by the bad economist, by the heedless, by the spendthrift.—A second difficulty lies in this, that the basic idea of the underestimate of the value of the prospective commodity could apply only in the case of interest upon a loan for consumptive purposes (a loan in which present articles of consumption are exchanged for future articles of consumption). As regards the interest payable on a loan for productive purposes, when we look into the matter closely we see that in such a loan no extant good (no article of immediate consumption) has been lent, but only a prospective good (that is to say an unripe extant good, such as a machine); and that therefore what is lent must itself, ex hypothesi, have its value underestimated, above all, when, as in the case of machine-making machinery, it is used to make, not actual, but prospective goods!—In the "three reasons" (see above, p. 270), ripe present goods and unripe present goods (really, future goods) are huddled together promiscuously.

Apart from the agio theory, the most important theories of interest are: the productivity theory; the utility theory, according to which usufruct must be taken into account as well as productivity (Menger and others); the exploitation theory of Marx, who regards interest as only one of the forms assumed by surplus value; and the "dynamic theory" of Schumpeter who considers that interest and entrepreneur's profit are the outcome of economic progress. The productivity theory has secured the most widespread acceptance, and among the classical economists Thünen elaborated it with especial thoroughness and insight. The central notion of this theory is that, by the aid of capital, labour becomes enabled to obtain or produce a larger quantity of goods. Thus a hunter with bow and arrows will kill more game than one not provided with such weapons. Böhm-Bawerk, however, raises the following objection. The theory, he says, can account for the increase in material productivity that results from the use of capital; but it does not explain the supplementary production of values, nor yet the supplementary value of the products, in which alone interest inheres. "Why is not the portion of capital worth as much as the expected product itself," asks Böhm-Bawerk, "seeing that according to the theory of marginal utility capital (cost goods or productive goods) derives its value from its fruits (see above, p. 259); why should it be worth less, so that the product of capital has enhanced value, and consequently interest accrues?

This objection is invalid because Menger's idea of cost, according to which costs cannot be regarded as independent elements, is itself unsound. But these questions cannot be followed up here, where nothing more has been possible than to trace the most recent developments of the concepts under consideration.

E. THE MATHEMATICAL SCHOOL

The mathematical school is not identical with the marginal-utility school, but is closely akin. Many of the exponents of the theory of marginal utility have tried to present the notion mathematically. The following have been the most notable representatives of the mathematical school: its founder, Cournot (1801–1877, *Recherches sur les principes mathématiques de la théorie des richesses*, 1838); Gossen (1810–1858, *Entwicklung der Gesetze des Menschlichen Verkehrs*, 1854); Jevons and Walras (works enumerated above, p. 256); Launhart (*Mathematische Begründung der Volkswirtschaftslehre*, 1885); Auspitz and Lieben (*Untersuchungen über die Theorie des Preises*, Leipzig, 1889); Schumpeter (*Wesen und Hauptinhalt der theoretischen Nationalökonomie*, Leipzig, 1908); Pareto (*Manuel d'économie politique*, Paris, 1909); Barone; Irving Fisher (*Mathematical Investigations in the Theory of Value and Prices*, Yale University Press, 1925).

The mathematical school must be commended for having emphasised more clearly than any previous school of economists the distinction between an immutable and a mutable, or as we now phrase it between a "static" and a "dynamic" economy— a distinction to which I alluded on p. 86.[1] Since there is no such thing as a completely immutable, a perfectly static economy, the differentiation is nothing more than a hypothesis

[1] Regarding this matter, see especially John Bates Clark, *The Distribution of Wealth*, New York, 1899. In German, consult Schumpeter (*op. cit.*) whose leading formulae are derived from Walras.

which has practical value for methodological purposes, and it is one which has at times misled those who have accepted it. In other respects the mathematical method in economics is barren, and can serve only for the vivid demonstration of results obtained in other ways. The main fallacy which invalidates it is the assumption that the magnitudes with which it deals are separately and individually variable. This is not the case in an organic aggregate, such as economic life, whose magnitudes, moreover, are not primary, but derivative. If, e.g., a double supply of iron appears in the market, this occurrence must have been preceded by more mining of ores, more smelting, more transport, the payment of more wages, and so on. There has not been an isolated "variable". All the factors of the problem have varied simultaneously; the whole economy has been modified. (It is otherwise in physics, where, for instance, volumes alone can be altered, with consequent mathematically calculable changes in pressure and temperature.) Besides, there are achievements that are not susceptible of quantitative statement and are inexhaustible, such as a commercial treaty or an invention. Cf. K. Faigl, *Ganzheit und Zahl*, Jena, 1926, p. 110, also pp. 95 et seq. (The application of mathematics to biology.)

CHAPTER TWELVE

PRESENT-DAY ECONOMIC SCIENCE

A. CERTAIN NEW TRENDS[1]

1. THE REALIST-DESCRIPTIVE SCHOOL

THE realist-descriptive school may be regarded as an outgrowth from the younger historical school (the school of Schmoller). The realist-descriptive school works, in fact, upon the same methodological principles as the historical school, but devotes more attention to the economic problems of the present day. Among investigators attached to this school who belonged to a somewhat earlier generation than our own, I may mention Albert Schäffle (ob. 1904, *Bau und Leben des sozialen Körpers*, second edition, 1896), and Lexis (ob. 1914, *Volkswirtschaftslehre*, second edition, 1915. Of contemporary representatives of the realist-descriptive school, I will enumerate in alphabetical order: B. Harms; H. Herkner (*Die Arbeiterfrage*, eighth edition, Berlin, 1923); Passow (editor of *Beiträge zur Lehre von den Unternehmungen*, Jena, 1925); J Pesch, S.J. (*Lehrbuch der Nationalökonomie*, five vols., Freiburg, 1904–1925); Schumacher (*Weltwirtschaftliche Studien*, 1911, and other works); Adolf Weber (*Der Kampf zwischen Kapital und Arbeit*, fourth edition, 1921); K. Wiedenfeld (*Das Persönliche im modernen Unternehmertum*, Leipzig, 1911, second edition, 1920); Zwiedineck-Südenhorst ("Lohntheorie und Lohnpolitik" in *Handwörterbuch der Staatswissenschaften*, fourth edition, Jena, 1923), who is also of note as a theoretician.

[1] Cf. in this connexion, Salin, *Die deutsche volkswirtschaftliche Theorie im zwanzigsten Jahrhundert*, "Schweizerische Zeitschrift für Statistik", 1921; Surányi-Unger, *Geschichte der Volkswirtschaftslehre im ersten Viertel des zwanzigsten Jahrhunderts*, Jena, 1926; Honegger, *Volkswirtschaftliche Gedankenströme*, etc., 1926.

Pesch, a disciple of Adolf Wagner, hopes for a "solidarity" that shall be an effective compromise between individualism and socialism, but is essentially individualist in the groundwork of his ideas. He seems to be acquainted only with the teachings of the classical economists and the socialists, for he ignores the views of the romanticists and the scholastics.—Nevertheless he has penned the most comprehensive economic treatise ever produced in the German language—a work instinct with true scholarship.

In the United States, since the war, as in Scandinavia, the marginal-utility school has been replaced by the "institutional school".[1]

The economists of this group are persons who have been disillusioned by the failure of every kind of neo-Ricardianism since the outbreak of the war. Like the members of the older historical school in Germany (Roscher and Knies), while still endeavouring to keep in touch with theory, they consider that economic investigation must centre in the study of "institutions" and of "human behaviour" (the theory of motivation), so that their method becomes historical, statistical, and psychological. The crucial question for this school will be, as it was in the case of the older and the younger historical schools in Germany, whether its representatives can keep in touch with economic theory, and avoid lapsing into positivism.

2. THE EPISTEMOLOGICAL GROUP

Since the turn of the century, or shortly before, there has gradually been developing a system of methodological writings in which (with clarified arguments) an attempt has been made to carry a stage further the old dispute about method between Menger and Schmoller, and to broaden the philosophical, social, and scientific foundations of economics.

[1] Cf. R. G. Tugwell, *The Trend of Economics*, New York, 1924. This is a symposium with contributions from many of the younger American professors of economics. See also the account of the institutional school by Allyn A. Young in the "Quarterly Journal of Economics", 1925; and Suranyi-Unger, *op. cit.*, pp. 33 et seq.

To this school belong: Rudolf Stammler (*Wirtschaft und Recht*, first edition, 1896, sixth edition, 1923), the first writer to apply neo-Kantian ideas to jurisprudence, and indirectly to economics; Max Weber ("Archiv für Sozialwissenschaft", 1902 and subsequent years, also 1920); Gottl ("Archiv für Sozialwissenschaft", 1906 and subsequent years); Andreas Voigt ("Zeitschrift für Sozialwissenschaft", 1906 and subsequent years, *Technische Oekonomik*, 1911, article "Volkswirtschaftslehre" in *Handwörterbuch der Staatswissenschaften*, fourth edition, Jena, 1923); Alfred Amonn (*Objekt und Grundbegriffe*, Vienna, 1911; important critical articles in "Archiv für Sozialwissenschaft"; also *Volkswohlstandslehre*, vol. i, 1926, see below, p. 279); Werner Sombart, *Die Ordnung des Wirtschaftslebens*, second edition, 1927. This book contains an elaborate study of economic systems. See also above, p. 242; also Karl Diehl (*Theoretische Nationalökonomie*, vol. i, second edition, 1916); also W. Mitscherlich (see below, p. 283).

3. THE NEO-LIBERAL TREND

The very existence of a neo-liberal trend to-day (when all the Ricardian schools have proved so sterile in the field of theory), and still more the fact that this school should recently have become dominant, are manifest indications that our science is still talking the language of the eighteenth century.

As leaders of the neo-liberal school (apart from the marginal-utility school, which is likewise neo-liberal) must be mentioned first of all the Swede, Gustav Cassel (*Theoretische Sozialökonomik*, first edition, 1918, fourth edition, 1927), whose textbook has had great influence in Germany, and who has endeavoured to give a mathematical explanation of the formation of prices, and of distribution, in terms of the "principle of scarcity", without having recourse to any theory of value. But Cassel's equations do not provide us with any fresh knowledge; they merely serve to express the general connexion between supply and demand, on the one hand, and price, on the other, which was presupposed. In fact, they are tautological.—Franz Oppenheimer tries to take up an intermediate position, professing a "liberal socialism" (*Grundriss der theoretischen Oekonomie*, 1926).[1] Earlier economists belonging to this trend are Adolf Wagner (see above, p. 244) and Heinrich Dietzel (*Theoretische Sozialökonomik*, 1925). Alfred Amonn's attitude towards Ricardo is ambiguous. On the one hand, he sharply criticises Ricardo (*Ricardo als Begründer der theoretischen Nationalökonomie*, Jena, 1924, also in *Volkswohlstandslehre*, 1926); on the other, he advocates a return to Ricardo. The explanation of this apparent inconsistency is that in the domain of "national economics" (the universalist economy of the social aggregate) Amonn renounces Ricardianism, but still accepts it in the narrower domain of "economics" (individualist economics). In his brilliant book *Volkswohlstandslehre* (1926), Amonn is still trying to rescue the old formal theory of exchange, and wants to keep it afoot side by side with the universalist doctrine of the interconnexion between means and ends.

4. Universalist Economics

a. The doctrine of the author of the present work starts from the assumption that first of all the sociological presuppositions of economic science must be safeguarded. These sociological postulates were briefly expounded in the fourth chapter of the present work, the chapter entitled "An Introduction to the Basic Problem of Sociology—Individualism versus Universalism". (See above, pp. 59 et seq.)

The doctrine of universalism, originally developed by myself, derives, moreover, from the principles that underlie the idealist philosophy, as formulated in my *Kategorienlehre*.

[1] See Amonn's criticism of Oppenheimer in the "Zeitschrift fur Volkswirtschaft", vol. v, 1925.

b. According to the universalist view, "economics" objectively considered is an interarticulation of means for ends (being subjectively the estimation of means, and the consecration of means to ends). From this outlook, all economic phenomena are, by their very nature, an interarticulated structure of achievements (seeing that the means achieve something on behalf of the ends). The land effects something; factory buildings, machines, raw materials, effect something; the activities of the workers effect something.—These achievements may be classed under three heads: direct achievements, those which directly result in the pleasures of consumption, as when we pluck a fruit; indirect achievements, as when we instal the instruments that will enable us to pluck fruit, i.e. instal capital; and achievements which, though still indirect, have a higher grade of intermediate effect (constitute capital of a higher grade), e.g. a commercial treaty which will help every one doing business with a foreign land.—But this idea of achievement must not be conceived in a technically causal sense; we must keep our minds fixed upon the quality of the achievement which makes of it the fulfilment of an aim, the quality which makes of it an interarticulated part of a larger whole; we must look at the matter structurally. The achievement is always a member of a more exalted and an articulated aggregate. Contraposed to the totality of all the ends is the totality or the articulated structure of all the achievements.—Hence there must be superadded to the idea of achievement the idea of the articulated ordination of the economic aggregates as the second fundamental notion. This articulated ordination is characterised by the partial aggregates and the grades. Things preparatory to ripeness (inventions and theories); things ripening through production (subdivisible into the materially ripe, the locally ripe, things ripe for the market, and things ripe for consumption); things communal that promote ripening (capital of a higher grade)—

these are the "partial aggregates" of all economies, whereof the world economy, the national economy, and its subordinate parts down to the individual enterprise and the domestic economy, are the "stages". As between the partial aggregates and the stages, there are relations of superiority and inferiority. Consider, for instance, what was said on p. 48, that "the total balance takes precedence of the individual balance"; and on p. 70, that "financial capital takes precedence of industrial capital".—All these concepts, for whose fuller elucidation I must refer the reader to my other works, are designed to make an end of the atomistic and mechanical way of regarding economic processes. For the first time they enable us to grasp alike the form and the substance, to understand both the anatomy and the physiology, of the economic life of all historical epochs.

The doctrine of achievement (in the traditional terminology it might better be called the doctrine of production) holds the premier place in the development of the system; and, just as "achievement takes precedence of price", so likewise "the doctrine of achievement takes precedence of the doctrine of price". For, in fact, "price" is only the expression of the articulation of achievements. Prices attach to goods in accordance with the grade of articulation of achievements. When precedence is thus given to achievement, and then only, we get quite beyond the economic system of Smith and Ricardo. (See above, pp. 109 et seq., and p. 268.)—Thenceforward, the leading principle in the formation of value and of price is, not marginal utility (though achievement in the widest sense is identical with utility in the widest sense), but equilibrium or equivalence. For price does not arise out of the encounter of subjective estimates of value in the market, nor yet out of the encounter of supply and demand (Menger, Cassel), but out of the relations of magnitude in the articulated structure of an economy, price being the expression of these relations in accordance with the principle of equilibrium. (Cf. pp. 91 and 268; also "just price", p. 255.)

From the methodological standpoint, these concepts embody the universalist outlook, and take us right away from the atomistic and individualist outlook of the classical economists and the champions of the doctrine of marginal utility. No one denies the comparative independence and individuality of the particular economic agent, but the primary reality is always that of the totality of the economy as an invariably antecedent datum. (See above pp. 115 et seq., "reason for articulation versus self-interest".)

Although the realm of means has its own laws (laws of ideal universalist articulation, not laws of mechanical causality), this theory is not abstractly isolative like the theory of Ricardo and Menger, for it does not set out from the "motives" of the individual, nor yet from the subjective at all; it sets out from the extant articulated objective totality of the body economic. Neither is it an unhistorical doctrine, seeing that the ends are always implicit in the articulated structure of the means, and that in these ends the whole living abundance of historical society finds expression.

c. Theory of Money. (See below, pp. 285 et seq.)

d. Doctrine of Crises. (See below, pp. 293 et seq.)

For further details, I refer to my other writings, which can best be read in the following order: *Vom Geiste der Volkswirtschaftslehre*, Jena, 1919 (now printed as appendix to the fourth edition of the *Fundament*); *Tote und lebendige Wissenschaft*, third edition, Jena, 1929 (read the second and third sections first); *Fundament der Volkswirtschaftslehre*, fourth edition, Jena, 1929.—To the foregoing economic works, a methodological foundation is supplied by my *Kategorienlehre*, Jena, 1924; a sociological, by my *Gesellschaftslehre*, second edition, Leipzig, 1923; a socio-political, by *Der wahre Staat*, second edition, Leipzig, 1923; and a philosophical, by my *Der Schöpfungsgang des Geistes*, part i, Jena, 1928.—Concerning the collections edited by me, "Herdflamme" and "Deutsche Beiträge zur Wirtschafts- und Gesellschaftslehre", see below, p. 301.

There exists to-day quite an imposing number of younger

investigators who are voicing the "organic" idea of economics. Collectively they make up what is now usually termed the "neo-romantic" or "universalist" school. Among them I may mention: W. Andreae, of Graz (translations of Plato in the collection "Herdflamme", vols. v, vi, and xiii; *Bausteine zu einer universalistischen Steuerlehre*, Jena, 1927); J. Baxa, of Vienna (*Geschichte der Produktivitätstheorie*, Jena, 1926; editions of the works of Adam Müller and the other romanticists in the collection "Herdflamme", vols. i, viii, and xviii); Karl Faigl, of Znaim (*Ganzheit und Zahl*, Jena, 1926); Walter Heinrich, of Vienna (*Grundlagen einer universalistischen Krisenlehre*, Jena, 1928); Hans Riehl, of Graz (editor of *Fichtes Schriften zur Gesellschaftsphilosophie*, in the collection "Herdflamme", vol. xv, Jena, 1928); G. Seidler-Schmid, of Prague (*Systemgedanken der sogenannten klassischen Volkswirtschaftslehre*, Jena, 1926); J. Sauter, of Vienna (editor of the writings of Baader, in the collection "Herdflamme", vol. xiv; *Baader und Kant*, Jena, 1928); H. Wagenführ, of Jena (*Die neuromantische Schule*, Jena, 1928). Besides the foregoing, there are many economists who in general accept the organic-universalist idea, though with certain reservations. Among these I may mention: Alfred Amonn (see above, p. 278); Below (*Zum Streit um das Wesen der Soziologie*, "Jahrbücher für Nationalökonomie, vol. cxxiv, 1926; *Othmar Spann*, "Deutschlands Erneuerung", 1924); J. Dunkmann (*Der Kampf um Othmar Spann*, Leipzig, 1928); Wolfgang Heller (*Theoretische Volkswirtschaftslehre*, Leipzig, 1926); Friedrich Lenz (*Aufriss der politischen Oekonomie*, 1927); Waldemar Mitscherlich (*Wirtschaftswissenschaft*, "Schmollers Jahrbuch", 1926; *Der wirtschaftliche Fortschritt*, second edition, 1923; *Moderne Arbeiterpolitik*, 1927); E. Salin (*Geschichte der Volkswirtschaftslehre*, Berlin, 1923); Sartorius von Waltershausen (*Die Weltwirtschaft*, Leipzig, 1926; *Weltwirtschaft und Weltanschauung*, Jena, 1927); Egon Scheffer (*Oesterreichs wirtschaftliche Sendung*, Vienna, 1927); Suranyi-Unger (see above, p. 276, and below, p. 301); Andreas Voigt ("Volkswirtschaft und Volkswirtschaftslehre", *Handwörterbuch der Staatswissenschaften*, fourth edition); Weddigen, of Breslau (*Theorie des Ertrages*, Jena, 1927; *Ertragstheorie und Verteilungstheorie*, "Jahrbücher für Nationalökonomie", vol. cxxviii, 1928).

I have not, so far, come across any serious criticisms of my doctrines, and I have no intention of replying at any length to unworthy (if not positively morbid) onslaughts such as those of Mr. Liefmann and Mr. Sander. Liefmann has understood my teaching so little that he actually describes as "nonsense" the proposition "the whole comes before the part"—which derives from Aristotle. Being utterly incapable of even beginning to grasp the idea of totality, he inevitably finds my theory of exchange, of achievement, of the ordination of articulation, of partial aggregates, etc., a book with seven seals. It is the same with Sander, who, since my doctrine of the categories is beyond his comprehension, finds it easy to despise it. But I am sorry for the periodicals which descend to so low a level.

Other opponents, more well-meaning, have tried to find a "middle course" between individualism and universalism. They should, however, begin by proving that these oppositions are not mutually exclusive, for then only can any sort of compromise be possible. Otherwise their attempts will be shattered against the elementary logical rule, "Inter duo contradictoria non est medium", they will vainly try to evade the law of excluded middle. I have dealt with these and other criticisms at sufficient length in my article *Ein Wort an meine Gegner auf dem Wiener Soziologentag*, which appeared in the "Kölner Vierteljahresschrift", sixth year of issue, 1927, pp. 311 et seq.

Finally, I have little taste for discussing the question of priority raised by Stolzmann (*Die Krisis in der heutigen National-ökonomie*, Jena, 1925), though in other respects I am glad to recognise the value of this author's writings. After all, the main thing is that the ideas in question should live and work, and it does not matter very much who first voiced them. But Stolzmann overlooks the immense difference between his "ethical purposive concept" (which is incapable of serving as foundation for the general notions of economic science) and my idea of achievement and totality. A further vital distinction between my views and Stolzmann's is that the forcible severance of the basic notions of our science into "natural" or purely economic categories, on the one hand, and "social" categories on the other—a severance which Stolzmann and Adolf Wagner attempt—is incompatible with my postulates and cannot be deduced from them; for according to my understanding of economics the "social" ends are already implicit in the means. Such a severance of the purely economic from the social is liberalism.—Furthermore, any one can ascertain for himself the dates of our respective publications. My enunciation of the idea of achievement goes back to 1904. (See *Kategorienlehre*, pp. 6 et seq.)

B. SOME OF THE MOST RECENT DOCTRINES

1. THEORY OF MONEY

For Ricardo, the essential nature of money seemed to inhere in its commodity character, in its value as a metal. But his attitude towards the problem was inconsistent. On the one hand, he regarded the value of money as the expression of the labour that had been incorporated in it (cost of mining plus cost of transport), the money being thus looked upon simply as so much metal, as a commodity on a similar footing to commodities in general; on the other hand, like Hume before him, he considered that the value of money must vary inversely as the quantity of it at any time available, so that if (for instance) the quantity money were doubled, its value would be halved, and prices would consequently be doubled— the "quantity theory" of money.[1] But in this latter way of regarding the question, money is thought of only as medium of exchange, and not as commodity at all; for if the objective doctrine of value be accepted without reserve, the value of a commodity cannot change enduringly because its quantity changes.—Nor was John Stuart Mill,[2] who restated the theories of the classical economists in a clarified and systematised way, able to escape this contradiction.—To those who held the quantity theory of money, and believed that prices necessarily rise when the quantity of money increases, the mercantilist doctrine of the balance of trade seemed absurd. An influx of money due to a "favourable balance of trade" would, they said, lead to a rise in prices; this would result in more imports being made, with a consequent outflow of money.

Here we come to the crux of the theory of money—to the fact that money is not simply a commodity like any other, but a commodity distinguished from all others by its function as medium of exchange. This quality of being a commodity which functions only as an intermediary between others makes it open

[1] Cf. Ricardo's *Principles*; also *The High Price of Bullion*, 1809.
[2] *Principles of Political Economy*, London, 1848.

to question whether and how far the commodity-quality of ordinary metals still attaches to metals when used as money, The view that the metallic commodity-quality still persists is termed "metallism"; the view that it has been lost is termed "chartalism", but has also (somewhat infelicitously) been termed monetary "nominalism".

By the classical economists, and by many economists on into our own day, money was mainly regarded as still possessing the ordinary commodity-quality; but Knapp has recently advocated an uncompromising chartalism, which has secured wide acceptance. According to this form of chartalism, money is State-made.[1] Already a hundred years ago and more, in *Elemente der Staatskunst*, 1809, and *Versuche einer neuen Theorie des Geldes*, 1816,[2] Adam Müller had formulated a non-metallist theory of money, and the canonists had long ere this expressed similar ideas. Adam Müller dissented from the view of the classical economists that money had developed out of the adoption of the most marketable commodity as a medium of exchange, declaring money to be a "primary need of economic life". Müller's theory, inasmuch as it regards money as "preeminently the sociable material" (for a further explanation see above, p. 164), centres in the trustworthiness of economic cooperation, in the relationship of money to the community. Nevertheless, Müller does not regard metallic money from an exclusively chartalist outlook, does not look upon it as something endowed with a purely symbolic value that is quite independent of its material value; for him, it is money endowed with an all-round validity, is "preeminently the sociable material". On the other hand, Knapp, taking a much narrower view than Müller, says that money is a "creation of the extant juridical order", and nothing more. The essence of money, according to this authority, inheres in its form, and has no concern with its substance. (Think, for instance, of paper money, which according to Knapp is not a "useful good" at all.) Nor has this essence of money anything to do with custom. What makes up the essence of money, says Knapp, is simply and solely the decree of the State that this, that, or the other shall be valid as means of payment.—Following Knapp, Bendixen[3] (ob. 1920) regards

---

[1] Knapp, *Staatliche Theorie des Geldes*, Leipzig, 1905, fourth edition, 1923.

[2] Both books republished, Jena, 1922.

[3] *Wesen des Geldes*, 1908, third edition, Munich, 1922; *Das Inflations-problem*, Stuttgart, 1917.

money as legally nothing more than a means of payment, but economically it is "that which entitles one who has previously done something for another, or for others, to have something done for him in return". On this view, money is a lien upon goods, a lien whose nature resembles that of a bill of exchange. The same idea was given an apter economic phrasing at an earlier date by Adolf Wagner (ob. 1920), and earlier still by Adam Müller, for they considered that the origin of money was connected with the production of goods, was connected with the economic process itself; and it follows from this that the nature of the substance out of which money is made is a matter of little moment. (But Adam Müller transcends this notion by introducing the factor of mutuality into his conception of money).—Schumpeter's outlook resembles Bendixen's.[1]— According to the present author, money is "capital of higher grade", and is therefore a guiding, and organising, economic instrument, whose essence is not necessarily associated with the commodity-quality of the substance out of which money happens to be made. Only when this is understood, does the position of money in the body economic become comprehensible. Whereas hitherto it has been customary to distinguish between "means of production, means of consumption, and means of exchange",[2] so that money was considered apart from the world of commodities properly speaking, in the new light the productive role of money grows clear. Money is not productive capital in the sense in which (e.g.) a machine is productive capital; it is productive in a higher sense, seeing that (like a commercial treaty or other capital of higher grade) it cooperates in the production of machinery as well as in that of articles of consumption—that it is at work in this process as an invisible agent, so to say.[3] See also, above, what was said under Law, regarding the creation of money, pp. 73 et seq.; also, below, pp. 289 et seq.

Midway between the metallist view and the chartalist is the outlook of Friedrich von Wieser[4], who ascribes only a historical

[1] Schumpeter, *Das Sozialprodukt und die Rechenpfennige*, "Archiv für Sozialwissenschaft", 1918, vol. xliv.

[2] Knies, *Das Geld*, second edition, 1885, p. 20; and other writers.

[3] Cf. my *Fundament der Volkswirtschaftslehre*, third edition, pp. 181 et seq., et passim.

[4] *Der Geldwert und seine Veränderungen*, "Schriften des Vereins für Sozialpolitik", Leipzig, 1910, vol. cxxxii; *Theorie der gesellschaftlichen Wirtschaft*, "Grundriss der Nationalökonomik", Tübingen, 1914.

role to the material or substantial nature of money, but considers that paper money owes its entity to "mass custom" (and not, therefore, to the juridical order)—an idea which likewise found earlier expression in the writings of Adolf Wagner.[1] The same opinion is voiced by Mises.[2]—When we take a general survey of the modern development of the theory of money, we see that this theory has been fruitful only in so far as (unconsciously, hitherto!) it has followed Adam Müller.

The champions of metallism consider that the essence of money is to be found in its commodity-nature. There can be no doubt that uncompromising metallism contains atomistic and individualist elements, since its supporters hold that the qualities of money are an offshoot of those of the particular commodity gold. But there are very few metallists in this rigid sense of the term. All the noted "metallists" have looked upon metallic money (coined money) as a sort of "credit instrument" (the phrase is used from time to time by Dühring, though he is one of the strictest of the metallists), as symbolic money. This means that money is only the most intensified form of wealth, and a form in which wealth is guaranteed by the possession of the commodity-quality—an idea already implicit·in Ricardo's and Menger's notion of money as the "most marketable" of commodities. In the sense that for them the essence of money is anchored in the qualities of the precious metals, the following are, with more or fewer reserves, to be reckoned as metallists: Knies (*Geld und Kredit, I, Das Geld*, second edition, 1885); Eugen Dühring (*Kursus der National- und Sozialökonomie*, fourth edition, 1925; see above, p. 209); Richard Hildebrand, *Theorie des Geldes*, Jena, 1883; *Wesen des Geldes*, Jena, 1914); Karl Menger ("Geld", in *Handwörterbuch der Staatswissenschaften*, third edition); Karl Helfferich (*Das Geld*, Leipzig, sixth edition, 1923); Jevons; Laughlin; Pareto; and others. As to Walras, see above, p. 256.

The main theories concerning the value of money are: the cost-of-production theory (Senior, Helfferich); the quantity theory (see above, p. 140, and immediately below on the present and ensuing pages); a subjective modification of the foregoing, known as the income theory (Zwiedineck, Wieser), according to which the value of money is deducible from its

[1] *Die russische Papierwährung*, Riga, 1868; *Die Geld- und Kredittheorie der Peel'schen Bankakte*, Vienna, 1862.
[2] *Theorie des Geldes und der Umlaufsmittel*, second edition, Leipzig, 1924.

quality as income, that is to say from its use in income; and, finally, the organic theory of the value of money (Adam Müller; my own theory concerning the channels of inflation, see below, p. 290).—The most famous among the earlier exponents of the quantity theory of money were Hume, Ricardo, and John Stuart Mill. Among more recent economists who have espoused it, though critically, may be mentioned: the writers on the "banking principle" (see below, p. 291); Sombart (*Der moderne Kapitalismus*, sixth edition, Munich, 1924, vol. i); Wicksell (*Geldzins und Güterpreise*, Jena, 1898); Gide (*Principes d'économie politique*, 1884, and many subsequent editions; English translation from the twenty-third edition, by Ernest F. Row, *Principles of Political Economy*, Harrap, London, 1924); Marshall; Levasseur (*Le coût de la vie*, "Revue Economique Internationale", vol. iv, 1910); Kemmerer (*Money and Credit Instruments in their Relation to General Prices*, New York, 1907); Cassel; Mises; Irving Fisher (*The Purchasing Power of Money*, New York, 1911; *Stabilizing the Dollar*, New York, 1920); Keynes (*A Tract on Monetary Reform*, Macmillan, London, 1923); Hawtrey (*Monetary Reconstruction*, London, 1923; *Currency and Credit*, London, 1919).—Among the before-mentioned, Irving Fisher, Cassel, Keynes, and Hawtrey advocate the stabilisation of the domestic purchasing power of money and of the course of exchange.

Irving Fisher's doctrine forms the climax of the "critical" quantity theory. Fisher improves on the old quantity theory, in that he wishes also to take into account the velocity of the circulation of money (as shown by the average annual number of exchanges of goods for money) and the "volume of trade" (this meaning the quantity of goods bought with money). He says that the main tenet of the quantity theory, that prices rise and fall in direct ratio with the quantity of money in circulation, is sound, assuming the velocity of the circulation of money and the volume of trade to remain constant. Consequently we get the equation

$$MV = \Sigma pQ$$

this meaning that the product of the quantity of money, M, and the velocity of circulation, V, is equal to the product of the sum of prices, Σp, and the volume of trade, Q.—From this equation it follows that prices vary directly as the quantity of money, M, and as the velocity of circulation, V; and inversely as the volume of trade, Q. In M, Fisher includes the bank deposits, M^1, and their turnover, V^1.—The formula will not hold water, for the right-hand term, ΣpQ, is a pure tautology. In pQ there is implicit an assumption of what has to be explained, for p (price) is not put forward as a mathematical function of the quantity of money, M, nor yet of the velocity of circulation, V.[1]

For the rest, the general fallacy inherent in any quantity theory of money is the assumption that when the quantity of money doubles, there will necessarily be a doubling of the demand for all commodities. What really happens is a manifold increase in the demand for certain goods, accompanied by a notable decline in the demand for others; this will mean a transformation of demand and production, with a resulting change in price relations. The transformation will vary as the kind or quality of increase in the quantity of money varies (as the channels of outflow vary): taking either the form of a broadening of the basis of production, as happened in the case of inflation during the war; or else the form of an increase in consumption, as happened in Germany, in the case of inflation after the defeat. In the former instance there is an excess of ready money available for production, with consequent slackening of credit and reduction in the velocity of the circulation of money; in the latter, there is a scarcity of ready money for production, with a resulting extension of demands for credit and an increase in the velocity of the circulation of money.— What really matters is, not the quantity of money per se, but the power of money to effect the reorganisation of economic life. Here, too, the principle applies, "achievement takes precedence of price". (See above, p. 281.) The channel of outflow determines the function assigned to money; only in an indirect fashion does the quantity of money concern us. (Theory of the channels of outflow.) These considerations enable us to transcend the mechanics of the quantity theory, and to recognise that there is a qualitative factor at work to decide the value of money.[2]

I need mention the names of only a few of the opponents of

[1] See Fisher, *The Purchasing Power of Money*, New York, 1911, pp. 24, et seq.; and for further details, see my article *Bemerkungen zu Irving Fishers Geldlehre*, "Schmollers Jahrbuch", vol. xli, 1917, pp. 443 et seq.

[2] Further details in my *Fundament der Volkswirtschaftslehre*, fourth edition, Jena, 1929, pp. 292 et seq.

the quantity theory of money: Jevons, Richard Hildebrand, Lexis[1], Lotz, and Spiethoff.

Historically there is a close connexion between metallism and the quantity theory of money. Hence we find the quantity theory developing into the "currency theory"—known also as the "currency doctrine" or "currency principle"—(Ricardo; Samuel Jones Loyd, subsequently Baron Overstone, 1840; Peel's Bank Act of 1844), according to which the issue of bank-notes must be fully covered by a reserve of metallic money, since an increase in the former has just the same effect as an increase in the latter. In criticism of and in opposition to the foregoing we have the so-called "bank theory" or "banking principle",[2] according to which an increase in bank-notes secured by bills of exchange does not raise prices as does an increase in the amount of coined money in circulation, seeing that the economic process (the handing over of commodities) has preceded the issue of the notes. The champions of this principle are therefore content that only a fraction of the note issue should be covered by specie, the rest being secured by negotiable paper.—On principle, those who have espoused the "nominalist" theory of money are entitled to repudiate the need for a coined monetary reserve, so that their doctrine becomes unqualified chartalism.

2. Theory of the Rate of Exchange

A contentious point in connexion with all the theories of money is the explanation of the price of any particular country's money in foreign markets—the rate of exchange. At the present time, two theories are current.

a. The Balance of Payments Theory[3]

The metallists, regarding money as simply a commodity, consider that the price of money must be closely associated with the balance of payments; that is to say it must regulate

---

[1] *Allgemeine Volkswirtschaftslehre*, Leipzig, 1913; third edition, 1926.

[2] See Fullarton, *On the Regulation of Currencies*, third edition, London, 1845; Thomas Tooke, *An Inquiry into the Currency Principle*, London, 1844; Adolf Wagner, *System der Zettelbankpolitik*, second edition, 1873.

[3] See Goschen, *The Theory of the Foreign Exchanges*, London, 1861; also Thomas Tooke and W. Newmarch, *A History of Prices*, etc., six vols., London, 1836–1857.

itself strictly in accordance with supply and demand on the monetary exchange. The condition of the balance of payments finds expression in the international ratio of exchange. The main process runs as follows. Let us suppose that a Berlin merchant has delivered goods to a Viennese merchant. He then draws upon the latter a bill of exchange, and, before it is due for payment, tries to sell it on the Berlin bourse, hoping to find there some one who will "discount" it (buy it at a little less than its face value) in order to make payments in Vienna, because it is easier and cheaper to send a bill of exchange than to send specie. In like manner, a Viennese merchant who sends goods to Berlin draws on Berlin and sells the bill of exchange to some one in Vienna who has a payment to make in Berlin. If now, as a result of deliveries of goods from Berlin to Vienna (or of services rendered, or what not) there are so many bills on Vienna offered for sale on the Berlin bourse that the aggregate amount is more than the total of the sum which Berlin debtors wish to pay to Viennese creditors, the demand for these instruments of payment lags behind the supply, and the rate of exchange falls. Correspondingly, Vienna will have more payments to make to Berlin than can be made by the bills of exchange drawn on Berlin that are at this time available in Vienna, and the price of these bills in Vienna will rise. In such a case, therefore, the balance of payments is unfavourable to Vienna. Since Vienna has more to pay (more bills of exchange to meet) than Berlin, specie will flow from Vienna to Berlin. Specie must be moved from one city to the other, for as soon as the rate of exchange exceeds the cost of sending specie, a merchant will naturally find it expedient to have recourse to the latter.—But if (as is necessarily the case when a country has only a paper currency) no coined gold is available for this purpose, the rate of exchange may go on rising indefinitely. Then the currency is disturbed. It becomes necessary to pay for bills drawn on foreign countries (and therewith for all other means of making payments abroad, and above all for gold) more than corresponds to the metallic ratios between the respective currencies.—During the recent war, all the belligerent countries (wishing to keep a sufficient gold reserve) found it necessary to prohibit the export of gold, and thus their currencies became paper ones. (Incidentally, the Swedish currency likewise became a paper currency; Sweden had to suspend free coinage—for an opposite reason, because there was a menace of gold inflation.) In all these countries, foreign currencies were at a premium corresponding to the "balance of payments."

b. THE PURCHASING-POWER THEORY

The purchasing-power theory was formulated by the Swedish economist Cassel, building upon a Ricardian foundation.[1] The price of a country's money in foreign money markets cannot (says Cassel) depend, like the price of other commodities, upon supply and demand. Money is not, like other commodities, used by being consumed; it is used in the purchase of other commodities, to make payments. The decisive factor in determining the price of money in a foreign market is, therefore, the ratio between the purchasing power of foreign money in the foreign country and native money in the native country. On this view, the home value of money determines the foreign value, and takes precedence of the balance of payments.

The purchasing-power theory of the rate of exchange, which is necessarily associated with the quantity theory of money, is not, however, competent to explain the whole matter—though in many respects it certainly marks an advance when compared with the mechanical balance-of-payments theory. Even before the war, the rate of exchange between Vienna and Berlin could never be completely expressed in a purchasing-power equation; nor has the world ever been one undivided monetary exchange. The level of prices as between the various national economies is perforce and permanently diversified. This is because each national economy occupies its own particular organic position in the aggregate world economy. An organic theory of the value of money upon foreign exchanges must start from the peculiarities of the articulation of the distinct national economies into the world economy as a whole, and from the fact that prices are not perfectly commensurable.

3. THEORY OF CRISES[2]

No economy remains always the same in its articulation; none is perfectly "static". A rearticulation, a "dynamic" change, is

---

[1] Cassel, *Deutschlands wirtschaftliche Widerstandskraft*, Berlin, 1916.—Subsequently Keynes expressed similar views.

[2] See W. Heinrich, *Grundlagen einer universalistischen Krisenlehre*, Jena, 1928.

continually going on, thanks to increase of population, changes in technique, in the supply of raw materials, in capital of higher grade, in wants, etc.; also thanks to changes in the way in which various subordinate parts of economic structure are articulated into superordinate parts. In every such process of rearticulation two factors are at work: on the one hand, the development and the increasing importance of the new constituents of the economy; and, on the other, the retrogression; the diminishing importance, and in certain cases the disappearance, of some of the old constituents. When retrogressive features are predominant, we have a "crisis" or a "slump"; when developing features are predominant, we have a period of "good trade", or a "boom".—It follows from these considerations: (1) that there can be no crisis affecting all branches of industry simultaneously, and that crises can be classified as agricultural, industrial, monetary (money market), speculative (stock market), etc., according to the nature of the predominant element in the disturbance; but (2) that certain rearticulations of the body economic may have extensive repercussions upon numerous and important provinces of economic life—these constituting "crises" in the narrower sense of that term. A widespread crisis will be especially apt to occur in a national economy when its articulation into the world economy is suddenly altered. Notably does this happen after great wars. It happened after the Napoleonic wars; also after the war of 1870–1871; and we are now, above all in Germany, Austria, and Great Britain, passing through a lengthy period of crisis as a sequel to the war of 1914–1918.

As regards the theories of crises hitherto formulated, it is usual to classify them as follows:

a. Say's "théorie des débouchés" (theory of openings for trade), which is fundamentally sound, but not sufficiently comprehensive. (See above, p. 108.)

b. The theory of over-production (Sismondi, Malthus). The leading thought here is that the increase of capitalist production is not attended by a corresponding increase in the purchasing power of the workers, and that, for this reason, difficulty arises in disposing of the surplus. (But, as previously shown, general over-production is impossible.)

c. The theory of under-consumption. This develops the same notion as the theory of over-production, but looks at the matter chiefly from the consumer's standpoint, and lays the chief stress on defective distribution. (See under Rodbertus, p. 217, "law of the falling share of wages"; also under Marx, p. 220.)

d. The quantity-theory explanation of crises (the explanation of the "currency school"), according to which unfavourable conditions in the market and the occurrence of crises depend upon changes in the quantity of money in circulation—for instance, upon inflation, and upon too low a bank-rate.

e. The theory of over-capitalisation, which has been developed above all by Cassel. According to this theory, the main cause of crises is an unduly rapid increase in fixed capital during periods of "good trade".—The theory of over-capitalisation is masked Marxism. (See above, p. 222, the theory of the concentration of capital.) It suffices to explain certain "market crises", but is not an all-round explanation of crises. Indeed, under-capitalisation is just as potent a cause of these as over-capitalisation. Often enough, a crisis can only be liquidated by a plentiful supply of new capital, as we learn from the history of crises, and from a study of what is to-day termed "rationalisation" in Germany.

f. The explanation of crises as due to a cyclical movement, to an alternation of "booms" and "slumps" in the market, was given a good while ago by, among others, Jevons. The periodicity of crises was supposed to harmonise with the periodicity of sun-spots, the intermediate link being the quality of the harvests! Recently the cyclical theory has been revived by Spiethoff, Pohle[1], Sombart[2], E. Vogel, etc. In a capitalist economy with a free market, over-production has hitherto always been the destiny lying in wait for "good trade", and has usually led to a sudden collapse, to a crisis.[3]—The kernel of Spiethoff's doctrine is over-capitalisation in the domain of "goods of indirect consumption" (iron, coal, bricks, cement, timber), which Spiethoff classifies apart from "producing goods" (mines, brickfields, factories where machinery is made, and the like) and from goods for direct consumption, with the raw materials from which they are derived.

[1] *Bevölkerungsbewegung Kapitalbildung und periodische Wirtschaftskrisen,* 1902.

[2] *Versuch einer Systematik der Wirtschaftskrisen,* "Archiv für Sozialwissenschaft", vol. xix, 1904, p. 25.

[3] Spiethoff, "Krise", *Handwörterbuch der Staatswissenschaften,* fourth edition, vol. vi.

All the foregoing theories of crises are more or less individualistic. But the phenomena of crises really lie beyond the
conceptual range of individualism. Self-interest, supply and
demand, and over-capitalisation (supposed to be the outcome
of self-seeking, Marx in especial taking this view—see above,
p. 222), are concepts in which the collectivist nature of the
phenomena of crises is ignored. (The monetary theory of
crises, considered under *d*, is to some extent an exception here.)
Furthermore, the individualists are mistaken in regarding the
processes of crises as merely mechanical. The outcome of such
a way of looking at the matter is the modern "market baro-
meter".[1]—Those who hold the "organic" theory of economic
life look upon a crisis as something which, at the very outset,
derives from and concerns the social aggregate. Their concepts
of the partial aggregates, gradation, achievement, ordination,
articulation (sound or unsound, as the case may be), etc.,
enable them to grasp the essence of the whole process.

g. The organic theory, the one held by the author of the
present work, involves a repudiation of the idea of a quasi-
automatic recurrence of "booms" and "slumps". As previously
explained in connexion with any economic rearticulation, there
must be correlated movements in both these directions. For
instance, when one thing "comes into fashion", another must
"go out". If a boom is followed by a slump, this is not because
of over-capitalisation, but because of other flaws in the process
—such flaws as I have myself analysed in my *Theorie der
Preisverschiebung als Grundlage zur Erklärung der Teuerungen*,
Vienna, 1913, in which I discuss the way in which a cyclical
rise in prices is brought about by progressive changes in production and modifications of price.[2]

The distinction usually drawn between endogenous and
exogenous crises is likewise untenable, for the aims or ends that
must be described as "exogenous" are always "endogenous"
too, in so far as they are reflected in the choice of means. Such
subdivisions as market crises, credit crises, stock-exchange
crises, money-market crises, industrial crises, are not without
value, but the classification keeps to the surface of things.—If
the body economic is an articulated structure of means to an
end, then a crisis must be regarded as a disturbance of this

---

[1] Further details in Heinrich, *op. cit.*, pp. 144 et seq.

[2] Further details regarding this matter will be found in Heinrich, *op. cit.*,
pp. 210 et seq., 293 et seq., and 330 et seq.

articulated structure; and an analysis, a dissection, of the articulated structure must furnish the basis of a classification of crises. We have therefore to distinguish between: a. disturbances that arise from a change of aim (as when teetotalism and vegetarianism lead to a crisis in the vine-growing industry, and encourage the cultivation of edible plants to the detriment of stock-raising); and b. disturbances that arise from a change in the way in which the means are articulated.

Considering the latter in fuller detail, if in the articulated structure of means we distinguish "grades" and "partial aggregates" (see above, pp. 280–281), we get:

a. A group of crises which arise mainly out of a disturbance of the gradational structure of the body economic (these being the most important crises of which we have any record). For the most part they are due to a modification of the way in which the national economics are graded in and articulated into the world economy. Of this nature are our contemporary crises, by which some of the national economies always gain, though others lose.

β. Within the partial aggregates of the body economic, crises arise because of inventions; because of the discovery of new deposits of ore and new sources of other raw materials (the opening of new coalmines—the enduring crisis in the Austrian smelting industry—the replacement of coal by petroleum and by water-power as a motive force); because of changes in methods of transport and in trade routes; and so on. —Then there are changes in the partial domains of "commerce", "financial capital", etc., which are just as well able as are technical changes to cause a boom in one field and a slump in the next. Changes in credit and speculation (inflation, for example) are extremely conspicuous, and their importance in this connexion is for that reason apt to be overrated to-day. In actual fact they are more often effects of crises than causes, for the root of the trouble generally lies elsewhere, in the gradational structure, in the partial aggregate, or in the aims.— Especial reference must be made here to the crises that result from changes in capital of higher grade (new taxes, new laws to regulate economic life, administrative measures, commercial treaties, etc.)—changes which help or hinder this or that technical method, this or that branch of industry. In the world economy, the effect of commercial treaties in the cause or cure of crises is plain to all men's eyes.

The most important ways of preventing and curing crises will be: on the one hand, to ensure a certain fixity of aims, and to consolidate these aims; and, on the other hand, to ensure a certain fixity of means, and to coordinate these means. But if the means are to acquire the qualities of constancy and coordination, they must be interarticulated into a fairly well-rounded structure, this implying, above all, that in the main a country shall produce for itself and shall be able to satisfy its consumers' needs by home productions. Such a strengthening of the independence of the national economy does not signify a repudiation of the ultimate supremacy of the world economy; all that it means is that the articulated position of the national economy in the world economy must be as constant and as stable as possible.

A SURVEY OF THE COMPARATIVE VALIDITY OF THE VARIOUS SCHOOLS AND TRENDS

WHEN we take a general survey of all the trends of economic science that have been expounded in the present work; ranging through the individualists from Quesnay to Ricardo, with their successors, including the champions of the doctrine of marginal utility; through the universalists from Adam Müller to the historical school, not forgetting the mercantilists; and, finally, through the socialists who are partly individualist and partly universalist in their outlook—we are led to the general conclusion that, from the historical standpoint, there is no unified body of economic doctrine, but that the trends must be classified as individualist and universalist, respectively, according as the attitude to the fundamental problem of individualism versus universalism may vary. Nay more, as our whole study of the subject has shown, a modern critic's own attitude towards the mercantilists, the physiocrats, the classical economists, Adam Müller, List, and Carey, will be modified according as he himself is an individualist or a universalist.

Nevertheless, there are certain economic doctrines common to all schools. For instance, the law of diminishing returns, and Thünen's theory of localisation, have a place in every one of them. The doctrines which can thus find acceptance in all the schools are those which imply, more or less, the operation of self-determining or self-governing economic forces. This is possible as regards the theories of value, price, money, and output. But the individualists see such atomistic forces at work everywhere and without reserve. For them, the actions of the particular economic agent are the result of the automatic force of self-interest; commodities are self-determining concrete portions of value, each of them representing so much congealed labour; money is the embodiment of metallic value; supply and demand behave as self-governing entities, each having a given magnitude at any particular time. For the universalists this idea of automatic or self-governing forces has only a restricted applicability in economics; it is but a working hypothesis for use on appropriate occasions, and does not cover the whole of economic life. Necessarily, therefore, in many matters the universalists reach conclusions differing from those reached by the individualists. That is why the individualists start their concatenation of economic reasoning from value and price, whereas the universalists set out from achievement and from the articulated structure of the aggregate of all achievements.— Common to all trends, likewise, are those doctrines which entail the recognition of the mutual organic interdependence of means and ends. This applies to Thünen's law, to Gresham's law (that bad money drives good money out of circulation), to Fullarton's law of the reflux of banknotes, to the doctrine of fruitfulness or theory of productivity (supra, pp. 88 and 163), and to the theory of the functions of money—though in these cases, too, the point from which an economist starts his analysis will greatly influence his views on such particulars.

Nevertheless, the recognition that hitherto there has not existed any uniform system of economic doctrine, must not lead us to doubt the possibility of a science of economics. The controversy between the individualists and the universalists must be conducted upon a purely scientific, a purely analytical plane. To us universalists it seems unquestionable, after our critical survey of the whole field, that truth lies on the side of universalism, and that the universalist doctrine will ultimately prevail.

APPENDIX ONE

LITERATURE

WORKS ON THE HISTORY OF ECONOMICS

THE two following are of primary importance: August Oncken, *Geschichte der Nationalökonomie*, vol. i, Leipzig, 1902, reprinted 1922 (extends only to Adam Smith); and Roscher, *Geschichte der Nationalökonomik in Deutschland*, Munich, 1874.—Among other recent works, the most notable are: Gide and Rist, *Histoire des doctrines économiques*, Paris, 1909, third edition, 1920 (English translation from the second edition, 1913, by R. Richards, *A History of Economic Doctrines from the Time of the Physiocrats to the Present Day*, Harrap, London, 1915); John Kells Ingram, *A History of Political Economy*, first edition, 1888, second, 1907, third, 1915; Eugen Dühring, *Kritische Geschichte der Nationalökonomie und des Sozialismus*, Berlin, 1871, fourth edition, 1900; Böhm-Bawerk, *Geschichte und Kritik der Kapitalzinstheorien*, fourth edition, Innsbruck, 1921 *Die Entwicklung der deutschen Volkswirtschaftslehre im neunzehnten Jahrhundert*, two parts, Leipzig, 1908 (a symposium in honour of Gustav Schmoller); E. Salin, *Geschichte der Volkswirtschaftslehre*, Berlin, 1923.—Mombert, *Geschichte der Nationalökonomie*, Jena, 1927.—Surányi-Unger, *Philosophie in der Volkswirtschaftslehre*, vol. i, Jena, 1923, vol. ii, Jena, 1926.—Volumes on the history of economics will also be found in the *Deutsche Beiträge zur Wirtschafts- und Gesellschaftslehre*, Jena, 1926 and subsequent years (edited by Spann, Below, H. Dorn, H. Freyer, F. Lenz, and W. Andreae).—Of earlier works on the history of our science, I may mention: Contzen, *Geschichte der volkswirtschaftlichen Literatur im Mittelalter*, second edition, Berlin, 1872; Eisenhart, *Geschichte der Nationalökonomik*, Jena, 1881, reprinted, Jena, 1910.

WORKS OF THE CLASSICAL ECONOMISTS

I earnestly commend the study of these to all who wish to gain any real insight into economic science. In Germany there are two outstanding collections. The universalist writers will be found in the "Herdflamme" collection, edited by myself and published by Gustav Fischer of Jena. Notably it contains the works of Adam Müller, List, Baader, Fichte, Hegel, Plato, Augustine, and Thomas Aquinas. The individualist writers will be found in the "Sammlung sozialwissenschaftlicher Meister", edited by Waentig and likewise published by Gustav Fischer. It contains the works (among others) of Quesnay, Adam Smith, and Ricardo; also those of Thünen and List.— Other collections are: "Sammlung älterer und neuerer staatswissenschaftlicher Schriftsteller", edited by Brentano and Leser, Leipzig, 1893 and subsequent years; "Bibliothek der Volkswirtschaftslehre und Gesellschaftswissenschaft", originated by Nikolas Stöpel and carried on by R. Prager (contains about twenty volumes); and, finally, the "Hauptwerke des Sozialismus und der Sozialpolitik", originated by the late Georg Adler, carried on by C. Grünberg, and published by Hirschfeld, Leipzig, 1904 and subsequent years.—Good extracts from the classical economists will be found in Diehl and Mombert, *Ausgewählte Lesestücke zum Studium der politischen Oekonomie*, Karlsruhe, 1912 and subsequent years.

TEXTBOOKS

The leading [German] textbooks are (authors' names in alphabetical order): Amonn, *Grundzüge der Volkswohlstandslehre*, vol. i, Jena, 1926; Cassel, *Theoretische Sozialökonomik*, fourth edition, 1927 (English translation by Joseph McCabe, *The Theory of Social Economy*, two vols., Fisher Unwin, London, 1923), written from the individualist outlook, and in accordance with the mathematical method; Wolfgang Heller, *Theoretische Volkswirtschaftslehre*, Leipzig, 1926; Philippovich, *Grundriss der politischen Oekonomie*, vol. i, *Allgemeine Volkswirtschaftslehre*, fifteenth edition, 1920 (eclectic); Roscher, *Grundlagen der Nationalökonomie*, twenty-sixth edition, edited by Pöhlmann, 1922 (English translation by J. J. Lalor, from thirteenth German edition, *Principles of Political Economy*, New York, 1878), in some respects out of date, but extremely readable, and on many topics still admirable; Schmoller, *Allgemeine Volkswirtschaftslehre*, two vols., third edition, 1919 (the most important work produced by the historical school, and the ripe fruit of a scholar's life); Spann, *Fundament der Volkswirtschaftslehre*, third edition, Jena, 1923.—Works penned from the universalist outlook are reissued in the before-mentioned collection, "Deutsche Beiträge, etc."

DICTIONARIES

Handwörterbuch der Staatswissenschaften, fourth edition, edited by Elster, Weber, and Wieser, Jena, 1922 and subsequent years; Schönberg's *Handbuch der politischen Oekonomie*, fourth edition, Tübingen, 1896 and subsequent years; *Handwörterbuch des Kaufmanns*, five vols., Hamburg, 1925 and subsequent years; *Grundriss der Sozialökonomik*, Tübingen, 1914 and subsequent years (six vols. issued so far); Palgrave's *Dictionary of Political Economy*, new edition, edited by Henry Higgs, three vols., Macmillan, London, 1925–1926; *Politisches Handwörterbuch*, edited by P. Herre, 2 vols., Leipzig, 1923.

HISTORY OF ECONOMIC DEVELOPMENT

Häpke, *Wirtschaftsgeschichte*, Leipzig, 1922 (a good introduction to the study); Below, *Probleme der Wirtschaftsgeschichte*, third edition, 1925; Sombart, *Der moderne Kapitalismus*, four vols., sixth edition, Munich, 1924–1927 (a monumental product of German science); Dopsch, *Die wirtschaftliche und soziale Entwicklung Europas*, two vols., second edition, Vienna, 1923–1924; Brodnitz, *Englische Wirtschaftsgeschichte*, Jena, 1918; Sartorius von Waltershausen, *Deutsche Wirtschaftsgeschichte*, 1815–1914, second edition, 1923; same author, *Zeittafel zur Wirtschaftsgeschichte*, third edition, Halberstadt, 1928; Wilhelm Bauer, *Einführung in das Studium der Geschichte*, second edition, Tübingen, 1928. [For England, read Charlotte M. Waters, *An Economic History of England*, 1066–1874, with 221 illustrations, Oxford University Press, 1920.]

APPENDIX TWO

HOW TO STUDY ECONOMICS

> "Not again shall I rest until nothing
> is to me any longer word and tra-
> dition, until everything has become
> living concept."
>
> GOETHE
> at Rome, June 27, 1787

IN view of the cleavage of our science into conflicting trends
(a cleavage which makes it impossible to be content with
simply following the lead of this or that standard textbook),
it is desirable to give the student of economics certain counsels
regarding the course of his studies.

This advice must be divided into two sections, for it is necessary to distinguish between those who want nothing more
than an elementary general grasp of the principles of economics,
and those who aim at a profound and exhaustive study of the
subject.

I. THE ACQUIREMENT OF A GENERAL GRASP

One who desires to get a general grasp of the elements of economic doctrine, should pass from the study of the present
volume to that of a little book in the Göschen collection, Fuchs'
Volkswirtschaftslehre, fourth edition, Berlin, 1922. A student
who wishes to proceed from this to an understanding of the
domain where economics passes into politics (that is to say,
applied economics) should read Conrad's *Volkswirtschafts-
politik*, tenth edition, edited by Hesse, published by Fischer,
Jena, 1924.

Should he then wish to go a step farther, and to gain an
insight into the opposition of the two main trends and methods,

he will do well to read my inaugural address at Vienna, *Vom Geist der Volkswirtschaftslehre*, Jena, 1919, reprinted as an appendix to the third edition (1923) of my *Fundament der Volkswirtschaftslehre*; and also my little book entitled *Tote und lebendige Wissenschaft*, Jena, 1925, of which the second and third sections are the most important. Should he now wish to study one of the easier classical economists, let him turn to List's *Das nationale System der politischen Oekonomie* (two English translations, as *The National System of Political Economy*, see above, p. 190).—The reader who wants to understand economic reports in the newspapers will find much help in R. Wagner's *Der Handels- und Wirtschaftsteil der Tageszeitung*, Hamburg, 1922.—A very useful work is W. Heller's *Wörterbuch der Nationalökonomie*, 1926.

The first seventy pages of my book *Der wahre Staat*, second edition, Leipzig, 1923, contain a summary of the main doctrines of sociology.

II. SYSTEMATIC STUDY

German university students to-day are prone, after attending a general course of lectures, to use a subject-index for the selection of works that will enable them to compile a dissertation upon some special topic. This method is not to be commended. It will enable one who has acquired a mere smattering of the subject to make a sterile assemblage of facts—about as valuable as a postage-stamp collection!

Whoever wishes to gain a profound and systematic knowledge of economic science, and aspires to something more thorough than the crude information deemed sufficient for immediate "practical purposes", will need to undertake the following accessory studies in addition to the general economic course: (1) a methodological, philosophical, and sociological course of reading, that he may acquaint himself with the

U

spiritual and social nature of the field of enquiry; (2) a statistical and economico-historical course; and (3) a course that will enlighten him regarding everyday business life and technology, that he may acquire a sound knowledge of the facts and thus become enabled to walk confidently among them. As regards the specialised study of economics, that must certainly be built upon a general scientific knowledge of economic theory. In support of this contention, I may venture the following remarks.

It is utterly wrongheaded (though usual nowadays) to make applied economics the foundation of economic study. As regards the economics of agriculture, for instance, what the student first needs to know is, not the sort of things that will be of especial value to the managing official of an agricultural cooperative, but such general principles as Thünen's theory of localisation, the theory of landrent, the theory of protection, and the like. These theories must be mastered from start to finish. If nothing more than "practice" were required, the student could be apprenticed to the aforesaid managing official, and could dispense with a university course. The university must not try to compete with the practising expert, nor the student to vie with the apprentice. Practice can only be learned by practice, and for that all the after years of life are open; but the time for learning theory is usually short, is in most cases restricted to the undergraduate years. (Besides, in the vacations the student can, if he likes, devote himself to gaining the practical knowledge he will never learn from books.) The study of economics, therefore, must centre in the theory, the philosophy, and the history of the subject. One who thinks otherwise need aspire no more than to become a book-keeper, and would be better at a commercial school than at a university. Above all, however, one who lacks grounding in the theoretical concepts of a science, can never be more than a rule-of-thumb practitioner, a mere empiric. I wish to utter a most emphatic protest against the modern tendency to set "practice" above theory. Conceptual knowledge, theoretical knowledge, is essential, if the mind is to raise itself above the matter it contemplates. But to-day the historical and realistic trend has been so successful in economics, as to lead right away from theory, away from science, with the paradoxical result that those who wished to escape from Marxism and individualism find themselves more defenceless than ever against these types of economic theory. Economics, aware of its own poverty and perplexity, is degenerating into jurisprudence or even mere book-keeping, having little more to offer than useful descriptions of economic fact. In such circumstances, zealous students must pluck up courage for themselves, and spontaneously devote themselves to theory. Let them choose as topics for their graduating theses, not the "condition" of this or that branch of industry, but questions of pure theory. Now, the appropriate method of theoretical study is the historical. Whatever subject you select, you should broaden the basis of investigation by an exhaustive study of its history.

The main difficulty at the present time attaching to the study of economic theory is that it is so hard to transcend the narrow individualist Anglo-French doctrine which dominates the textbooks and economic literature in general. The essential thing is that the student should make himself acquainted with universalist theory no less than with individualist!

When entering upon the systematic study of economic theory, the student should begin by reading an introductory book like the present one. Then let him work through my *Tote und lebendige Wissenschaft* (beginning with the second and third sections), and from that go on to my *Fundament der Volkswirtschaftslehre*, fourth edition, Jena, 1929. Next he should devote himself to a systematic textbook, and cannot do better than read Amonn's *Volkswohlstandslehre* (1926) or W. Heller's *Volkswirtschaftslehre* (1927), both of these works being written, in part at least, from the universalist standpoint. As to other textbooks, see above, p. 302.

Now should come the study of the classical economists, for only with this does the real entry into the science begin. At least List's *Nationale System* should be read, followed by Adam Müller's *Elemente* and *Abhandlungen*, and then by Adam Smith's *Wealth of Nations* or Ricardo's *Principles of Political Economy and Taxation*. It will next be useful to read John Stuart Mill's *Principles of Political Economy*, for Mill, the last in the line of succession of the individualist classical economists, gives a comprehensive general exposition of their views. But beyond question the writings of List and Adam Müller demand close attention.—Now, if time permits, the student should read Thünen (see above, p. 171) and the romanticists, and he will find the requisite material in J. Baxa's *Staat und Gesellschaft im Spiegel der deutschen Romantik*, Jena, 1923.—Nor should Marx's chief socialist work, *Das Kapital*[1] (vol. i), be forgotten, for this author's theories—though their fallaciousness is obvious enough to any one who has thoroughly mastered the principles of economics—still play a great part in the world to-day. (That this has been possible and is still possible, the Germans owe, above all, to the aridity of economic theory as expounded by the historical and realistic schools of yesterday and to-day.)

Among British and American textbooks, I should like to recommend: Marshall's *Principles of Economics* and John Bates Clark's *The Distribution of Wealth* (see above, p. 261); Seligmann's *Principles of Economics*, eleventh edition, New York, 1926; Tugwell's *The Trend of Economics* (see above, p. 277).

---

[1] *Capital*, newly translated by Eden and Cedar Paul, George Allen & Unwin, Ltd., London, 1928.

In French, read Leroy-Beaulieu's *Traité théorique et pratique d'économie politique*, fifth edition, Paris, 1909.

From the very first, philosophical, historical, and then methodological economic study should be associated with the study of pure theory.

[In the German original there now follow seven pages devoted to the study of special economic disciplines: applied economics, the science of finance, method, philosophy, sociology, history, statistics, business affairs, jurisprudence, etc. Under each head, the author gives the student copious advice as to the books he should read. Since these books are almost exclusively German, and since very few of them have been translated, it would be a waste of space to reproduce the lists here. Advice as to suitable literature under any or all of these heads will be found in Palgrave's *Dictionary of Political Economy* and other standard English works of reference. It seems expedient, however, to reproduce from the suppressed pages all the passages which embody Othmar Spann's specific views.

Under *Method*, the author writes: "As soon as the student's mastery of economic theory has gone far enough, he should devote himself to the study of method. He cannot possibly attain to an independent standpoint until he has gained an insight into methodological problems. (The failure to recognise this was the most grievous fault of the historical school, and has been the main cause of the present decay of economic science.)"

Under *Philosophy*, Spann writes: "But methodological study is impossible to one who has failed to master the logical and philosophical foundations of economics. Were it only for this reason (though the fact that political economy is one of the abstract sciences must also be taken into the reckoning), philosophical study must from the first go hand in hand with economic. Indeed, it is best that economics should be taught under the auspices of the philosophical faculty."

Again, under the same head: "The history of philosophy is no mere jumble of opinions, as people are apt to think to-day, but a magnificently unified aggregate of a restricted number of thought-trends. (From this generalisation I except the empiricists, who are not philosophers in the true sense of the term, but ignoramuses in philosophy.) Fundamentally, there are but two closely interconnected thought-trends, upon a thorough knowledge of which everything turns, the trend of Plato and Aristotle, and the trend of German idealism from Kant to Hegel."

Further (still under the same head): "I must expressly warn the beginner against Haeckel, Ostwald, Büchner, and similar vagrant philosophers. Masters in their own field, in philosophy they are tyros, and must not be taken seriously. The student should also be on his guard against Schopenhauer and Nietzsche. They were both of them men of outstanding genius, but were morbid and eccentric, so that their works are not appropriate reading for one who has still his way to make in philosophy."

Under *Sociology*: "After he has gained a sufficient grasp of economic theory and of philosophy (not before!), the student must without fail begin to acquire a knowledge of sociology, for this is essential to the full understanding of economics."

Under *Statistics*: "A thorough grounding in statistics is indispensable to the modern political economist. Though he may never completely master the historical method, statistics form the inductive means proper to his subject. Statistics are not necessarily dry, being very much alive for one who contemplates them with insight. In many instances, figures well chosen and well arranged afford the only way of obtaining a precise and, still more important, a plastic knowledge of reality. Of course, in the right use of statistics, everything depends on method, and the statistics of population are especially instructive in this respect."

Under *Business Affairs*: "Another essential aid to the study of economics is a knowledge of business affairs and technology. One who does not know what a bill of exchange is or the meaning of such terms as 'arbitrage' and 'discount', one who does not know how to read a balance sheet or the signification of rates of exchange, will remain in the dark about credit and banking, currency and the money market, and he will therefore be incompetent to understand the mechanism of modern business life. This does not mean that we must fall into the mistake of regarding the theory of business as a science. Book-keeping and the conduct of enterprises are not sciences but arts. . . . Nevertheless, the student will do well to take a course in practical book-keeping; . . . to learn book-keeping by double entry, the keeping of business accounts, the methods of commerce, etc. . . . The regular reading of the market reports and the commercial articles in a great daily newspaper is desirable to give knowledge in these fields a practical turn."

Concluding this section on Systematic Study, Spann writes:

"The guiding principle must be to pass from the general to the particular, and not conversely. It is of the first importance that the study of applied economics should follow, not precede, the study of theory.

"Moreover, alike in his theoretical and in his practical work, the student should always seek the great interconnexions of things, should keep his gaze fixed upon the whole and upon the living—in accordance with Eckehart's saying:

"*A master of life is more worthy of commendation than a thousand masters of books.*"]

INDEX

THE EVOLUTION
OF CAPITALISM

Allen, Zachariah. **The Practical Tourist,** Or Sketches of the State of the Useful Arts, and of Society, Scenery, &c. &c. in Great-Britain, France and Holland. Providence, R.I., 1832. Two volumes in one.

Bridge, James Howard. **The Inside History of the Carnegie Steel Company:** A Romance of Millions. New York, 1903.

Brodrick, J[ames]. **The Economic Morals of the Jesuits:** An Answer to Dr. H. M. Robertson. London, 1934.

Burlamaqui, J[ean-] J[acques]. **The Principles of Natural and Politic Law.** Cambridge, Mass., 1807. Two volumes in one.

Capitalism and Fascism: Three Right-Wing Tracts, 1937-1941. New York, 1972.

Corey, Lewis. **The Decline of American Capitalism.** New York, 1934.

[Court, Pieter de la]. **The True Interest and Political Maxims, of the Republic of Holland.** Written by that Great Statesman and Patriot, John de Witt. To which is prefixed, (never before printed) Historical Memoirs of the Illustrious Brothers Cornelius and John de Witt, by John Campbell. London, 1746.

Dos Passos, John R. **Commercial Trusts:** The Growth and Rights of Aggregated Capital. An Argument Delivered Before the Industrial Commission at Washington, D.C., December 12, 1899. New York, 1901.

Fanfani, Amintore. **Catholicism, Protestantism and Capitalism.** London, 1935.

Gaskell, P[eter]. **The Manufacturing Population of England:** Its Moral, Social, and Physical Conditions, and the Changes Which Have Arisen From the Use of Steam Machinery; With an Examination of Infant Labour. London, 1833.

Göhre, Paul. **Three Months in a Workshop:** A Practical Study. London, 1895.

Greeley, Horace. **Essays Designed to Elucidate the Science of Political Economy,** While Serving to Explain and Defend the Policy of Protection to Home Industry, As a System of National Cooperation for the Elevation of Labor. Boston, 1870.

Grotius, Hugo. **The Freedom of the Seas,** Or, The Right Which Belongs to the Dutch to Take Part in the East Indian Trade. Translated with Revision of the Latin Text of 1633 by Ralph Van Deman Magoffin. New York, 1916.

Hadley, Arthur Twining. **Economics:** An Account of the Relations Between Private Property and Public Welfare. New York, 1896.

Knight, Charles. **Capital and Labour;** Including *The Results of Machinery*. London, 1845.

de Malynes, Gerrard. **Englands View, in the Unmasking of Two Paradoxes:** With a Replication unto the Answer of Maister John Bodine. London, 1603. New Introduction by Mark Silk.

Marquand, H. A. **The Dynamics of Industrial Combination.** London, 1931.

Mercantilist Views of Trade and Monopoly: Four Essays, 1645-1720. New York, 1972.

Morrison, C[harles]. **An Essay on the Relations Between Labour and Capital.** London, 1854.

Nicholson, J. Shield. **The Effects of Machinery on Wages.** London, 1892.

One Hundred Years' Progress of the United States: With an Appendix Entitled Marvels That Our Grandchildren Will See; or, One Hundred Years' Progress in the Future. By Eminent Literary Men, Who Have Made the Subjects on Which They Have Written Their Special Study. Hartford, Conn., 1870.

The Poetry of Industry: Two Literary Reactions to the Industrial Revolution, 1755/1757. New York, 1972.

Pre-Capitalist Economic Thought: Three Modern Interpretations. New York, 1972.

Promoting Prosperity: Two Eighteenth Century Tracts. New York, 1972.

Proudhon, P[ierre-] J[oseph]. **System of Economical Contradictions:** Or, The Philosophy of Misery. (Reprinted from *The Works of P. J. Proudhon*, Vol. IV, Part I.) Translated by Benj. R. Tucker. Boston, 1888.

Religious Attitudes Toward Usury: Two Early Polemics. New York, 1972.

Roscher, William. **Principles of Political Economy.** New York, 1878. Two volumes in one.

Scoville, Warren C. **Revolution in Glassmaking:** Entrepreneurship and Technological Change in the American Industry, 1880-1920. Cambridge, Mass., 1948.

Selden, John. **Of the Dominion, Or, Ownership of the Sea.** Written at First in Latin, and Entituled *Mare Clausum.* Translated by Marchamont Nedham. London, 1652.

Senior, Nassau W. **Industrial Efficiency and Social Economy.** Original Manuscript Arranged and Edited by S. Leon Levy. New York, 1928. Revised Preface by S. Leon Levy. Two volumes in one.

Spann, Othmar. **The History of Economics.** Translated from the 19th German Edition by Eden and Cedar Paul. New York, 1930.

The Usury Debate After Adam Smith: Two Nineteenth Century Essays. New York, 1972. New Introduction by Mark Silk.

The Usury Debate in the Seventeenth Century: Three Arguments. New York, 1972.

Varga, E[ugen]. **Twentieth Century Capitalism.** Translated from the Russian by George H. Hanna. Moscow, [1964].

Young, Arthur. **Arthur Young on Industry and Economics:** Being Excerpts from Arthur Young's Observations on the State of Manufactures and His Economic Opinions on Problems Related to Contemporary Industry in England. Arranged by Elizabeth Pinney Hunt. Bryn Mawr, Pa., 1926.